THE NEGOTIATOR

THE GUARDIAN

DANGER IN THE SHADOWS

"Dee Henderson had me shivering as her stalker got closer and closer to his victim. The message that we have nothing to fear as long as God is in control was skillfully handled, but I got scared, anyway! I highly recommend this book to anyone who likes suspense."

TERRI BLACKSTOCK, BESTSELLING AUTHOR OF
WORD OF HONOR AND SHADOW OF DOUBT

"Dee Henderson is quickly rising to the top of Christian suspense! Ms. Henderson's sparkling characters and superb plotting in *Danger in the Shadows* sweeps the reader along to a breathless conclusion. You'll want to keep the light on for this one!"

LORI COPELAND, AUTHOR OF THE BRIDES OF THE WEST SERIES

"A masterstroke!! In *Danger in the Shadows* author Dee Henderson gives the reader not one but two irresistible heroes."

COMPUSERVE REVIEWS

"An excellent read for those looking for a nail-biting read with lots of heart."

ALL ABOUT ROMANCE

TRUE DEVOTION

"Action, adventure, and romance! *True Devotion* has everything a reader could want!"

ANGELA ELWELL HUNT, BESTSELLING AUTHOR OF THE IMMORTAL

"Dee Henderson has done a splendid job mixing romance with the fast-paced action of a Navy SEAL platoon. *True Devotion* captures the qualities of intrigue, suspense, and intimacy within the setting of America's elite waterborne commandos."

STEVE WATKINS, FORMER NAVY SEAL

"Another fast-paced romantic suspense....A great read!"

ROMANTIC TIMES MAGAZINE

"A wonderful story with real and entertaining characters. Ms. Henderson's gift with words makes this book impossible to put down."

WRITER'S CLUB ROMANCE GROUP ON AOL

the Negotiator

BOOK ONE—THE O'MALLEY SERIES

DEE HENDERSON

Multnomah® Publishers *Sisters, Oregon*

THE NEGOTIATOR
published by Multnomah Publishers, Inc.

© 2000, 2001 by Dee Henderson
International Standard Book Number: 1-59052-243-5

Cover photo by David Kroland/Tony Stone Images

Scripture quotations are from: *Revised Standard Version Bible* (RSV)
© 1946, 1952 by the Division of Christian Education
of the National Council of the Churches of Christ
in the United States of America

Multnomah is a trademark of Multnomah Publishers, Inc., and is registered in the
U.S. Patent and Trademark Office.
The colophon is a trademark of Multnomah Publishers, Inc.

Printed in the United States of America

For information:
MULTNOMAH PUBLISHERS, INC.
POST OFFICE BOX 1720
SISTERS, OREGON 97759

Library of Congress Cataloging-in-Publication Data:
Henderson, Dee. The negotiator / by Dee Henderson
    p.cm.—(O'Malley series ; bk.1)
    ISBN 1-57673-608-3 (mass paper)
    ISBN 1-57673-819-1 (trade paper)
    1. Government investigators—United States—Fiction. 2. Hostage negotiations—
United States— Fiction. I. Title
    PS3558.E4829 N44 2000   813'.54–dc21   99-058861

03 04 05 06 —16 15 14 13 12

TITLES BY DEE HENDERSON

THE O'MALLEY SERIES:
Danger in the Shadows (prequel)
The Negotiator
The Guardian
The Truth Seeker
The Protector
The Healer
The Rescuer (March 2003)

UNCOMMON HEROES SERIES:
True Devotion
True Valor
True Honor (October 2002)
True Courage (March 2003)

"For the Son of man came to seek and to save the lost."
LUKE 19:10

Prologue

D ynamite.

Where had he put the dynamite? He shoved aside cobwebs striking his face, moving deeper on his belly into a crawl space that only rats should inhabit. His flashlight lit the area like a Roman candle: It had come from the construction site and could illuminate half a mile. Twenty-eight years of hard work had come down to a pink slip, an insincere *"I'm sorry"* from the young brat, and a flashlight. He was apologizing to no one for taking the flashlight.

That young brat of a boss would have his own trouble soon. Even a blue-collar guy like himself could figure that out. Some guy tells him to look the other way when he was doing his nightly rounds; something was getting planned.

But the bank manager…he would have to take care of that problem himself. The bank manager was going to be more than just sorry.

The rage ate inside him like the cancer did, and he felt no remorse for deciding he had been pushed around long enough. To take a man's job, to take a man's home, was to take the last of his dignity. If he let them get away with it, he would die a coward. He would rather die a man.

There it was. He pulled the wooden crate toward him, pushed aside the dust, popped the lid with a screwdriver, and looked inside. The sticks of dynamite lay in neat rows. Plenty. They were old, but they would still go boom.

One

Kate O'Malley had been in the dungeon since dawn.

The members of the emergency response group comprising the SWAT and hostage-rescue teams had been relegated to the basement of the county building during the last department reorganization. The metal desks were crammed together; the concrete walls needed repainting; the old case files made the room smell musty; and the hot and cold water pipes coming from the boiler room rumbled overhead.

The team was proud of its little hovel even if the plants did die within days. The location allowed for relaxed rules. The only evidence of bureaucracy was a time clock by the steel door so those not on salary could get paid for all their overtime.

Despite the dirt on her tennis shoes, Kate had her feet propped up on the corner of her desk, her fingers steepled, her eyes half closed, as she listened to the sound of her own voice over the headphones, careful not to let the turmoil of her thoughts reflect in her expression. She was reviewing the last of four negotiation tapes. Case 2214 from last week haunted her. A domestic violence call with shots fired. It had taken six hours to negotiate a peaceful conclusion. Six agonizing hours for the mother and two children held in the house. Had there been any way to end it earlier?

As Kate listened to the husband's drunken threats and her own calm replies, she automatically slowed her breathing to suppress her rising emotions. She hated domestic violence cases. They revived unwanted memories…memories Kate had buried away from the light of day.

The cassette tape reversed sides. She sipped her hot coffee and grimaced. Graham must have made this pot. She didn't mind strong coffee, but this was Navy coffee. Kate tugged open her middle desk drawer and pushed aside chocolate bars and two heavy silver medals for bravery to find sugar packets.

She found it odd to be considered something of a legend on the force at the age of thirty-six, but she understood it. She was a negotiator known for one thing—being willing to walk into any situation. Domestic violence, botched robberies, kidnappings, even airline hijackings—she had worked them all.

Kate let people see what she wanted them to see. She could sit in the middle of a crisis for hours or days if that's what it took to negotiate a peace. She could do it with a relaxed demeanor. Detached. Most often, apparently bored.

It worked. Her apparent boredom in a crisis kept people alive. She dealt with the emotions later, after the situation was over—and far away from work. She played a lot of basketball, using the game to cultivate her focus, let go of the tension.

This was her fourth review of the tapes. Her case notes appeared complete. Kate didn't hear anything she could have done differently. She stopped the tape playback, relieved to have the review done. She pushed back the headphones and ran her hand through her ruffled hair.

"O'Malley."

She turned to see Graham holding up his phone.

"Line three. Your brother."

"Which one?"

"The paramedic."

She punched the blinking light. "Hi, Stephen."

"Let me guess; you're screening your calls."

She was, but it was an amusing first observation. "I'm ducking the media for a few days. Are you off duty?"

"Just wrapping up. Had breakfast yet?"

Kate picked up the tension in his voice. "I could go for some good coffee and a stack of pancakes."

"I'll meet you across the street at Quinn's."

"Deal."

Kate glanced at her pager, confirming she was on group call. She slid her cellular phone into her shirt pocket as she stood. "I'm heading to breakfast. Anyone want a Danish brought back?" Quinn's was a popular stopping point for all of them.

Requests came in from all over the room. Her tally ended with three raspberry, four cherry, and two apple Danishes. "Page me if you need me."

The stairs out of the dungeon were concrete and hand railed so they could be traversed with speed. Security doors were located at both ends. The stairway opened into the secure access portion of the parking garage. The team's specially equipped communications vans gleamed. They'd just been polished yesterday.

Kate slid on her sunglasses. June had begun as a month of glaring sun and little rain. It parched even the downtown Chicago concrete, coating the ground with crumbling dust. Traffic was heavy in this tight narrow corridor. She crossed against the traffic light.

Quinn's was a mix of new interior and old building, the restaurant able to comfortably seat seventy. Kate waved to the owner, took two menus, and headed to her usual table at the back of the restaurant, choosing the chair that put her back to the wall. It was always an amusing dance when there were two or more cops coming to Quinn's. No cop liked to sit with his back to an open room.

She accepted a cup of coffee, skimming the menu though she knew it by heart. Blueberry pancakes. She was a lady of habit. That decision made, she relaxed back in her seat to enjoy the coffee and tune into the conversations going on around her. The ladies by the window were talking about a baby shower. The businessmen to her left were discussing a fishing trip. Two teenagers were debating where to begin their shopping excursion.

Kate stirred two sugar packets into her coffee. Normal life. After ten years as a negotiator, there wasn't much normalcy left in her own life. The mundane details that most people cared about had ceased to cause the slightest blip on her radar screen. Normal people cared about clothes, vacations, holidays. Kate cared about staying alive. If it weren't such a stark dichotomy, it would be amusing.

Stephen arrived as she was nursing her second cup of coffee. Kate smiled when she saw the interest he attracted as he came to join her. She couldn't blame the ladies. His sports jacket and blue jeans didn't hide his muscles. He could walk off the cover of nearly any men's fashion magazine. Not bad for someone who spent his days dealing with car accidents, fire victims, gang shootings, and drug overdoses.

He wouldn't stay in this city forever—he talked occasionally about moving northwest to some small town with a lake, good fishing, and a job where he would finally get to treat more heart attacks than gunshot victims—but for now he stayed. Kate knew it was primarily because of her. Stephen had designated himself her watchdog. He had never asked; he'd just taken the role. She loved him for it, even if she did tease him on occasion about it.

He pulled out the chair across from her. "Thanks for making time, Kate."

"Mention food and you've got my attention." She pushed over the second cup of coffee the waitress had filled, not commenting on the strain in his eyes despite his smile. That look hadn't been there yesterday when he'd joined her for a one-on-one basketball game. She hoped it was only the aftereffects of a hard shift. He would tell her if he needed to. Within the O'Malley family, secrets were rare.

At the orphanage—Trevor House—where family was nonexistent, the seven of them had chosen to become their own family, had chosen the last name O'Malley. Stephen was one of the three special ones in the family: a true orphan, not one of the abandoned or abused.

They might not share a blood connection, but that didn't matter; what they did share was far stronger. They were loyal, faithful, and committed to each other. Some twenty-two years after their decision, the group was as unified and strong as ever.

They had, in a sense, adopted each other.

"Did you see the news?" Stephen asked once the waitress had taken their orders.

Kate shook her head. She had left early for the gym and then gone straight to the office.

"There was a five-car pileup on the tollway. A three-year-old was in the front seat of a sedan. He died en route to County General Hospital."

Kids. The toughest victims for any O'Malley to deal with. "I'm sorry, Stephen." He decompressed like she did. Slowly. After he left work.

"So am I." He set aside his coffee cup. "But that's not why I called you. Jennifer's coming to town."

Jennifer O'Malley was the youngest in the family, everyone's favorite. She was a pediatrician in Dallas. "Oh?"

"I got a call from her this morning. She's got a Sunday flight into O'Hare."

Kate frowned. It wasn't easy for any doctor to leave her practice on such short notice. "Did she say what it was about?"

"No. Just asked which day I was off. She was trying to set up a family gathering. There's probably a message on your answering machine."

Kate didn't wait to find out. She picked up her cellular phone and called her home number, listening to the ring; then the answering machine kicked on. She punched a button to override, added her code, and listened as the messages began to play.

Their breakfasts arrived.

Jennifer had left a message. It didn't say much. Dinner Sunday evening at Lisa's. Kate closed her phone. "I don't like this."

"It gets worse. Marcus is flying back from Washington for the gathering."

Kate let that information sink in as she started on her hot blueberry pancakes. Their oldest brother, a U.S. Marshal, was interrupting his schedule to fly back to Chicago. "Jennifer is one step away from saying it's a family emergency." Let any member of the family say those words and the others dropped everything and came.

Stephen reached for his orange juice. "That's how I would read it."

"Any ideas?"

"None. I talked to Jennifer last Friday. She didn't say anything."

"Did she sound tense?"

"Tired maybe; unusual for her, but given the schedule she keeps, not unexpected."

Kate's pager went off. She glanced at the return number and grimaced. One of these days she was actually going to get to finish a meal. She set down her linen napkin as she got to her feet. "Work is calling. Can you join me for dinner? I'm off at six. I was planning to grill steaks."

"Glad to. Stay safe, Kate."

She grinned. "Always, Stephen. Put breakfast on my tab."

"I've got it covered."

She didn't have time to protest. It was an old debate. She smiled and let him win this round. "See you at six."

FBI special agent Dave Richman dealt with crises every day of his life. However, being a customer when a bank holdup went down was not one he would recommend.

His heart pounding, he rested his back against the reception desk and prayed the gunman stayed on the other side of the room.

The man had come in through the front door, shot four holes in the ceiling with a handgun, and ordered some of the customers and staff to leave, specific others to stay.

Dave had nearly shot him in the first few seconds of the assault, but the dynamite around the man's chest had halted that idea. The FBI playbook was simple: When facing dynamite, a loaded gun, and a lot of frightened people—don't get anyone killed.

In the initial commotion, Dave had managed to drop to the floor and get out of sight. He had about six feet of customer counter space that ended in an L that made up the reception desk he was hiding behind. So far, it was sufficient. The gunman had the hostages clustered together on the other side of the open room. He hadn't bothered to search the offices or the rest of the room. That most likely meant he was proceeding on emotion—and that, Dave knew, made him more dangerous than ever.

Dave would give anything to have his FBI team on-site. When the local cops surrounding the building ran the license plates for the cars in the parking lot, the trace on his own blue sedan would raise a flag at the FBI office. His team would be deployed because he was present. He had trusted his life to their actions in the past; it looked like he would be doing so again. The sound of sirens and the commotion outside had died down; by now he was sure they had the perimeter formed.

He leaned his head back. This was not exactly how he had planned to spend his birthday. His sister, Sara, was expecting him for lunch. When he didn't show up, she was going to start to worry.

There would be no simple solution to this crisis.

He was grateful God was sovereign.

From the tirade going on behind him, it was obvious this man had not come to rob the bank.

They had a bank robber that had not bothered to get any money. Kate was already assuming the worst.

The security camera video feeds had just been tapped and routed to the communications van. Four different camera angles. Two were static pictures of empty areas, the front glass doors, and the teller area for the drive up. One was focused high, covering the front windows, but it did show the hostages: five men and four women seated against the wall.

The fourth camera held Kate's attention. The man paced the center of the room. He was big and burly, his stride impatient.

The dynamite trigger held in his right hand worried her. It looked like a compression switch. Let go, and the bomb went off. There was no audio, but he was clearly in a tirade about something. His focus seemed to be on one of the nine hostages in particular, the third man from the end.

This man had come with a purpose. Since it apparently wasn't to rob the bank, that left more ugly possibilities.

He wasn't answering the phone.

Kate looked over at her boss, Jim Walker. She had worked for him for eight years. He trusted her judgment; she trusted him to keep her alive if things went south. "Jim, we've got to calm this situation down quickly. If he won't answer the phone, then we'll have to talk the old-fashioned way."

He studied the monitors. "Agreed."

Kate looked at the building blueprints. The entrance was a double set of glass doors with about six feet in between them. They were designed to be energy efficient in both winter and summer. Kate wished the architects had thought about security first. She had already marked those double doors and those six feet of open space as her worst headache. A no-man's-land. Six feet without cover.

"Graham, if I stay here—" she pointed—"just inside the double glass doors, can you keep me in line of sight?" He was one of the few people she would trust to take a shot over her shoulder if it were required.

He studied the blueprint. "Yes."

"Have Olsen and Franklin set up to cover here and here." She marked two sweeps of the interior. It would be enough. If they had to take the gun-man down, there would be limited ways to do it without blowing up a city block in the process.

Kate turned up the sleeves of her flannel shirt. Her working wardrobe at a scene was casual. She did not wear a bulletproof vest; she didn't even carry a gun. The last thing she wanted was to look or sound like a cop. Her gender, size, and clothing were designed to keep her from being perceived as one more threat. In reality, she was the worst threat the gunman had. The snipers were under her control. To save lives, she would take one if necessary.

Kate glanced again at the security monitors. There was a lot of the bank floor plan not covered by the cameras. There might be another gunman, more hostages—both were slim but potential realities. The risks were inevitable.

"Ian, try the phones one more time."

Kate watched the gunman's reaction. He turned to glare at the ringing phone, paced toward it, but didn't answer. Okay. It wouldn't get him to answer, but it did capture his attention. That might be useful.

It was time to go.

"Stay safe, Kate."

She smiled. "Always, Jim."

The parking lot had been paved recently; spots on the asphalt were sticky under her tennis shoes. Kate assessed the cops in the perimeter as she walked around the squad cars toward the bank entrance. Some of the rookies looked nervous. A few veterans she recognized had been through this with her before.

Her focus turned to the glass doors. The bank name was done in a bold white stencil on the clear glass; a smaller sign below listed the lobby and drive-up teller hours. Kate put her hand on the glass door and smoothly pulled it open, prepared sometime in the next six feet to get shot.

Dave saw the woman as she reached the front doors of the bank and couldn't believe what he was seeing. She came in, no bulletproof vest, apparently no gun, not even a radio. She just walked in.

God, have mercy. He had never prayed so intently for someone in his life, not counting his sister. Absolutely nothing was preventing that gunman from shooting her.

He pulled back from the end of the desk, knowing that if she saw him, her surprise would give away his presence. He moved rapidly toward the other end of the counter, his hand tight around his gun, knowing he was likely going to have to intervene.

"Stay there!" The gunman's voice had just jumped an octave.

She had certainly gotten the gunman's attention.

If she had followed protocol and worn a vest, Dave could have taken the gunman down while his attention was diverted. Instead, she had walked in without following the basic rules of safety, and his opportunity filtered away in the process. He silently chewed out the local scene commander. The city cops should have waited for the professional negotiators to arrive instead of overreacting and sending in a plainclothes cop, creating more of a problem than they solved.

Lady, don't you dare make things worse! Listen, say little, and at the first opportunity: Get out of here!

"You didn't answer the phone. Jim Walker would like to know what it is you want."

She had a calm, unhurried, Southern voice. Not what Dave was expecting. His initial assessment had certainly not fit his image of a hostage negotiator, but that calmness didn't sound forced. His attention sharpened. The negotiators he had worked with in the past had been focused, intense, purposeful men. This lady looked like everything about her was fluid. Tall. Slender. A nice tan. Long, auburn hair. Casual clothes. Too exotically beautiful to ever make it in undercover work, she wasn't someone you would forget meeting. She even stood relaxed. That convinced him. She had to be a negotiator; either that or a fool. Since his life was in her hands, he preferred to be optimistic.

"I've got exactly what I want. You can turn around and go back the way you came."

"Of course. But would you mind if I just sat right here for a few minutes first? If I come right back out, my boss will get ticked off."

It was how she said it. She actually made the guy laugh. "Sit down but shut up."

"Glad to."

Dave breathed a silent sigh of relief and eased his finger off the trigger. They wouldn't send a rookie into a situation like this, after all; but who was she? Not FBI, that much was certain.

Kate sat down where she stood in one graceful move and rested her head against the glass doors. Her heart rate slowly decelerated. She hadn't gotten herself shot in the first minute. That was always a good sign.

She scanned the faces of the hostages. They were all nervous, three of the women crying. The gunman was probably not enjoying that. The man the gunman was focused on looked about ready to have a coronary.

At least there were no heroics going on here. These nine folks were scared, nervous, ordinary people. Seeing it on the monitor had been one thing, confirming it directly was a relief. No athletes. No military types. She had lost hostages before who acted on their own.

She wished she could tell them to stay put, but the only communication she could make with them was in her actions. The more bored she appeared with the situation, the better. The goal was to get the gunman to relax a little. His barked humor had been a minor, very good sign. She would take it and every other one she could get.

Kate studied the bomb as the gunman paced. It was everything she had feared. Manning, her counterpart on the bomb squad, was going to have a challenge.

It was a pity God didn't exist. Someone, God if no one else, should have solved this man's problems before he decided to walk into this bank with dynamite and a gun. The gunman wouldn't agree with her, but options now were limited—he would end up in jail or dead. Not exactly happy alternatives. She had to make sure he didn't take nine innocent lives along with him.

Ten, counting hers.

She couldn't have the guy shot; his hand would come off the bomb trigger. She couldn't rush the guy; she would get herself shot. If she got shot, her family would descend on her like a ton of bricks for being so stupid. As she knew from firsthand experience, it was difficult enough recovering from an injury without having the entire O'Malley clan breathing down her neck as she did so.

Negotiating to get the hostages released was going to be a challenge. He didn't appear to want anything beyond control of the bank manager's fate—and he had that. Releasing hostages took something to exchange. She could go for sympathy for the crying women, but that would probably get her tossed out as well.

As time wore on, bargaining chips would appear she could use—food, water, the practical reality of how he would handle controlling this many people when faced with the need for restroom visits.

She could wait the situation out indefinitely, and slowly it would turn in her favor. But would he let that much time pass? Or would he escalate before then?

Dave had a difficult decision to make. Did he alert the cop of his presence and risk her giving away his position with her expression, or did he stay silent and watch the situation develop? He finally accepted that he had no choice. It would take more than one person to end this standoff. That was the reality. He eased his badge out of his pocket and flipped it open.

He moved forward, leaning around the end of the desk.

There was not even a twitch to indicate her surprise. No emotion across her face, no movement of her head, no quick glance in his direction. She flicked her index finger at him, just like she would strike an agate in a game of marbles.

An irritated flick at that, ordering him back.

Dave sat back on his heels. He would have been amused at her reaction had the situation been different. That total control of her emotions, her facial expression, her demeanor was a two-edged sword—it would keep his location safe, but it also meant it would be very hard to judge what she was thinking.

Her response told him a lot about her though. That silent flick of her finger had conveyed a definite order—one she expected to be obeyed without question. She knew how to get her point across. He felt sorry for anyone who would ever question her in a court of law. She must give defense attorneys fits.

He had to find some way to talk to her.

He opened the receptionist's desk drawer a fraction at a time and peered inside. He found what he hoped for—paper. He silently slid out several sheets and took out his pen. He had to make the message simple and the letters large and dark enough so she could read them with a mere glance.

What did he say first?

4 SHOTS. 2 LEFT.

She adjusted her sunglasses.

Okay, message received.

The best way to take this gunman down was from behind, by surprise. But the gunman would need to be close so that Dave could put his hand around that bomb trigger.

MOVE HIM TO ME.

She read the message. Several moments passed. When the gunman paced away from her, she shook her head ever so slightly.

Why not? His frustration was acute. There was no way for her to answer that.

RELEASE HOSTAGES.

She gave no response.

Dave grimaced. This was the equivalent of passing notes in high school, and he had done all of that he would ever like to do when he was a teen. Why had she not even tried to start a dialogue with the man?

TALK TO HIM!

Her fingers curled into a fist.

Dave backed off. Whatever she was considering, at the moment she didn't want to take suggestions. Frustration and annoyance competed for dominance within him. She had better have a great plan in mind. His life was in her hands.

He had no choice but to settle back and wait.

Kate flexed her fingers, forced to bury all her emotions into that one gesture. She would give her next paycheck to be able to go outside for about ten minutes and pound something. She not only had a cop in her midst, she had a would-be hero who wanted to give her backseat advice!

Someone had a federal badge; he thought he understood how to deal with any crisis he faced. That suggestion she move the gunman toward him had been truly stupid: Before any negotiations had been tried, he wanted to force a tactical conclusion. There was one word that defined her job: patience. This cop didn't have any, and he was going to get them all killed.

She had two people to keep calm: the gunman and the Fed. Right now it looked like the FBI agent was going to be the bigger problem. If he got it in his head to act, some innocent person was going to get killed, and she was the one sitting in the direct line of fire.

She never should have gotten up this morning.

Deal with it. Do the job.

Kate drew a quiet breath and turned her full attention to the man pacing away from her.

Dave shifted to ease a leg cramp as he listened to the conversation between the negotiator and the gunman. He knew her name now. Kate O'Malley. A nice Irish name for someone who didn't sound Irish.

The conversation had begun slowly, but over the last hour it had become a running dialogue. So far the topics had touched on nothing of significance to the situation. It was all small talk, and she had that down to an art form. It was too well controlled for it to be an accident. Dave wondered how long she could talk about nothing before she drove herself crazy. He knew very few cops who could tolerate such small talk. They were too factual, cut to the bottom line, take-charge people.

The gunman was still pacing, but his stride had slowed. Her constant soft cadence was beginning to work. Dave knew what she was doing, but he could still feel himself responding to that calm, quiet voice as well, his own tension easing. The stress of the situation was giving way to the fatigue that came from an overload of adrenaline fading from his system. He could only imagine how she was managing that energy drain. The last hour and a half felt like the longest day of his life.

He no longer wondered if she was the right person for this task; she had convinced him. She had a voice that could mesmerize a man. Soft, Southern, smooth. Dave enjoyed the sound. It conjured up images of candlelight dinners and intimate conversations.

This lady was controlling events with just her voice; it was something impressive to observe. Part of her plan was obvious. Wear the other side down; remove the sense of threat; build some equity that could be used later when it would matter.

He was learning a lot of minor information about her. She loved the Cubs. Disliked sitcoms. Thought the potholes in the neighborhood were atrocious. When she went for takeout, her first choice was spicy Chinese.

The topic shifted to which local restaurant made the best pizza. Dave

knew what she was doing, trying to convince the gunman to request food
be sent in. It would probably be laced with something designed to calm
the man down. He had to admire how she was working toward even that
minor objective with patience. He reached for his pen again. She was making him hungry, if not the gunman. He had been trying to figure out what
he could do to help her out. This kind of negotiation was tiring work. He
might as well make this a three-way conversation.

YOU FORGOT THE MUSHROOMS.

She never dropped the conversational ball as she smoothly mentioned
what exactly was inside a mushroom cap, if anyone wanted to know.

Dave smiled.

Since her plan was to sit there and talk, he could think of a few more
questions for her. She had to be running out of topics. He was more than
a little curious to learn about Kate O'Malley. She had him fascinated. She
was sitting in the midst of a stressful situation, accomplishing a nearly
impossible task, and yet looking and sounding like she didn't have a care
in the world. Her conversation was casual, her smile quick to appear. If
this was what she was like on the job, what was she like off duty?

FAVORITE MOVIE.

His query was met with the glimmer of a smile. Minutes later, she
smoothly changed the subject of the conversation to movies.

He had to stifle a laugh when she said her favorite movie was *Bugs
Bunny's Great Adventure*. It didn't matter if she actually meant it or was
simply showing an exquisitely refined sense of humor. It was the perfect
answer.

IS THIS OUR GREAT ADVENTURE?

High Noon.

Dave leaned his head back, not sure how to top that one. Kate
O'Malley was apparently a movie buff. It was nice to know they had something in common. If she could get them out of this safely, he would buy
the tickets and popcorn to whatever movie she wanted to see. He was certainly going to owe her. The idea was enough to bring a smile. It was one
debt he would enjoy paying.

Two

Kate watched the gunman pace away. Henry Lott was divorced, fighting cancer, had recently lost his job, and the bank manager had foreclosed on his home Monday. In the hour since she had convinced him to release the four women hostages, his anger had repeatedly flared, volatile and unpredictable. Wilshire Construction and First Union Bank were getting equal amounts of his hate.

She watched, her face impassive, as he waved the bomb trigger in front of the bank manager's face and pealed back one finger, then another, threatening to let go. One of these times it was not going to be an act. Henry would blow that dynamite.

Every couple months there was a case like this, one that actually scared her. She prepared for them, but she was never really ready. Going up against someone who was dying, who wanted to end his life by making a statement, left her little room to maneuver. She knew that. She didn't have to like it, but she did have to accept it.

She had bought them five hours and four hostages. If they were going to get the remaining hostages out alive, they would have to do it by force. The decision didn't come easy, for it was failure on her part, but protecting her pride wasn't part of her job. Henry Lott had finished talking, and it was time she made the recommendation. The bank manager whimpered, and the sound made her want to flinch.

The growing tension in the room had seeped into her muscles and bones; no matter how she tried to mentally divert for a moment and visualize herself somewhere else to get back a sense of distance and calm, the pressure inside didn't abate. Was this the day her family got the phone call they dreaded? Kate closed her eyes for a moment, took a deep breath, and accepted what was going to happen was going to happen.

I'm sorry, guys. I did my best.

She rested her weight back against her hand and tapped her finger twice.

A red dot blinked on the top of her left tennis shoe. She had been talking with Graham most of the day. Morse code was low tech, but it let them pass information back and forth. She tapped out a terse message for Jim.

The present assault plan called for a breach that would come from two directions—they'd blow the steel security door by the teller windows; two seconds later they'd shatter the front glass doors. Flash grenades would come in to freeze the situation. She would have two seconds to clear the glass doors, reach Henry Lott, and close her hands around the bomb trigger.

High risk. She could get shot. She could fail, which was worse.

Her peripheral vision scanned the place where the FBI agent hid. What was he thinking? The notes had ceased during the last twenty minutes. The risk of his being discovered increased with the passing of time; another good reason they should act sooner versus later. She wished she had a way to coordinate with him, warn him. He had turned out to be surprisingly good company during the last few hours. She wanted a chance to say thanks for the notes. His humor was sharp and dry; it came across even in his two- or three-word shorthand. He had stayed relaxed in this tense situation, a fact she appreciated.

It didn't take long for her boss to reach a decision. The teams were moving into position.

She needed Henry Lott to be within five feet. She planned to hit him and take him down, pinning the trigger between them. He had seventy pounds on her; she was going to have a fight on her hands in the few moments before her team could reach them. The frustration of not being able to talk him into giving up would solve some of that disparity. The FBI agent should be able to close the distance to help. She would do whatever it took to win.

She got the signal from Graham. The teams were in position, ready for her mark.

She knew exactly where she would like Henry to be when she made her move. She tapped out another request: Ring the phone.

Henry started across the room toward the ringing phone on the receptionist desk. Kate toned out his words, looking only at the distance. Eight feet, seven feet, six feet...in range. Her fingers began to fold one by one, controlling the first blast. Three. Two. One. Fist.

The steel door blew apart.

Kate surged forward, ignoring the gun, going down with the man, her forearm across his windpipe. Her hand closed around his on the trigger release.

They hit the marble floor hard, pelted by exploding glass.

Henry tried to toss her off him. Her shin took a kick from a steel-tipped boot. She felt her wrist going around and fought back with desperate energy. With both hands around his to keep the bomb trigger down, her face was exposed. She saw his left hand coming around and braced for the broken nose. It wouldn't be the first punch she had taken. His blow connected, but it wasn't with her. The FBI agent grunted in pain, threw a short jab back.

She forgave the agent the elbow to her ribs. It was a fight between two equals with her sandwiched between them. She did her best to keep her head down. Wires slid up around her fingers; dynamite wedged against her abdomen.

Henry Lott stopped moving.

She hung suspended in time for a moment, wondering if it was over, waiting for Henry to move. Then she was hearing again, feeling again. The rushing sound of the assault teams, of hostages being pulled clear, made it into her consciousness; muscles quivered from the sudden stress release; forming bruises demanded attention.

"Do you have it?" The FBI agent demanded, his weight still sandwiching her.

"Got it." She was literally curled around the bomb trigger, clutching it like a treasure. Her hands were slick with sweat, and her fingers were cramping, but she had it.

"Don't move."

What did he think she was going to do? Get up and dance? Something sharp was digging into her chest, and she could feel wires pinching her fingers. "Fine. I won't move. But you could," she replied, letting her tone of voice carry a fine bite to it for the first time since she had entered the bank.

He shifted to the side, and she got her first full breath since the fight had begun. She closed her eyes to enjoy it. She was quivering with the fatigue. A wave of nausea swept over her as her body literally shook off the stress. The entire situation had been too close for comfort.

Teammates crowded around, surrounding them, her boss in the front of the group. "Franklin, get that syringe from the doc; make sure this guy stays out. Let's get bomb disposal in here."

"Hostages?" Kate asked, forcing her head to clear and her voice to firm.

"All fine." Jim was looking at the device. "Can you hold that trigger for a few minutes while Manning takes this apart?"

"I'm not planning to let go."

Somebody laughed.

"Okay," Jim said. "Let's clear this place of nonessential personnel. Good job, Kate. I'll see you again in a few minutes. Dave, your team is waiting for you outside."

The FBI agent shook his head. "I'll be out with Kate."

Her boss considered him for a moment, then nodded. He got to his feet. The room began to clear.

Kate was not so willing to concede the point. "I appreciate the thought. Now would you get out of here?"

He sat on the floor beside Henry, breathing hard, looking at her. She frankly enjoyed looking back; he was a good-looking man. His sandy hair was ruffled and the split lip had to hurt. He had the sleek look of an athlete, and she had learned firsthand that his bulk was well-conditioned muscle. This was not an FBI agent who spent his days behind a desk.

"What's the matter? Tired of my company?" The twinkle in his eyes said he was humoring her. She had no hope of getting him to leave. The fact he told her no with a smile didn't lessen her irritation with his answer; it increased it. He was cocky and wrong again. He didn't belong in here. She sighed silently. That was the problem with guys; they always had to be heroes.

The only danger for him at the moment was if she let go of the bomb trigger; the realization made her silently chuckle. She wondered if he had given more than a passing thought to the fact she was the one still protecting him as he sat there keeping her company.

Accents were a hobby, and his was a delight. He was British. Her sister Jennifer was going to be so jealous. If he insisted on staying, then she was going to enjoy it. "Keep talking."

"About what?"

"Anything. I like your accent."

His grin was quick. "Don't knock yours, Southern. I could listen to you all day."

"You have."

"I enjoyed it, too, despite the circumstances." He reached over and feathered a hand through her hair. "You've got glass slivers in your hair."

His touch made her freeze. In any other situation, she would have slapped his hand away, but she couldn't move, and she was suddenly glad she had to remain motionless. She had already shown this man too much of herself in the past hours of conversation, letting him know how prickly she was about being touched by any man other than her brothers would have been humiliating. As his fingers brushed through her hair, she took a deep breath and unexpectedly felt herself relax; it was a comforting touch. "I'm sure I sparkle."

He chuckled. "Actually, you do." He leaned over to brush glass fragments from her shoulder and tensed. "I should have hit the guy harder. You're bleeding."

"It was quite a shower of glass. A few cuts were inevitable." Kate could feel them across her shoulders, her arms. They were beginning to sting.

"You've got more than a few." He moved to let Manning take his place and came around to her side. "Don't lean back." He brushed aside the glass fragments on her shirt with care.

"The cuts are not that big a deal." He ignored her comment. "You never did tell me your name."

"Dave Richman."

"Cute notes."

He leaned over to see her face. "Nice small talk."

She narrowed her gaze but found nothing in his expression to contradict his words. The last Fed she had worked with had panned what she did as being trivial chitchat. Dave had just moved a step out of the hole he had dug for himself with that MOVE HIM TO ME ridiculous note. "It's my specialty."

"It saved lives, including mine. I owe you."

She scowled at the idea. "Don't get too grateful. It was my job. I didn't do it specifically for you."

He laughed, and it was a nice sound. Kate let herself smile. With all Dave's notes asking questions, she might have been chatting more than usual; it was hard to tell after the fact. Her abused muscles cramped. She closed her eyes against the pain, walling it off.

"Another minute and the paramedics will be in here."

"Manning, is Stephen out there?"

"Pacing."

Anticipating the lecture, she winced. "Don't hurry." She saw Dave's look of curiosity. "My brother is one of those paramedics you mentioned."

"Ahh. Be glad you've got family to get on your case."

He had no idea. "Three brothers, three sisters. I'm going to get killed." She had given them cause to worry, which was what annoyed her the most.

"It should be an interesting evening."

"You have a knack for understatements." Remaining motionless was hard work. "You know what I would really like right now?" She knew she was starting to ramble, but the fatigue felt like a heavy blanket, and words had always been her first defense.

"What?"

"A good steak, a cold drink, and a nap, not necessarily in that order."

"Sorry, but what I think you're going to get is an ambulance ride, a couple needles, and some stitches."

Great. Just how she wanted to spend her evening. "What an unappealing thought."

Manning set aside the wire clippers. "You can let go, Kate; it's defused."

The sense of relief was intense but not quite complete. "You're sure?" She wasn't passing judgment, but she was the one holding the trigger.

"It won't go boom," Manning promised.

She eased open her grip on the trigger, heard the faint click of open contacts.

Now she felt the relief. She gladly moved away from Henry Lott. Manning started moving the dynamite to an explosive ordinance box. As soon as it was clear, cops were waiting to handcuff Henry and carry him outside.

Kate sat on the marble floor, content to wait for Manning to finish. It felt better than just good to have this situation over with. She didn't even cringe as she thought about all the paperwork the tactical response would demand. For the moment she was just going to savor the fact it had ended with the gunman and all the hostages still alive.

She draped her arms across her knees and looked around at all the damage. "What a mess."

Dave nodded. "Looks like a bomb went off. Doors blown in, a couple ceiling tiles down, glass everywhere."

She looked over at him. "You have a wicked sense of humor."

"Thanks."

"Don't mention it."

Humor was too rare a commodity in this business not to pause and enjoy having found it in an unexpected place. She could really get to like this guy, despite his charge-right-in attitude and his annoying habit of not listening to her when she was right. They were grinning at each other when they were interrupted. "This is not a good way to start the weekend, Kate."

"Stephen, it's a great way to start the weekend. Go away."

Beside her, Dave choked back a laugh. "Behave."

She reluctantly turned her attention to her brother. "I'm only banged up, I promise."

Stephen set down the case he carried and surveyed her. "At least you didn't get yourself shot. What did you do, go swimming in the broken glass?"

"It's not as bad as it looks."

He gave her a skeptical look. "What else hurts besides the cuts?" He used sterile gauze to wipe away the blood so he could look at the cut on her right arm.

"My tailbone. I've been sitting on this marble floor all day."

"Seriously."

"My left shoulder. I hit the marble floor hard. And my headache is a killer."

Because she had no choice, she sat still as he and his partner dealt with the cuts; she winced when gentle hands hit bruises. Stephen frowned as he touched the back of her head. "Nice goose egg."

"He got in a lucky blow."

"How's the vision?"

"Fine."

"Hmm."

She looked at the gurney that was wheeled in with suspicion. "Stephen, I'm walking out of here."

"If you want to pass out in front of your team, you can. Your blood pressure is low even for you."

"Fading adrenaline. Give me a break."

He accepted something from his partner. "Close your eyes; you don't like needles."

"Stick me with that and you'll be fixing your own steak tonight."

"Would you rather me do it or a nurse you don't know?"

"You play dirty." She turned her head and squeezed her eyes closed.

"It's done." He taped down the IV line. "You want a grape or cherry lollipop?"

She considered hitting him. She plucked a cherry one from his pocket. "You know the only reason I let you get away with the needle is so I can get one of these."

"Jennifer bribes her patients with them."

"Her patients are two years old. I don't like the inference."

"You're the one who made it."

She retrieved the grape one and handed it to Dave. "Eat this and be quiet." She had heard his stifled chuckle.

"Stephen," Dave interceded as he unwrapped the sucker, "you'd better quit while you're ahead."

Her brother looked over at him. "Probably. Would you?"

Dave considered the question for a moment. "No. She's too cute when she's annoyed."

"I knew I would like you."

Kate scowled. "Gentlemen, now that you've bonded, can we go?"

"Sure. But you're taking the gurney." Stephen moved it beside her and grinned. "Just sit on it, Kate. I won't make you go out with the straps and the blanket."

She knew it was going to be a rough afternoon when getting up to move to the stretcher made her light-headed. Dave didn't release his grip on her arm until she was seated and her legs were up.

She saw his concern despite their lighthearted banter, and it bothered her. She didn't want his final impression of her to be one of weakness. It wasn't pride; it was the reality of her job. Managing impressions was critical to keeping her reputation intact—a reputation that insured her voice carried weight when she was called into a crisis situation. If the consensus about her around the FBI offices six months from now was *got hurt* rather than *solved it,* the next time she worked a case with them she would be playing from a weak hand.

Stephen squeezed her hand. She returned the pressure. She knew what he had been doing, the cad. He'd raised her blood sugar level, got an IV line in place, stopped the bleeding, and kept her mind off what he and his partner were doing. He had always been excellent at his job. Stephen was born to the role of rescuer.

There were days she would give anything to trade in her role of nego- tiator for something more along Stephen's role of white knight. She had to live and work with gray, in the middle of the violence, right at the edge of the grim reaper's hand of death. Getting banged up occasionally in the process just went with her territory.

"Dave, there's room if you want to ride along," Stephen offered.

"I'll take it."

"There's no need," Kate protested, not liking the idea.

Dave's frown silenced her. Having been silenced by a look from some of the best, she changed her profile of him, privately amused. He could simply cool his eyes to convey he didn't like your answer as easily as he could warm them to share humor. It was a trait a good leader perfected.

"Kate, the media is all over this. Be prepared." Stephen warned.

The media would likely make her life miserable for days to come. The two newspapers, not to mention the local newscasts, vied with each other for the most dramatic presentation of a crisis like this. Ignoring the press was becoming her second occupation. "Let's see how many pictures they can take of your back," she suggested to Stephen. That solution to the problem was one of her favorites.

"My pleasure. The squad will love the publicity."

"This is not a steak." Kate used the plastic fork to check the suspicious entree. It was bad enough she had lost the debate and been admitted to the hospital for the night; meatloaf for dinner was adding insult to injury.

Stephen got to his feet. "Want me to go get you a cheeseburger?"

"Make it two and a vanilla shake."

"Eat your salad."

She poked at the limp lettuce. "It's dead." She reached for the sealed pudding cup. "At least they can't ruin dessert."

Stephen tweaked her foot. "I'll be back shortly. Behave yourself while I'm gone."

"You want good behavior, too?" She grinned. "You're pushing it, Stephen. You already overruled me on staying here for the night."

"I managed to stop the family from descending on you, so we're even."

She opened the pudding cup. "It's a brief reprieve and you know it," she countered. "Sunday's dinner is going to be interesting. I sure hope Jennifer has earth-shaking news to share or I'm going to be toast."

Stephen laughed. "You walked into it. I'll head the family off for a few days, but after that you're on your own." They had been calling from the moment she reached the hospital.

"I hate being the center of attention."

"Next time don't get hurt."

She couldn't exactly argue that point.

There was a tap on the door. "May I come in?"

"Hi, Dave. Sure." Kate pushed away the tray. "Stephen's smuggling in real food. You want something?"

Stephen paused by the door as he reached Dave. "Cheeseburger, Polish, chili? I'm heading across the street."

"A Polish with the works would be great."

Stephen nodded. "I'll be back in a few minutes. She's getting feisty, so watch yourself."

"Thanks a lot, Stephen." Kate settled back on the pillows and watched Dave take a seat. He looked tired. She wasn't surprised. It was after 7 P.M., and his afternoon must have been much like hers, full of doctors and official statements. She hadn't seen him since she had entered the ER and the medical community had surrounded her.

He stretched his legs out. "You look better than I expected."

"Feisty." She shook her head. "Stephen needs to work on his adjectives."

"I don't know. It fits," he replied easily, taking Stephen's side, probably just because he could. He glanced around at all the flowers. "It looks like you have had some company."

Kate looked at the bouquets, embarrassed at all the attention they represented. "I was just doing my job. You would think I got shot or something."

"The cops like you. It's not like they can bring flowers when one of the guys gets hurt."

"Your sister sent me a bouquet—the orchids."

"Did she?" Dave grinned. "You mean she limited it just to flowers? I was afraid she was going to drown you in gifts, she was so relieved to get my phone call."

"This is so embarrassing. I even got flowers from the owner of the bank."

Dave looked over the arrangements. "Which one?"

"Care to guess?"

He thought about it. "Zealous mortgage management. Rather stale donuts for 9 A.M. We have an owner who doesn't like to spend his money on others. The wildflower bouquet."

"You're good."

"I'm right?" He got up to retrieve the card and grinned as he read it. "Nathan Young. Owner, First Union Bank."

He put down the card, gestured to the two dozen red roses. "Who's your beau?"

She wondered if it was his British side that made the abrupt question come out sounding so stiff. Or was he just irked? She buried the smile fighting to be released. "Marcus. Check out the card."

He hesitated.

"Go ahead. You'll appreciate it."

"Lecture to come, Ladybug." He tapped the card. "Sounds like family."

He did sound relieved. Kate stored that pleasure away to enjoy later. She didn't want him to be interested in her, but she had to admit it felt good to know he was. "Oldest brother. And no, I don't want to explain the nickname." The roses were just like Marcus. Extravagant. Unnecessary. Wonderfully sweet. He knew her too well. She would look at them all night and know if he was not a thousand miles away, he would be sprawled in that chair for the night. The friendship went so deep she wondered at times if Marcus could read her mind. Today had shaken her up more than she cared to admit.

Dave settled back in the chair and stretched his legs out. "You've got a great family."

"Yes, I do." It was a subject that could make her sappy when she was tired. "I heard a rumor it's your birthday today."

"I couldn't think of a nicer person to spend it with."

She couldn't prevent the smile. He was smooth. "Seriously, I'm sorry your plans for the day got so messed up."

He shrugged. "I'm alive to enjoy it, mainly thanks to you. Have they told you how long you will be here?"

"I've been promised I can leave tomorrow morning." She held up the hand with the IV. "The antibiotics will be done in another hour; the doctors are just being cautious. All that glass was covered with flash grenade residue."

"How often do days like this happen?"

Why did he want to know? Concern was nice; worry was another way of smothering. She gave him the benefit of the doubt for now. "Days when you wonder if you will walk away in one piece?"

"Something like that."

"Nothing is routine, but every couple months there's a case like this one that tests the edge."

"That often?"

Definitely a frown. She sighed. Next he was going to be critiquing how she did her job. She couldn't prevent it from being dangerous, but someone had to do it. "In the decade I've been doing this, I've seen it change for the worse. People choose violence as their first course of action these days."

The door pushed open as Stephen backed in, carrying a sack and a cardboard container holding three drinks, rescuing her from telling Dave, *Thank you, but I know how to do my job.* Stephen sat on the edge of the bed and distributed the food. "Two cheeseburgers, Kate. I loaded them with hot stuff for you."

"This is great. Thanks." Her interrupted breakfast had been a long time ago. She listened to the guys talk while she focused on her dinner.

Stephen caught her in a yawn as she finished the second sandwich. "Ready to call it a day?"

Stiff, sore, and feeling every minute of the very long day, she reluctantly admitted the obvious. "Getting there. Are you picking me up tomorrow morning?"

"Ten o'clock, unless you page me earlier," he confirmed.

"Make it nine."

"Okay, nine."

She wasn't sure what to say to Dave. She wasn't interested in saying good-bye and yet to suggest something else…this was awkward. "Thanks for your help today."

She held still as his hand brushed down her cheek, and she saw her surprise briefly reflected on his own face. Clearly he hadn't thought before he made the gesture, had startled himself as much as her. It was nice to know she wasn't the only one feeling off balance at the moment. They were work acquaintances, and yet it kept jumping across to something more personal.

She had little experience deciphering the emotions reflected in his blue eyes; gentleness wasn't common in her world.

"It was my pleasure. Maybe next time we can meet by simply saying hello?" Dave said softly.

"I would like that."

His eyes held hers, searching for something. When he moved his hand to his back pocket and broke eye contact to look at his wallet, she blinked at the abrupt loss she felt. "Good. Give me a call, let me know how you're doing." He put a business card by the phone. "My cellular phone number is on the back."

Kate nodded, well aware of Stephen's speculation. "Good night, guys."

The FBI regional offices were on the eighteenth floor of the east tower in the business complex. Dave tossed his keys on his desk and went to brew a pot of coffee. It was 8:45 P.M. He had some questions regarding Henry Lott that needed answers. He was too on edge to consider going home.

There was such a contradiction in Kate. Who was the real Kate—the cop who had been coolly assessing the situation, prepared if necessary to call for a sniper shot? Or the woman who had been defusing the situation with her chatter—who liked pepperoni pizza, her steak cooked to just a hint of pink, mystery novels, basketball, marathon races, and chocolate chip ice cream?

The two images didn't mix.

He stirred sugar into his coffee and half smiled. He liked her. Despite the contradiction, he really liked her. She could keep her sense of humor in a crisis.

She was going to be hard to get to really know. One moment she was open and easy to read, the next impossible to fathom. Given the nature of her job, he should have expected that. He had crossed a line in those last few moments at the hospital, sensing an unexpected loneliness in her, wanting to comfort and not knowing how to reach her with words. He owed her. He couldn't dismiss that fact even if it did annoy her when he expressed it.

At least they had both come out of the day relatively unhurt. He touched his split lip and grimaced. It stung—he could only imagine what she must be feeling about now. He walked back to his office, set down his coffee cup, and turned on his desk lamp.

It didn't take a name on the door for the office to be recognizable as his. He liked a clear desk, organized files, large white boards, and space to pace and think. The whimsical sketches on the wall, done by his sister, were worth a minor fortune. A signed football from his brother-in-law was under glass on the credenza.

He did not appreciate almost getting killed on his thirty-seventh birthday. The situation had scared his sister. Sara, having been stalked for years by a man trying to kill her, had already taken enough scares in her lifetime. He wanted a few questions answered. He would start with Henry Lott's former employer, Wilshire Construction, then take a look at First Union Bank.

Night had descended. The shadows around the hospital room had finally disappeared into true darkness. Kate preferred the night over dusk. There was a little more truth in the darkness; it at least didn't pretend to hide danger. She reached over and turned on the bedside light.

It was after ten. Her shoulder ached. She was tired of staring at the ceiling. Fatigue had crossed into the zone where it now denied sleep. Normally after a crisis, she would go shoot baskets for a while, bleed off the stress. Denied the release, it was hard to settle for the night.

Accustomed to thinking in the quiet of the night, she reached for the pad of paper Stephen had brought her.

Why was Jennifer coming to town?

Kate wrote the question on the pad of paper and flared several lines out. Work opportunity? Boyfriend? Problem in the practice? Someone giving her trouble? Someone she wants us to help?

It could be practically anything. Kate didn't like not knowing. She couldn't fix it until she knew the problem. Family mattered. Intensely. She looked across the room at the roses. She was glad Marcus was coming.

Staring at the phone, she considered calling him. It was late on the East Coast, but Marcus never cared what time she called. If she woke him up, she'd hear the amused, warm sleepy tone in his voice that someday would delight a wife. He would talk for as long as she liked. She let down her guard with him. He knew it. They were the oldest two of the O'Malley clan and had been friends a very long time. In the quiet of the night they had talked about many things. He worried about her just like she worried about him. It went with the jobs they had.

If she called tonight, he would know she couldn't unwind. It would be better to call tomorrow.

She wished she knew how the case investigation was going. Her teammates were busy while she sat in a hospital. She had never been one to enjoy sitting on the sidelines of an investigation. They had to find the source of the dynamite, how Henry had procured it, where he had built the device. There was a good chance there were more explosives than the amount he had used. If she called the office at this time of night, from the hospital, she would never hear the end of it.

Kate dropped the pad of paper back on the table, causing Dave's business card to flutter to the floor. It took some careful maneuvering to pick it up. She didn't want to lose it.

She turned the business card over in her hand. Bothering him at home was not an option, but the card gave his direct number at work. What were the odds she was not the only one with questions?

The phone call surprised him. Dave glanced up from the printout he held and considered letting his voice mail answer it. His sister Sara would have called his cellular number.

It was his private line. He reached over and took the call. "Dave Richman."

"I hoped you would be at the office."

The sound of her voice was unexpected. "Kate. What's wrong?"

"Relax. I just can't sleep."

Some of his tension faded but not the concern. "The cuts bothering you?"

"They are itching like mad. Listen, can you pull the EOC records for Wilshire Construction?"

"Kate, come on. You're in the hospital. What are you doing working?"

"I need the overtime," she replied dryly. "I bet the data is somewhere on your desk."

Dave shifted printouts even as he smiled. "What are you looking for?"

"Was his termination from Wilshire Construction with cause, or was it age discrimination?"

He flipped through the Equal Opportunity Commission records. "Henry didn't file a formal complaint, but several others from the company have in the last six months. It's possible."

"I thought so. Have you looked at the mortgage?"

She was asking the same questions he was. It was nice to know they worked a case the same way. "Not yet. I'm still checking out the bank."

"Anything interesting?"

"Possibly. First Union's foreclosure rate is about triple that of last year. The bank is one of several owned by Nathan Young. He has a group here in Chicago, another group in New York, and recently bought his first one in Denver. It looks like the same trend is in place at all the banks."

"He's building up cash," Kate concluded.

"It looks that way."

"So Henry's complaint might have some basis in fact."

"We'll keep digging," Dave agreed. "His financial records should be available tomorrow. If there was something irregular in his foreclosure, we'll find it."

"Thanks for starting the search."

"We both want the answers. ATF is working on tracing the explosives. An initial search of his home did not reveal where the device had been built. They sealed the place to do a more thorough search tomorrow."

"Good. I'll touch base with Manning."

She was decompressing. He should have realized it earlier. "I wish I had more to offer."

"This helps."

The silence on the phone crossed the subtle line from a pause to being too long. "Kate, you did a good job today."

"Maybe. At least everyone walked away alive."

"Ease up on yourself. Some situations don't lend themselves to peaceful endings."

"I know. Ignore the whining. I don't normally second-guess myself." He heard her muffle the phone and speak to someone. "The nurse is here."

"I'll hold on."

"Oh. Okay, thanks."

His answer had thrown her. Studying the sketch on the wall across from him, Dave smiled as he waited for her to return.

"I'm back."

"What else do you want to talk about?"

"It's late. I ought to let you go."

He wasn't going to let her go that easily. He enjoyed talking with her. "We're both old enough not to have curfews. Enough about work. Tell me about where you lived to acquire that accent."

"I've heard it sounds good over the phone."

"Quit flirting." He meant it, but still he smiled. She would thank him in the morning. She was tired, on painkillers, and it had been an emotional day for them both; another day, a better time, and his answer would be different.

Her laugh was as nice as her voice. "You know when you dream as a kid about what you want to be?"

"Sure. I wanted to be a pilot, fly fighter jets off an aircraft carrier."

"You would. I just wanted to be different than everyone around me. The South seems as different as you could get. So I decided to change even my voice."

"You grew up here in Chicago?"

"Elm and Forty-seventh."

"You're serious."

"It's hard not to have the accent." She had turned it off like a switch.

"You're good."

"I'll take that as a compliment. So, did you ever learn to fly?"

Why had she wanted to change everything about herself? He let her change the subject rather than ask the question. He had a feeling it would stir painful memories. "As a matter of fact, yes. It's the best place to be in the world, the open sky."

"How so?"

"Freedom, speed, control of an intricate machine."

"You're a good pilot?"

"Yes. Would you like to go up sometime? The jet is at O'Hare."

"Just like that, the jet is at O'Hare."

"I have to fly something. I outgrew the piper cub when I was in high school."

"Maybe I'll take you up on that."

"You should." He didn't like the image of her awake, alone, in a hospital room. "Would you like me to come over? We could watch an old movie; I could smuggle in dessert." He never would have made the suggestion under ordinary circumstances, preferring to keep his work and private life separate, but the events of the afternoon had shredded that normal reticence, left him feeling very protective about her. She mattered to him.

"Tempting."

"But you are passing." The disappointment was intense.

"Taking a rain check. It's late. You need to go home."

Truth or politeness? He wasn't sure. He'd have to make sure she didn't politely file and forget about that rain check. "What time will you be at your office tomorrow?" If she were working from her hospital room, she would not be taking the day off, not with the open questions in this case.

"Ten."

"Call me then, and I'll fill you in on anything else I've found. I'm meeting my sister and her husband for a late lunch, but I'll be here in the morning."

"I'll call you. Go home."

The order made him smile. Normally only his sister bothered to fuss about such things. "Soon. Good night, Kate."

Three

There was no place like home. Kate walked in the front door of her apartment Wednesday night, kicked it shut, and gave a welcomed sigh of relief. A long day at work had resulted in more questions than answers. Nothing about this case with Henry Lott was proving simple to solve. She had tossed in the towel half an hour ago, shoved work in her briefcase, and said good night to Graham. The second day soreness made movement painful and nagged a headache to life.

The rich smell of flowers lingered heavy in the still air in the apartment. Stephen had brought the flowers over after he dropped her off at work. The window air-conditioner unit in the bedroom rumbled to life, breaking the silence and stirring the air. Kate found the sound comforting.

The apartment was not large, but it was sufficient for her needs. She had taken her time to make it her own space, create herself a much-needed haven. The place was warm, comfortable, cozy. Her sister Lisa called it beautiful. Kate had tried. Hardwood floors. Plush furniture. Bold fabric on wingback chairs. She needed someplace in her life where she could relax.

Kate dropped her gym bag by her bedroom door and nudged off her tennis shoes. She went looking for dinner, too tired to really care what she found.

A new note under the smile face magnet on the refrigerator caught her attention. "Ice cream in the freezer, caramel sauce in the refrigerator." *Bless you, Lisa.*

Dessert sounded good.

She fixed a sundae, licking the spoon as she walked back to the living room. She pushed the play button on her answering machine as she walked by.

Reporter. Reporter. Yet another reporter. It was time to change her unlisted number again; it always managed to eventually leak. She was faintly surprised they hadn't staked out her apartment.

She flipped through two days worth of mail—bills, magazines, junk mail. The bills she dropped on the small desk, the magazines went on the coffee table, and the rest she tossed without opening.

Marcus.

Kate paused to listen. Good, his flight was due in Sunday afternoon.

Reporter.

The next message stopped her in her tracks. "Hello, Kate O'Malley. I've been looking for you, and what do I see—you made the news last night. We'll have to meet soon."

It was not a voice she recognized. Puzzled, she played the message again. The words were innocuous, but the tone wasn't. She did not want to meet this guy. His voice had a sinister edge. Probably someone recently released from jail. She sighed and ejected the cassette. She would make a copy of the tape, as she did with all questionable calls. There were several dozen in the archives.

It fit the kind of day it had been.

She opened her briefcase on the coffee table and pulled out the work she had brought home. Henry Lott's financial records. Dave had sent copies over that morning. She closed the briefcase so she didn't have to look at the copies of the negotiation tapes. Listening to hours of dialogue, knowing she had failed to resolve the situation short of a tactical conclusion, was not something she wanted to face tonight.

She turned on the television to catch the late news.

The third news story was another segment on the bank incident yesterday. She had hoped it would have a one-day shelf life.

Kate watched tonight's clip, knowing in advance that it was going to make her mad. Reporter Floyd Tucker and the police department mixed together like oil and water. This was one of his more blatant accusations of police incompetence. Two of the hostages claimed the police had put their lives at risk. A former member of the National Association of Hostage Negotiators critiqued what was known about the case and declared the tactical conclusion to be a use of excessive force.

She shut off the television and tossed the remote control on the table. "Floyd, your expert lost 28 percent of his hostages during the three years he worked in Georgia." She wished Floyd would become some other city's menace, but no one else would hire him.

The police PR department declared the case under review. Floyd made a big deal of that fact. Kate wished he were at least an accurate reporter. A review was always done when a tactical response was taken. She wasn't looking at spending her weekend working for the pleasure of it.

She had dreamed about the bank last night, had watched the bomb go off in her hands. She didn't need the news to remind her. The news story would create more work for her. Case notes were never easy to write when a tactical conclusion was required. It became a psychological assessment of Henry Lott—observations, rationale, an after-the-fact review of the tapes. She would be questioned on her decision; and the more complete she could make her case notes, the less time she would be under scrutiny. These notes would be read more widely than most. The bank's insurance company was already hounding her boss to produce the report.

The phone rang.

She considered ignoring it, then realized she had failed to replace the cassette in the answering machine.

"Hello?"

"I guess I don't need to ask if you saw the news."

Kate relaxed. Dave. "Floyd Tucker is not on my Christmas card list."

"I can see why. It was a very unflattering piece. Ignore him."

She wedged the phone against her shoulder as she got up and rummaged through the desk drawer to find another tape for the answering machine. "With pleasure. How was lunch with your sister?"

"Considering the shock I gave her yesterday, not bad."

"It's always hard on those who have to wait and worry, who can't affect the outcome."

"Yes. Sara has been there before. She's tough. I think you would like her."

"Probably. I like her brother."

"Flirting, now flattery. You're good for my ego."

She could hear the amusement in Dave's voice. This was the third time he had deflected a comment rather than follow up on it. She was glad he wasn't taking her too seriously. He was too much a threat to her peace of mind, and she didn't have time for a relationship. But an interaction like this—lighthearted, fun—was okay. She could live with the line he was drawing. Her heart had been mangled enough in the past. She settled back on the couch. "I think I had best change the subject. Thanks for sending over the information this morning."

"I hope some of it will be useful. I hear Manning found more dynamite."

"A partially filled crate in the crawl space under Henry's home. ATF has the crate numbers to trace, but the markings are old. It will take them some time."

She had spent the day working with Manning trying to figure out where it had come from. Henry wasn't talking. Wilshire Construction, the most obvious place it could have been obtained, claimed nothing was missing from its inventory. Did Henry have help obtaining the explosives? It was a critical question to get answered. She hoped she would find a clue in the financial data spread out before her.

"Did you see his correspondence with the bank?" She pushed the papers around until she found copies of the letters she sought.

The letters found in his home were enlightening. The correspondence stretched back about eight months and had gone as high as the bank owner, Nathan Young, although it was doubtful Mr. Young had ever seen the letter. The reply to that letter had come from a vice president, Mr. Peter Devlon.

The correspondence on one hand suggested a willingness by the bank to work with Henry, and on the other hand took a very hard-line stance. It looked like First Union Bank and the corporate offices had been acting at cross-purposes. It was clear Henry had felt he was being jerked around.

"They were faxed over a short time ago. Henry had been building toward the crisis for some time."

Because of the damage to the bank, employees had not been allowed back inside the building yet. Kate still hadn't seen the bank's version of the mortgage dispute. "I'm thinking about paying the bank president, Nathan Young, a visit. Ask him about the letters, follow up on that foreclosure rate trend you noticed."

"I would enjoy tagging along for that visit."

"I'll give you a call."

"Did you work all day?"

"Yes." She stretched out on the couch and leaned her head back against the padded armrest. Talking to Dave at the end of the day was a nice way to end the evening.

"Want to cash in that rain check? I'll bring over a pizza."

She looked at the bowl of ice cream and smiled. She was not going to feel guilty. "I'm lousy company at the moment. I've still got work to do."

"All the more reason to accept. If you're going to work on at home, you should at least have company. I'm a good sounding board."

After telling Stephen and Lisa she was looking forward to a quiet evening, the realization she didn't want to spend the evening alone surprised her. "What do you like on your pizza? I'll order one from Carla's down the street."

"Make it with onions so I'll only be tempted to kiss you good night."

Her heart fluttered hard, then settled. She couldn't prevent the soft laugh at his rueful tone and carefully chosen words. "You would have to disarm me first anyway. I don't date cops."

"And here I thought that was my line."

Her amusement deepened. "Do you have my address?"

"And your phone number."

"Cute. Come over and I'll put you to work."

"Expect me in twenty-five minutes."

Kate called Carla's and placed an order for a large supreme pizza.

She had a cop coming over to share a pizza. Not exactly a common occurrence.

She had her cliff note reasons for why she didn't date cops: two people with pagers, long uncontrollable work hours, the dangers in each job. She didn't need to be smothered by someone trying to keep her safe. She had also learned with time that while it was wonderful to have someone available to talk with who understood her job, that also meant there was no place to escape work. And underneath those answers, was the real reason she rarely shared—she wanted to date someone safe. Cops were interesting, made good friends, but were far from safe. Cops brought the stress of their jobs home with them. She certainly did. That was a bad recipe for a good marriage.

She looked around the room, tired enough she was going to ignore the urge to straighten the clutter. It probably wouldn't hurt to change though. The jeans and top she wore had been pulled from her gym bag this morning. Groaning at the pain in her shoulder, Kate pushed herself off the couch. She was avoiding taking a painkiller and was paying for that stubbornness.

Her bedroom looked Southern, from the rich rose pattern in the wallpaper to the thick cream carpet under her bare feet. The bed was made; the sheets turned down over the comforter.

She found a white button-down shirt in the closet. She had probably swiped it from either Stephen or Marcus; it was several sizes too big. She slipped it on over a blue T-shirt and turned up the sleeves to above the elbows. There was little that could be done with her hair. She ran a brush through it and clicked off the bathroom light.

She was searching out plates and napkins in the kitchen when there was a knock on the door. After checking that Dave was alone, she turned the locks and opened the door. "What's this?" She grinned. He came bearing gifts.

"A hostess gift, so I'll get invited back."

She untied the ribbon on the sack. Red cherries. Hershey's Kisses. A paperback mystery she had mentioned yesterday. They weren't expensive gifts, but it had taken thought to make the purchases. She sampled one of the cherries, closing her eyes to savor the taste. It was sweet, juicy—delicious. "You'll get invited back."

He rocked back on his heels and chuckled. "Good."

She waved her hand. "Go on into the living room; make yourself at home. Can I get you something to drink? Soda? Iced tea?"

"Tea would be great."

Nodding, she put the gifts on the kitchen counter and opened the refrigerator to pour him a glass of tea.

Hostess gifts. The guy had class. She slid a finger over the cover of the book, reading the jacket text. She was already looking forward to reading the book.

"Here you go." She carried his glass of iced tea as well as the bag of Hershey's Kisses into the living room.

"Thanks. You have a beautiful home."

"I like it. It's my own little peaceful world." She had turned on the stereo shortly before he arrived; music filled the room. The roses from Marcus were prominently displayed on the end table. She filled the candy dish with the chocolates. "Thanks again for the gifts."

He smiled. "I wanted something as a thank-you, and you were already swimming in flowers." He settled comfortably on the couch. Picking up her bowl from the table, he raised his brow and gave her a wicked grin. "Ice cream, Kate?"

She had forgotten to return the bowl to the kitchen. She took it from him, feeling the blush his comment generated heat her face. "Guilty. I started with dessert."

"A great way to break the stress of the day."

A knock on the door saved her from having to come up with a comeback. "Pizza, coming up."

The pizza was fresh from the oven, piping hot, and the cheese still bubbling. She made a place for it on the coffee table. Choosing to leave the couch to Dave, she settled into the wingback chair across from him.

The pizza tasted great. She had been hungrier than she realized.

"This is excellent," Dave commented after a few bites.

"I've settled more than one dispute in the neighborhood over a pizza from Carla's."

"I can see why." He reached for a second piece. "Why don't you take something to kill that headache?"

That sharp eye made her uncomfortable. "I will if it lasts."

"Were you born stubborn?"

It was a teasing question, but the memories of voices from the past made her headache jump in intensity. "Probably."

He studied her thoughtfully, nodded, then turned his attention to the papers beside the pizza box. "Tell me what you're working on."

She was grateful for the change in subject. "I'm still trying to get a handle on the explosives, the detonator, any of the components. Henry had to get them somewhere. We need to know where and if he had help."

Dave scanned the printouts, set down his plate, and wiped his hands. He moved from the couch to the floor; pushed the coffee table down another foot. He started laying out the reports by date in a semicircle around him. "Let's see if we can track his movements, find out if Henry traveled."

It was a good approach. Kate wished she had thought of it. She reached for the stack of pages Dave offered, then looked at him when she realized he wasn't letting go.

"Add hard on herself to stubborn." He smiled. "Would you relax and let others help? Piecing together puzzles is my full-time job."

"You're right. I'm sorry."

He released the papers and frowned. "This case really shook you up, didn't it?"

"I don't like the ones that I dream about."

"How bad?"

She shook her head, declining to answer. "Anything in particular I should be looking for?"

"The general pattern first; did he travel much, where to."

Kate settled back in the chair and started to work. The quietness was broken only by the sound of pages turning. It was a comfortable silence. She looked up after a bit to watch Dave, focused on the task in front of him. He had been serious about coming over to help.

The phone rang. Dave looked up.

"The machine will get it; I'm screening calls."

He nodded and resumed turning pages.

She heard her own voice end and the beep that followed it. "Hello, Kate. I taped the news tonight."

Her hand curled the paper she held; she had heard that voice earlier in the evening. She took a deep breath, and the calm, detached front that hallmarked her work slid into place. *Give me a clue I can work with.*

"Sounds like you have trouble coming your way. Soon it will be more than you can handle."

The tape clicked off on an amused, deep laugh.

She forced herself to mark her place with a pen, set down the printouts, and not to let that voice invading her home get to her. It went with her job. The courts had reversed the truth-in-sentencing law, and the number of inmates being released swelled daily. This sounded like another one determined to harass her.

"I can see why you screen calls."

She could tell from Dave's expression that he was concerned. Having someone else showing a protective streak put her in an uncomfortable position. "Once a month on average, someone I need to avoid finds the number."

"That's a very high incident rate."

She bit her tongue not to reply it wasn't his concern. He didn't mean to step on a sore spot. She changed out the tape as she had done with the first one. She would keep screening calls. When she never answered, most callers stopped harassing her machine after a week. If this caller persisted, it would not be the first time she had requested a tap on her own phone line. "Most call just to show they can find the number," she finally replied. "The persistent callers get traced and dealt with. If there's an obvious threat, it bumps to my boss to decide how to handle it. Those are rare."

"When did you last change your phone number?"

"Dave—"

He held up his hand. "Sorry, consider it unasked. But if you do want some suggestions someday, I could probably make a few. Protecting people is what I do for a living."

"Really?"

"Yes."

"The offer is appreciated, but another time, okay?" She ran her hand through her hair. "I think I will take something to kill this headache." It was a retreat, but a needed one. She found the painkillers the doctor had prescribed that morning, knowing she needed something powerful enough to deal with the aching muscles as well as the headache.

Returning to the living room, she found she simply could not face another moment of work. She settled on the couch.

"Stretch out, get comfortable."

She hesitated, then did as he suggested.

"Kate, why do you do it, your job I mean? You live with so much risk."

He asked it without turning around, continuing to work, but she could tell it was not a throwaway question.

"I was nine when I decided that someone had to kick death in the teeth for the sake of justice."

He glanced back at her. "That's quite a descriptive phrase. You really decided to become a cop when you were nine?"

"Around then."

"What happened?"

Kate hesitated. "It's a long story, for another time."

"Okay. Why become a negotiator?" She was relieved he didn't pursue his previous question.

"It's the center of the action, and I've got the patience and control necessary to do the job well."

"I should have guessed that. You are good at the job, don't get me wrong, but I wish you wouldn't take quite so many risks doing it. When you came through those bank doors not wearing a vest, I was sure you were going to get shot. I was praying harder than I can remember doing in the recent past."

He believed in God? She might not, but she respected people who did. At least they had hope, misplaced she thought, but there. She was always curious. "Do you think it helped?"

He turned around at that question, resting his elbows on his knees as he considered her. "Yes, I do. You don't believe?"

"Does it seem logical to pray for God to stop a crisis when, if He existed, He should have never let it begin?"

He didn't give her an immediate answer, and that had her intrigued.

"Interesting observation."

"Since you believe, thank you for praying."

"You're welcome." He turned back to the paperwork.

Kate didn't raise an eyebrow, but she wanted to. He was letting her close the subject if she chose to without getting uptight about it. From her experience, that suggested three things: He read people well; he was very comfortable with what he believed; and he didn't preach when he talked about religion.

To some people who said they believed, religion was a word; to others, it defined who they were. She had a feeling Dave was in that second group. To understand him, she would have to eventually understand his religion. The fact it bothered him that she didn't believe was kind of nice. People that stood for something made the best friends.

She felt the need to offer a reassurance she rarely made. "Dave, the situation has to be pretty extreme for me to take the risk I did yesterday."

He glanced back at her. "I'm glad to hear that. You're not ready to die."

"Because I don't believe?" She spent the time on her job making small talk. She preferred to avoid it in friendships. And she didn't mind talking about religion when it wasn't going to get shoved down her throat.

He turned, and the concern in his eyes was very personal. "Yes."

His look was patient. He wanted to understand. "It's no secret why I don't believe." She shrugged, wondering if her answer would sound overly simplistic. "My job is to restore justice to an unjust situation. To stand between danger and innocent victims. If your God existed, my job should not."

"He should prevent situations like Tuesday's holdup."

"Yes." She could feel the painkiller kicking in. She braced her hand on his shoulder as she shifted to get a pillow behind her bruised shoulder.

"So where should His interference with free will end?"

"Graham and I debate that question occasionally, and I have a hard time accepting the answer that anything goes. If God is not big enough to figure out a way around free will, He's pretty much left our fates up to chance. I see too much evil, Dave. I don't want a God that lets that kind of destruction go on." She stifled a yawn. She was too tired to have this discussion, as fascinating as it might be. Dave didn't push when he talked about God, but it wasn't like he was going to change her opinion. The pain now easing off, she tucked her hand under her chin.

"You've got a large family. Did your parents have large families, too?"

Another subject shift. He would make a good negotiator. Either that, or he read body language very well. "I grew up in an orphanage." Whatever sympathy that word brought, it was easier to deal with than explaining the abuse that had taken her from her parents' home at age nine.

"You've got three brothers and three sisters."

She shook her head. "I was an only child." She knew the confusion that answer brought. "Can you reach the picture in the silver frame?"

He picked it up from the end table.

"The O'Malleys. We sort of adopted each other. Legally changed our last names, became our own family."

He studied the group photo. "I figured this was you hanging out with friends."

"It is. We were friends long before we became family. Stephen, you've met. Marcus, who sent the flowers. Lisa, Rachel, Jennifer. Jack." She looked at the picture and smiled. "We are constantly stepping in and out of each other's lives. An O'Malley can always count on an O'Malley."

"Sara and I are like that, too. I don't know if I should say I'm sorry you lost your parents or that I envy you what you've found."

"Both apply."

"I would like to meet them."

"Stick around and you will."

He draped his arms across his knees. "We've known each other, what, about thirty-six hours?"

Uncertain as to why he asked, she nodded. "Yes."

"That's long enough. It takes me about twenty-four to make a friend. You're stuck with me."

She couldn't stop the chuckle, then got caught by another yawn. "I think it's time I threw you out and went to bed."

"You do need some sleep." He got to his feet and offered her a hand up.

She walked with him to the door. "Thanks for coming over. I enjoyed it."

"So did I." He stopped, one hand on the doorknob. "If you have a bad dream tonight, call me."

"What?"

"You heard me."

"You're as bad as Marcus. I'm not going to call you in the middle of the night."

"Kate, I'm serious. If you need to talk, call. I won't mind if you wake me up."

This was a different Dave, the amusement gone, in its place real concern. She smiled hesitantly. "If I need to."

He squeezed her hand. "Do." He stepped out the door. "Good night, Kate."

"Good night."

She let the door close and turned the locks, leaning back against the wood. She had expected the emotions from yesterday would fade, not grow. She had seen gentleness in Dave's eyes last night, seen kindness tonight. He was an action-oriented cop, yet she had seen him pull back on three occasions tonight rather than push over her: when the phone call came in, when the subject of religion came up, when he asked about the risks she took in her job. He was a hard man to get a handle on; he was certainly not what she was expecting. There was patience when he wanted to show it.

He hadn't said anything about seeing her again. She wasn't ready to set aside her rule of not dating a cop, but she hoped he did call again soon. Her life was certainly more interesting with him in it.

Four

The bank assault and its aftermath were playing again on television. "Is that her?"

"Yes."

There was silence in the room as the clip ran to completion. "I think you're crazy to go after a cop." It was a quiet assessment, already made before, and said more for reflection than for discussion.

"I want her father, but he's dead. His two kids will have to do."

"Just killing them would be easier. Certainly less complicated."

"Not as sweet. I want to ruin them first."

The man behind the desk clicked off the television set with the remote. "Understandable. But we're going to have to wait a while longer than planned. They'll be looking at Wilshire Construction as the source of that dynamite. That old man just messed up a year of planning."

The man sprawled comfortably in the seat across from him smiled. "We want them looking at Wilshire Construction—this way they will already be suspicious. Rather than delay, we need to move up our timetable."

"We can't."

"Getting cold feet?"

"Hardly. You want the two Emerson kids; I want your brother. I just don't want to get caught."

"Didn't you say he's got a flight to New York next week?"

"Yes."

"So what's the problem?"

꘎꘎꘎

"Is that her?"

Dave glanced up at his sister Sara's question to see Kate's picture on the television screen; the noon newscast had come back from commercial. He closed the newspaper he had been scanning. "Yes, that's Kate." He watched the reporter's story.

Sitting on the couch in her husband's study, Sara leaned forward to look closer at the image. "What's she like?"

Dave searched to find the right word. "Intriguing."

"Really?"

He understood the reason for her interest. "She's not a believer, Sara," he cautioned gently. Those words left a deep void inside; he felt like a prize of great value had been snatched away. He had left Kate's house last night, bitterly disappointed. He had never even considered that possibility, an indication of how strongly he had hoped the evening would be a success. As he had put together the hostess gift for Kate, he had been thinking of plans, possibilities, looking forward to getting to know her better. Those ideas had been stillborn with the discovery she was not a Christian. It didn't change the things that had drawn him to her; it only complicated enormously what he could do about that interest.

He liked Kate. He had never even considered there would be such a problem. That fact surprised him, looking back. Faith was not something he normally took for granted.

His sister looked defeated for a moment, then smiled. "Well, at least you didn't say she was married—lack of belief can change."

Dave leaned back his head and roared with laughter. "You're priceless, Sara."

"I'm happily married."

"I've noticed," he replied dryly, "You keep hoping it becomes contagious."

"Well, my best efforts are coming to naught."

Because he loved her and it was the dream of her heart, he offered— "I'll let you introduce me to another one of your friends." He accepted the reality that with Kate, a relationship beyond a friendship was not likely, and he really did want to settle down. Sara still carried the guilt of having tied up so many years of his life with her security needs. He had been focused on finding the man stalking her, the man responsible for killing their sister, Kim. Having a relationship had been far down on his priorities. Now that Sara was safe, married, and blissfully happy, she was determined to see his situation change. Dave was willing to admit it had become one of his priorities. He wanted to share his life with someone.

"I think I would rather meet Kate."

"Friendship evangelism takes time, Sara."

"But she saved your life."

He set aside his paper and sighed. "It's not that simple. You know that." He had thought about it a lot last night, worried about it, the fact Kate didn't believe. She walked into situations where a guy had a bomb. It made him shudder. But after praying a long time, he had accepted the fact there was really very little he could do. With a guy, it was different. He could get close as a friend, understand the issues preventing a decision of faith, talk through them one by one. Friendship evangelism worked if given enough time.

He couldn't do that with Kate. It was one thing to be friends with a woman, another to get close enough to influence her heart. One of them would likely end up with bruised emotions, and he had the gut feeling it would be him. The way she moved, the way she acted…and that voice of hers—that soft, captivating voice…he shook his head. Kate was trouble for him. The emotions she generated would not easily be contained to friendship.

She wouldn't be an easy person to approach with the gospel, either. Her own words told him she already thought enough about the subject to have some deep reservations. To root out why, have the patience to convince her to reconsider, would be a difficult task, and there would be no guarantee of success.

Sara crossed over to take a seat on the armrest of his chair. "Maybe it won't be simple. But you could use a good friend. Unlike my friends, she might be able to understand your job."

Sara understood his job. She had lived under the security, lived in constant fear of a killer. The past had left her with a knowledge about good and evil that had destroyed her sense of innocence. Dave didn't want that to happen to others, so he rarely talked about his job, rarely shared that part of his life. Part of it was security—what he couldn't say—and part of it was his wall—the things he wouldn't say. He wanted a life, and that couldn't happen if work invaded conversations. He appreciated Sara's concerns that it left him lonely, and she was right, but it also gave him a corner of his life that was normal, and he guarded that corner tenaciously.

The fact Kate would understand his job was sad, for it meant she had also lost, like Sara, that freedom not to know what evil was like. Kate lived with the knowledge like he did. It showed in her eyes. Cop's eyes. Despite the humor, the voice, the charm, and the smile, at the back of her eyes was a reflection of what she had seen through the years. Black. Cold. Contained. Wary.

Dave sighed, accepting he was going to have to see Kate soon, if only to try and shake that image. He glanced at Sara and let himself smile. "I thought I was the one who looked out after you."

"You did—magnificently. I think it's time for me to return the favor."

He locked his arms around her waist and tugged her into his lap, triggering a fit of giggles from her. "Listen, Squirt…"

"I thought I heard you two in here."

Dave looked up as his brother-in-law entered the room. "Hi, Adam."

"Dave." Adam smiled and leaned down to kiss his wife, still trapped in Dave's arms. "If you were planning to change before we leave, you've got eight minutes," he mentioned to her, amused.

She scrambled back to her feet. "I'll be ready in four."

Dave watched her go, content in a way he had not been in ages. "She looks happy, Adam. Thanks." There had been years he had wondered if this day would ever come for her.

"It's mutual." His friend took a seat on the couch, leaned back and stretched and grinned. "So—fill me in on this Kate I've been hearing about."

Sara and Adam had so smoothly tag teamed him into talking about Kate that Dave was almost willing to speculate their ambush had been planned. He smiled as he cut across traffic to reach his car. The wind had picked up as the day progressed, but there were only small clouds to be blown across the sky; the hoped for rain had still not appeared. He was about to do something he might regret in the morning.

He had the preliminary bank report on Henry Lott's mortgage with him. He had called Kate's office to fax her a copy, but Franklin had said she had already left for the day. The report could wait until tomorrow. Dave knew that, but he had decided to seize the moment and see if Kate happened to be home.

As he drove toward Kate's neighborhood, he tried to decide what he would say when he saw her. He wasn't sure how he had left it last night after she said she didn't believe. He thought he had handled it with tact, not shown his disappointment, but he wasn't going to assume that fact; he couldn't. He would soon know, maybe. Given the way Kate could control her voice and expression, clues to what she was thinking could be subtle at best if she decided to play it cool.

Dave ran his hand through his hair, admitting to himself he had no idea why he was doing this. To hear her voice again. Coax out another smile. He groaned at the realization he had just jumped again in his thoughts to something well beyond friendship and seriously considered abandoning this idea. He didn't need this kind of emotional quicksand.

His jaw firmed. He would keep it friendly. Brief.

He liked her, really liked her; he would just have to start treating her like a cousin or something.

Right. That was easier said than done.

Dave turned onto her block and slammed on his brakes.

There were three squad cars, lights flashing, parked at an angle in front her building.

That call. Kate was in trouble.

He should never have let her blow off that threatening phone call. He had known it wasn't something to ignore, and he had backed off when she got annoyed with him. He didn't do that! Evaluating threats, protecting people was his job. Someone's feelings had to be secondary to her safety, and he had overruled that basic mandate because he wanted to stay in her good graces. If Kate was hurt…

Dave pulled in behind a squad car, grabbed his keys, and hit the pavement at a run. Manning was coming down the building's front steps. "What happened?" Dave demanded.

"Kate got a package."

"Inside her apartment?"

Manning shook his head. "Leaning against the front door."

"Where is she?"

"Inside. We're just wrapping up."

Dave stepped past the lab technician dusting the front door. There was barely room to maneuver in the crowded apartment. Dave knew from the normal tones of voice that the immediate crisis was past, but his heart still pounded. Graham, talking to one of the other officers, spotted him, and waved him back into the living room.

Kate was on the other side of the room. Everything else going on slid into the background.

She looked furious.

That realization stunned him. He had been braced for hurt; prepared, if she wasn't hurt, to see rigid control hiding her thoughts. He hadn't anticipated seeing emotions full blown. Halfway across the room he could feel the emotions shimmering off of her. She sizzled. With her arms crossed, attention on her boss, she paced in three feet of open real estate like a caged tiger.

She hadn't seen him yet, and he was momentarily glad for that.

Stephen came up behind him, carrying a cup of hot coffee.

"There was a package delivered, left leaning against her front door," Stephen told him quietly. "We had gone to dinner at the Italian place around the corner; I walked her home. The florist box was leaning against the door. I reached for it, and Kate slammed me onto my back by instinct, nearly gave me a concussion."

"What was in it?"

"A black rose. Her friend is back."

Kate looked over and saw him before he could follow up on Stephen's last comment. Dave watched her expression change, harden, then clear. He buried a sigh. So much for wondering how she would react to seeing him here.

He moved past Graham to join her. "Kate."

"Dave." She didn't look pleased to see him, but he tried not to take it personally. This place had become Grand Central Station, a fact that had to be frustrating for her. She needed some space. As a cop, that would be even more true than for someone else. For the same reason she would sit in a restaurant with her back to the wall to keep people in front of her, she would be looking for space around her now.

Her boss closed his notebook. "The lab will put a rush on this. We should hear from the Indiana PD in a couple hours, find out if your friend has indeed managed to slip out of his supervised release. In the meantime, patrols are shifted for the night."

"He won't be back tonight. His MO looks the same, down to the ribbon used on the gift."

"Assuming it's him," Jim replied. "We should know something by midnight anyway." He lightly squeezed her shoulder. "At least this time it wasn't a gift-wrapped snake."

Kate chuckled softly. "Hey, I've got first class admirers."

It took about fifteen minutes for the cops and technicians to finish work, pack up their cases. Dave stayed out of their way, watching Stephen and Kate. Stephen was good with her, able to distract her. Or rather she let him distract her, Dave amended. The apartment door closed, leaving just the three of them.

Kate was looking around her apartment, looking unexpectedly lost. Dave crossed the room and placed his hand on her shoulder, felt the tremor. She was still so angry she was quivering.

"Go get your keys. We'll take a walk," he said calmly.

"It's going to rain."

"The forecast was wrong, and even if it did rain, it would just cool off that temper." He chuckled at the look she shot him. "Don't argue, Kate; you'll regret it in the morning." He turned her toward the bedroom. "Better yet, find a hat. It's windy."

She must have bitten her tongue not to argue, but she stalked away toward her bedroom.

"Kate following orders without a debate, that has got to be a first," Stephen commented after Kate's door closed. "Thanks. I'll get this place put back together while you're gone."

"You sure?"

"Once the fingerprint dust is gone from the front door and all the windows they checked, it won't look quite so invaded."

Dave agreed with him. "Sounds like a plan. Now tell me about this friend that likes to leave black roses."

"Bobby Tersh. Five years ago, Kate talked him out of ending his life. He fixated on her when he got out of the hospital a couple weeks later; it escalated through phone calls to the office, gifts, then took a nasty turn when he felt ignored and disintegrated into threats and to black roses being left on her car, and finally at her doorstep. He was eventually committed to a hospital in Indiana by his family. He's been out of the hospital about a year now on supervised release. This is the first indication there might be trouble again."

"Any history of violence in his background?" Dave asked, wishing he had access to the files. Maybe Jim would help him out there.

"No, just words, not that it necessarily means anything. And we're guessing that it is him."

Dave had already factored that in. "Okay."

They heard Kate's door open. She had changed into a gray sweatshirt with a hood. She looked calmer to the extent it was possible to read her.

"Stephen, we won't be gone long. Don't answer the phone; let the machine get it," Kate said, checking her pockets, avoiding looking at Dave.

Stephen crossed over to her and wrapped his arm around her shoulders. "Get out of here. You don't want to see how I clean your place."

"Thanks."

Dave closed the front door behind them and scanned the street before walking down the steps, alert to anything out of place. It looked normal and quiet, but that didn't mean much. "Which way?"

"North."

He fell into step beside her, not bothered by the silence.

"I've had black roses before," she finally said.

"Stephen told me."

"If his MO holds, I won't receive another one for weeks."

She was looking for an excuse to make that assumption; stupid of her, but he wasn't about to argue the point. "Okay."

Kate didn't say anything else. Dave eventually decided she had brooded long enough and changed the subject. "Did you hear about the Cubs game this afternoon?"

"What?"

"The baseball game. It was a perfect game through the eighth inning."

She stopped walking to look at him incredulously. "No comments about that scene back there? No advice?"

"What do you need to know that you haven't already heard?" he asked quietly.

She scowled.

"You just want someone to fight with so you can blow off steam," he said calmly. "Sorry, you'll have to settle for walking it off."

"Thanks a lot."

"My pleasure."

"You are so annoying." She sighed. "Tell me about the game."

Twenty minutes into the walk, Dave reached out and took her hand. Her fingers were cold, and he grasped them reassuringly. It didn't matter what anyone said, or that this situation was one of the realities that came with the job; it was her home that had been invaded. She had needed a night to relax and instead was being thrust back into a situation that must have been a nightmare. He could tell the memories were back by the shuttered weariness in her face and the fact she had responded with so much emotion—it had been anger, but it had been prompted by fear. And there was nothing he could do to make this go away. He hated not being able to help. He talked about the game, his visit with Sara and Adam, plans for the summer, anything but his work or hers.

"You're not that bad at making small talk," she commented.

He took it as a special compliment. "I spent a few hours listening to you."

She rolled her shoulders, and he saw the tension in her finally drain away. "It was a miserable day. I didn't need this on top of it."

"At least you didn't give Stephen a concussion. He would have been giving you grief about that for months."

"Months? It would have entered family lore." She shook her head. "You can't imagine the fear that hit when I saw him reach toward that package. I didn't even realize I had recognized it; I just reacted."

Having more than once taken his sister Sara to the ground in reaction to a threat, Dave knew exactly what that fear tasted like. It was much more powerful than facing a threat to yourself. "I know what that fear is like," he replied but didn't elaborate.

"It makes me *furious*. Someone wants to come after me, fine, but don't mess with my family. I saw Stephen reach for that package, and I had a sudden nasty image of a paramedic suddenly missing a hand." She visibly shuddered at the thought.

"Let it go, Kate. Stephen's fine. It was a false alarm. The adrenaline will eventually fade."

"Yeah."

She pushed her hands into her pockets, walked some more. "You will conveniently forget the fact you saw me lose my temper."

"Why? You're adorable mad."

"Dave—"

He held up his hands. "It's forgotten."

"Thank you. Now, why did you come over?"

She didn't want to talk about what had happened. He tried not to let his disappointment show. She deserved her privacy, but he had hoped they were on level enough ground as friends she would let him help her out. He would like to repay the debt he owed her.

Because he had no real choice, he let her change the subject. "I've got the preliminary bank report on Henry Lott's mortgage for you."

She pulled her hand out of her pocket to run it through her hair. "I had actually forgotten that case for a couple hours. Thanks for bringing it over."

"It was an excuse to see you."

She sneaked a glance at him, gave a small smile. "It's a pretty lame one."

"True." That smile cushioned her change of subject. He relaxed. She'd learn to share eventually; he'd be around until she realized it.

They had been walking for about forty minutes, had circled back around to her block again. "Stephen should be about done," he commented.

"Yes. Are you coming in?"

He wanted to, but she looked exhausted now under that contained front. "No. You need a hot shower and some sleep, not company."

"You just want to go meddle in this case, too."

He didn't bother to contradict her, just smiled. "Go on. I'll talk to you tomorrow."

"The Indiana PD have no leads on Bobby Tersh?" Dave asked, following Graham through the basement concrete hallways in the county building back to the emergency response group offices.

"He hasn't reported in to his release supervisor in five days; he hasn't been at his job in three. Officers interviewing the family reported they were very cooperative but had little to suggest. They haven't heard from Bobby either."

The steel door at the end of the hallway was locked and electronically coded. Graham paused to punch his code, then held open the heavy door for Dave. The quiet and coolness of the hallway disappeared in an assault of sound. The long open room was packed with desks and people. It was a stark contrast to the FBI offices where they had the luxury of individual offices and group conference rooms.

Dave scanned the room, disappointed not to see Kate. Maybe it was for the best. She might not appreciate having the FBI step across jurisdictions. He had called her boss late last night, and hadn't even needed to explain his credentials as a reason for why he was asking to take a look at the files. Her boss had granted his request and sounded relieved to do it. Dave knew that meant Jim was short handed or worried about the possible threat to one of his officers—probably both.

"Debbie, have those files on Tersh arrived from archives?" Graham asked.

The secretary working the phones paused the phone conversation she was on and pointed with her red pen to the cart on wheels pushed against a three-drawer file cabinet with a sprawling fern. They had tried to improvise greenhouse lights for the plant, but the fern still looked sick for lack of sunlight.

"Trust something to archives? That disaster waiting to happen? They are two years behind schedule to move and consolidate that warehouse, and it shows. I used my discretion and kept Tersh classified as an active file. It's the two-inch blue file on the left. I pulled it when I got in this morning and heard what had happened."

"What would we do without you?"

"Suffer the wrath of the system," Debbie replied with a smile. "Do you want me to pull her threat file, too?"

"You'd better," Graham picked up the Tersh file, leafed through it, then turned back to Debbie. "Three years ago, last name Edmond? If that's not in the threat file, pull it."

"Dead cat," Debbie said darkly. "It's there."

Graham indicated his desk halfway into the room, and Dave followed him to it. "Kate has a cat?"

Graham took a seat and glanced back up at him. "Not anymore." He gestured to a chair where a jacket and a briefcase were balanced. "Just put the stuff somewhere. Sorry, we're a little chaotic down here still. They haven't installed the lockers they promised us months ago."

Dave moved the jacket and briefcase, then settled down into a chair that was at least comfortable.

"Jim said to give you access to anything we had. I have to tell you, I don't like the idea of someone going after Kate again. Last year turned into a nightmare for her."

"That bad?"

"Kate is hard to read how something is affecting her, but by the end of the year you could see she was paying the price. She didn't want someone else in her building getting hurt if Tersh became confrontational."

"A case where the courts couldn't do anything."

"The DA tried, but it was hard to get more than a slap on the hands, and that wasn't going to do the trick. When Tersh's family committed him, you could see Kate's relief. If it had gone on much longer, she wouldn't have been able to stop her brothers from intervening."

Graham scanned pages. "It's going to be hard finding the guy if he's somewhere back in Chicago. He worked as a transit mechanic, knew the city very well." Graham handed over the file. "The initial report from Kate's intervention is in there, along with excerpts from that conversation. It was taped, so a full transcript is available, just ask Debbie for it. The rest of the files are the various incident reports regarding the gifts and calls."

Debbie joined them carrying two folders stuffed so full they were spilling over. "Kate's threat file." She handed it to Graham. "Anything else you need, just ask."

Dave was stunned at the size of it. "How many years does that encompass?"

"Two? Three? Most all of it is mail. She spends hours with people, they get sent to jail, and they think they know her, so they write—a lot. There is not much else to do in prison."

"And she's the type of lady that would stick in a guy's mind," Dave observed. She was too pretty, had too striking of a voice. He sighed just thinking about it.

"Exactly."

"Who else could this be besides Tersh?"

"At a guess, there are probably another six serious contenders in this stack."

"Where is Kate?"

"I haven't seen her this morning." Graham leaned back to see around him. "No gym bag sticking halfway out into the aisle, so she probably got paged while she was at the gym."

"She's a busy lady."

"Popular. They call her into situations earlier than they used to."

Graham picked up his phone to check the blinking message light. When he hung up a few moments later, he gestured to the files.

"Are you okay with going through this information on your own? I'm due over at the ATF office to talk about Henry's package. It will probably take me an hour."

"There's at least an hour of reading here before I'm ready to start asking questions," Dave agreed.

Graham's pager and two others in the room went off. "Change that," Graham glanced at his pager. "I'll be back whenever. Come on, Olsen."

"Can I drive?"

"Can you remember which streets are one-way?"

"It was an honest mistake."

"Sure it was."

The noise in the room dropped off as the guys headed out. Dave glanced at the open folder in his lap. Before he assumed it was Tersh as the others had, it would be better to know what they did regarding the other threats that had been made. He set the Tersh file on the desk and reached for the first of the threat files.

He looked up the Edmond case as a place to start.

Kate's cat had been shot through her living room window at 5:16 A.M. on a snowy winter day. Walter Edmond had eventually been charged with firearm violations, vandalism, and cruelty to animals. A cat. There was something more than just maliciousness at work when someone killed a pet. Walter's beef with Kate was over the fact she had talked his girlfriend into filing battery charges after he broke her arm. The sentence was not long enough given the threat Edmond represented.

Dave added the name to the list of individuals to check out. He picked up the next item in the file.

Kate, I wanted a chance to get to know you, but not like this. I didn't need more reasons to worry. And why didn't you ever get yourself another cat? You let him win.

"You like to stay out late," Dave said quietly, burying his emotions.

Kate whirled around on him. "Are you trying to get yourself killed?"

He stepped out of the shadows, not liking at all the fact he had been able to surprise her. He had been waiting for Kate to get home since 7 P.M., growing more concerned the later the hour became. The call she had been on had cleared shortly after six; he had heard Debbie take the call that Kate would not be back to the office. Kate was supposed to be going home, and he had left the station to meet her. And he had waited, wondering where she was and what was wrong. The only good thing the time had done was give him an opportunity to see the number of patrols passing by. He had spoken to several of them. Given the news he had received today, he was grateful to see them. "You assumed you would have time to react. You're a better cop than that Kate."

"Go away. It's been a horrible day." She turned back to the door.

"Hold it. Give me your keys."

"I can check my own home."

"You weren't even looking around as you walked down the block. Keys, Kate."

She handed them to him rather than argue the point. He pushed her back when she would have entered the apartment with him. "Dave—"

"Stay there," he ordered.

It took him four minutes to sweep her apartment, confirm it was empty, quiet, and nothing obvious waiting for her. "Okay. You can come in."

"Thanks," she said sarcastically, brushing past him.

"You're welcome," Dave replied, letting some of his own stress lash out at her.

"Why are you here?"

"Bobby Tersh has disappeared."

"So I heard." She collapsed on the couch. "Lock the door on your way out."

He watched her, his anger fading away to sharp concern. "Where were you today? Debbie just said you were out on a call."

"I was backup for a case on the south side."

"The family of four." He had heard about it on the radio. "An uncle barricaded himself with relatives. Shots were heard."

"The mother and two boys were dead before we arrived. He's facing three counts of first degree murder."

Dave squeezed her shoulder. "I'm sorry."

"So am I. Go away, Dave."

He tossed his suit jacket over a chair, undid his cuff links as he disappeared into her kitchen. It was an organized place, if rather sparse. Given the few choices, it limited what he could make. He brought her a mug of decaf coffee. She hadn't even stirred enough to kick off her shoes. "Don't take the blame for something you couldn't prevent."

She wearily sat up and took the mug. "I hate losing."

"I've figured that out." He watched her sip the drink. "Want to talk about it?"

"No."

"Feel like eating, or would you like to just go ahead and crash?" He asked, changing his plans. He had hoped to take her out to dinner, distract her, while he delivered the bad news about the details they had learned regarding Tersh.

She finished the drink, pushed the cup onto the table, and sank back down into the thick cushions of the couch. "I had a sandwich on the way home."

"You ate in the car."

"It's my car," she muttered into the pillow.

"Get to bed then."

"As soon as you're out the door."

Her irritation amused him. "Good night, Kate."

He waited until he heard Kate turn all the locks on her door before he walked down to his car. He was relieved to have her home. He'd been right about one thing: She had too much on her mind to pay adequate attention to her own safety. Given the choice, he supposed he would rather have her relaxed and let others worry about it; she couldn't be objective. Two days, three at the most, and they should have found Bobby Tersh.

After a day reading the files, he had to agree it did look like Bobby Tersh was back. There were too many similarities in the type of gift, how it was left, when, for it to be an accident. Those details were in the public domain, someone willing to go through all the court filings and the newspaper accounts could put it together, but the obvious candidate was Tersh. How much had he changed in a year? That was the tough assessment. Was it going to be roses and phone calls spread out across weeks, or something more aggressive this time?

Dave settled back in his car seat and reached for the thermos of coffee beside him. Kate's bedroom light eventually went out. Watching out for danger was his business, and he was good at the job, even if he had to do it without her full cooperation. Until they had some idea where Bobby Tersh was, he didn't mind killing a few hours outside her place.

If Bobby Tersh broke his MO, it would probably be in the first twenty-four to forty-eight hours. No use taking chances. Nothing was going to bother Kate tonight. In this case it wasn't even entirely personal, he always got ticked off when a cop was getting harassed. At least that's what he tried to tell himself as the clock slipped past midnight.

Five

Kate figured whoever was persistently ringing her doorbell at ten o'clock on a Saturday morning could live with the consequences. It wouldn't be an O'Malley. Family knew better. They would just let themselves in and make themselves at home. She flipped the locks and opened the door.

Dave. Smiling. On her doorstep.

"Here. Coffee. It looks like you need it."

She took the mug from his hand with a sigh. "I was asleep."

"I can tell."

He didn't look repentant about it. She continued to stand in the doorway even when he raised one eyebrow. His irresistible smile could probably charm even her elderly neighbor out of a snit. "The morning is half over, and I've got news." He tipped his head to one side. "Bad move?"

"I was asleep," she repeated, "and didn't I just see you?"

His instant grin was covered by a belated attempt to look sorry. He nudged the coffee mug up. "It's really good coffee."

Her lips twitched. It was wonderful coffee, and he knew it. It guaranteed she would not be going back to sleep. "What's your news?"

"Bobby's car was spotted at a rest stop in Indiana, but they didn't manage to take him into custody."

"Graham woke me up to tell me hours ago," she felt compelled to add. "Is that all?"

"It's a beautiful day."

She squinted at the sun. "It's sunny, dry, and hot. It looks like every other day has this month."

"Exactly. So come spend part of it with me."

"Why?"

He nudged the coffee mug up again. "Can we have this conversation inside?"

"No."

His grin widened. "We'll add ornery to that list. And cute. Your hair is a mess."

Kate ran a hand through it. It was going to be a mess to brush out. One foot idly went over the other as she let the doorpost take her weight. The coffee was helping, but not quickly enough. "I plan to spend today writing case notes."

"Let's go walk the beach instead."

"The beach."

"Sand, water, relaxation. I need it, and I bet you do, too. You've got a great tan. It had to be acquired somewhere."

She smirked. "One-on-one basketball with Stephen. The games move outdoors in April. I don't have enough free time to waste a day lazing around on a beach."

"I guess you don't play HORSE."

"No."

"You had a bad dream last night, didn't you?" The sudden change in subject threw her enough she wasn't able to entirely hide the answer that flickered in her eyes. His hand tipped her chin up so she looked directly into his eyes. "Why didn't you call me?"

"It was 4 A.M."

"And you were just getting back to sleep when I rang the doorbell."

She would give the man points for connecting the dots.

"I know what bad dreams are like, Kate. You should have called. It wasn't just a polite offer. Talking about it would have made it easier to get back to sleep."

"You sound pretty certain about that."

He gave a ghost of a smile. "The voice of much experience. Come on, Kate, you'll enjoy it. Shorts. Something loose and long sleeves you can slip on later so you won't burn."

"I'm on call."

"So am I. It will be the day of dueling beepers. I'll have my cellular phone with me, but bring yours along, too, if you'd like."

She gave in gracefully. Work was not exactly on par to spending a day outdoors. "Come in. I'll get changed."

She found blue shorts, a red cotton T-shirt, and matching red socks. The canvas tote of Lisa's was still in her closet. She slipped in a white shirt, tossed in the mystery Dave had given her, added suntan lotion, cash, her pager, and her phone.

"Okay, I'm ready to travel."

Dave turned from looking at the pictures on the bookshelf. "That was fast."

"If you had said wear a dress, I would have made you wait just for spite."

His rich laughter rolled around the quiet apartment. He took the now empty coffee mug she offered and waited as she locked the front door.

"The blue sedan." Dave indicated. He held open the passenger door for her. Kate slid inside with a murmured thanks. The O'Malley men had spoiled her. She had come to expect the old-fashioned courtesies.

"Nice car."

Dave found his sunglasses and slid them on. "Thanks."

Kate glanced through his cassette tapes as he pulled out into traffic. "Do you have anything besides country western?"

"Try the glove box."

She scanned his tapes until she found what she was looking for. This was more like it. She put in a Johnny Mathis tape.

"I thought you said you liked jazz."

"I lied."

"About something trivial?"

She chuckled. "Dave, I tell the bad guys I like them, too. If I don't have common ground with someone, I make it up."

She saw him frown. He obviously didn't like her lying. Why not? She considered it a necessary evil to doing her job. Common ground was critical, even if she had to invent it.

"What else did you make up?"

"In over four hours of small talk? Enough to keep the conversation going."

"You don't have an Aunt Gladys."

"Good guess."

"Now that I think about it, she sounds a little too eccentric to be true."

Kate looked at the Saturday traffic around them. "It's pretty early to be going to the beach."

Dave's lips twitched. "I think I'll feed you first."

"Smart man," she murmured.

"I gather making it a memorable breakfast might be in my best self-interest?"

"I'm hungry."

He glanced over at her and showed that wicked grin again. "That genteel Southern scold must have taken some practice."

The accent disappeared. "David."

He chuckled. "Sorry, it's just Dave. There's a great place in the north suburbs that makes everything from crepes to Belgian waffles. It's worth the time."

She was slightly mollified. "Strawberries?"

"And blueberries, probably even kiwi if you like."

Kate rested her head back and closed her eyes. "Sounds good. Wake me when we get there."

Dave let the waitress refill his coffee. They were lingering over breakfast. They had split a Dutch apple pancake and an order of strawberry crepes. He was full. Kate was still working on the strawberry crepes.

It felt good to be able to relax with her. He took the threat that black rose represented more seriously than she did; the news Bobby's car had been spotted in Indiana was a real relief. Hopefully by the time he took Kate home this afternoon they would have word that Bobby had been picked up. "Like a refill for the coffee?" the waitress asked.

"Please." Kate motioned to the last crepe. "Are you sure you don't want to split this?"

"Go ahead. I'm done."

"It's really good. You didn't answer my question."

"Which one?" The tongue-in-cheek answer earned him a look that made him laugh. "Okay. Why did I just show up on your doorstep this morning? It was a spur of the moment decision, and it's harder to say no when you are asked in person."

"True. But I was annoyed enough I was going to say no."

He shook his head. "You never considered saying no. Slamming the door in my face, maybe. But you never considered saying no."

"What would you have done if I had?"

"Walked back to my car and picked up my cellular phone. You would have had to eventually answer."

"So tell me again why you wanted to spend part of today with me?"

"Besides the fact Bobby is loose and you need someone to watch your back?"

"We'll consider that unsaid," she warned softly.

"Prickly, huh?" He didn't take it personally; he had already figured out she had an independent streak a mile wide. "Okay. You're fascinating company."

"Fascinating..." She considered the word. "Challenging, maybe. Unusual. Annoying. Aggravating. Fun. Why fascinating?"

The sparkle in her eyes made him smile. "Your humor."

His reply amused her. "That's fascinating?"

"It shows up in the midst of crisis. That's unexpected, therefore, fascinating."

"I wouldn't want to be predictable."

"That you will never be."

He watched her finish her coffee. "Ready to go?"

"Yes."

He picked up the bill and left a generous tip on the table.

He chose a stretch of beach near his home in Lake Forest. The wind off the lake made the sunny day comfortable. He dropped the blanket he had retrieved from the trunk at the beginning of the sand. "Come on; let's walk for a while."

The waves broke into white caps about ten feet off shore, rolling in on the sandy beach. Kate tipped her head back to enjoy the sun. "This is rather nice."

"Yes."

They walked the length of the beach and back. Dave enjoyed every minute of it. She was entranced with the birds flying out of the water. She stopped frequently to retrieve shell fragments, gathering them like a child would.

She rubbed the sand off her latest discovery. "Look at this one. It's got a touch of blue in it. It's pretty."

Dave took what she offered and turned it over in his hand. It was pretty. More so because she had noticed it. "Yes."

She took it back from him. "Odd souvenirs, I know."

"You're going to keep them?"

Her laugh was soft, indulgent. "Probably."

"In that case, let me help you look."

"No way. These are my memories. Collect your own."

Her protest amused him. "You like simple things."

She shrugged. "It's the value I place on something that matters, not what it cost. I like collecting memories of good days."

Dave started to smile; then what she had revealed registered. She was reaching for another shell fragment and didn't see his frown. When she stood, his hands settled lightly on her shoulders. "Have good days been rare?"

He was afraid she was going to sidestep the question. She was slow to answer, and when she did, her tone was serious. "I think everyone has stretches where the good days are rare." Her shoulders moved beneath his hands. "There was a bad stretch when I lost my first hostage, another very long one when I lost the first child."

"That's work. What about otherwise?"

She put her hand over his. Her smile was kind. "It's too early for history." She moved toward the water to wash off her shell collection.

"Too early today, or too early in our friendship?"

"Both."

"It doesn't feel like I've only known you five days."

"Check your calendar."

He enjoyed her grin as she came walking back to him. "I'll give you a week."

"To what?"

"Tell me all about yourself."

"That's generous of you."

"I thought so."

She stored her shells in the canvas bag. "I think I've said enough for today."

Dave smiled and changed the subject. "Where do you want the blanket spread out?"

She looked around. "Over there looks pretty level."

He spread it out.

Her laughter had him looking up. "I really don't think we want to be by an anthill. Try it a few more yards that way."

He didn't see what she was referring to, but picked up the blanket and moved it where she indicated.

"No. It's not level. Move it more to the left."

After the fourth move, Dave's eyes narrowed. She was doing this intentionally. He flicked his wrists, watched the blanket settle, and collapsed on it, wrinkles and all. When she sat down beside him, he tweaked her chin. "That was underhanded."

"You were the one buying it."

He buried the answering grin. Not many ladies had the nerve to try a practical joke. It was a shame, too. He was already thinking about how to retaliate.

She dug a book out of her canvas bag.

"Kate?"

"Hmm?"

"Thanks for coming today."

She settled back on her elbows and looked at him. "You're pretty good company."

"Better than good."

She laughed. "We'll have to see."

The sun was warm, Kate was quiet, and it had been a long week. Dave felt himself drifting to sleep and didn't fight it.

The sun was overhead when he awoke. He stretched; every muscle in his body was relaxed. He turned to look at Kate. She was sprawled on the blanket beside him, soaking in the sun. The book was set aside, about half read. Her beauty hit him again like a blow. He felt shaky inside at the suddenness of the emotion. Why did she have to be an unbeliever? A cop? He would love to have the freedom to lean over and kiss her. He looked away, took a deep breath. *Think cousin.* Right. He should have a cousin as good-looking as Kate. He glanced at his watch. It was past 2 P.M.

"We probably need to move into the shade."

"Later."

He chuckled. She was obviously quite comfortable where she was. "Come on, I'll spring for the cold sodas."

She reluctantly opened her eyes and sighed. "You are waking me up again."

He winced. "Sorry."

"That's okay." She glanced at her watch and groaned. "Let's find that cold drink; then I probably need to get home. Work is waiting."

"You're disappointing me, Kate. I hoped I could at least talk you into lunch."

His smile was rewarded with an answering grin. "You must be losing your touch."

"Ouch."

She laughed. "Seriously, I've got an O'Malley family gathering tomorrow. I've got no choice but to at least get started on reviewing the negotiation tapes."

He watched as she got to her feet and stretched. She was moving easier today, the cuts from the bank holdup having finally healed.

"Think you could find an ice-cream cone to go with that cold drink?"

"Probably." He was surprised at her choice and pleased that she had asked. "You're sure you wouldn't like something more exotic?"

"Just an ice-cream cone."

"How about Justins?" The locally owned ice cream shop was a regular at the Taste of Chicago, and it was near Kate's home.

"Now you're talking."

He looked at his beeper, confirmed again there had been no page. How hard was it to locate one man? Where was Bobby Tersh?

Six

You've been distracted all afternoon. Is everything okay?"

Lisa's question made Kate glance up and realize her sister was holding out a glass of lemonade. "Sorry." She reached to accept it. "Everything's fine." Except for the fact Bobby Tersh was still out there somewhere, now in Indianapolis according to the latest sighting; Dave had her flustered with his habit of showing up in her life; and Jennifer had called this gathering without indicating why. Kate shook her head and sipped at the cold drink. Dinner preparations were finished. Jennifer, Marcus, and the rest of the O'Malleys would be here within the hour.

"I tried to call you yesterday, but you weren't answering at home."

"You should have paged me."

"I knew I would see you today."

Kate settled deeper into the cushions of the sofa, resting the cold drink against her jeans. She had spent well into the evening hours yesterday beginning the review of the negotiation tapes from the bank. The tactical outcome had been necessary, but it still felt like a defeat.

"Kate." Lisa waved her hand. "See? Distracted."

Kate groaned. The last thing she wanted was for Lisa to know work was getting to her. The family already worried about her enough. Stephen had been sworn to silence about the black rose. "Sorry." Searching for a distraction, she offered one she knew would get Lisa's interest. "Dave Richman came over for pizza the other night. He seems to be there every time I turn around lately."

Lisa set down the glass she had just picked up. "Really?"

Kate looked over at her sister and half smiled. "Don't sound so surprised."

"You haven't exactly been dating much in the last year."

Lisa was being generous. She didn't think she had been out at all in the last year. "Don't get your hopes up. His interest is work related." She had noticed his frequent glances at his pager yesterday, waiting for the news that Bobby Tersh had been picked up. She had let it go because it was kind of nice to have him care enough to waste a Saturday covering her back. She would be inviting more attention than she wanted if she mentioned that to Lisa. "I think he'll make a good friend."

The doorbell rang and Lisa rose to answer it. "Don't let him slip out of your life, Kate. You need someone who can make you smile like that."

The O'Malleys spilled in through the door, laughing.

Setting her glass on the end table, Kate got to her feet. The energy that came into the room with their arrival was refreshing.

"Kate!"

She laughed as she was lifted off her feet in a hug. "Hi, Jack."

"It's good to see you're still in one piece."

"Rumors of my death were greatly exaggerated."

"Stephen ordered me not to come serenade you to sleep at the hospital."

"The way you sing, I'm grateful. Thanks for the e-mail gift. Manning is jealous. Where did you find the explosive screen saver?" She had laughed when she installed it. If she grabbed the mouse and cut the wires in time, the bomb would not go off.

"I was going to send you one of those electronic greeting cards, but when I saw the screen saver I knew you would appreciate it more."

"Absolutely."

Over Jack's shoulder, Kate saw Jennifer get swallowed up in a hug from Lisa. Jennifer was petite to begin with and appeared to have lost even more weight, but her smile was radiant, her color good. Kate lowered her voice. "Any idea what her news is?"

Jack lowered his head toward hers; the laughter in his voice disappeared as the serious side he so rarely showed came to the forefront. "We couldn't drag a thing out of her. It must be something pretty big."

Kate suppressed the desire to flinch. It was bad news; she just knew it. "Thanks for the warning." She took a deep breath. Whatever was coming couldn't be avoided. But it would help to stay busy. "Would you mind starting the grill? Marinated steaks are in the refrigerator."

"Consider it done. I'm starved."

"Of course you are. You're always hungry. I want mine pink, not dry."

"I notice, despite all the aspersions to my cooking, that you are still asking me to man the grill."

"Jack, you know Stephen will be out there to give you advice as soon as he sees the match in your hand."

"Just because we don't let you play around with the fire—"

She swatted his arm. "Go on." Jack laughed and moved toward the patio. "Stephen, Jack is going for the matches."

Stephen strode across the room, angling after Jack. "I'm on him. There is no way I am letting him burn *my* steak."

Grinning at the fact the two of them were so predictable, Kate turned to look for Rachel.

Her sister was hanging back half a step, observing it all with a smile. Kate headed toward her because her hugs were always the best. "Rachel. How was Florida?" The tan was there, but subtle.

"I went swimming with a porpoise." The quiet pleasure in her voice reflected the memory. She always had the positive to tell, even in a tragedy. She hadn't been in Florida for a vacation.

"Who'd you take?"

"Diane Faber, age ten. She was a much better swimmer."

"Did she lose one or both parents?" The tornado through Florida's Dade County three weeks ago had taken fourteen lives. As a trauma psychologist, Rachel got called in for the tough cases.

"Her father. He had promised her the trip for her birthday."

Rebuilding positive memories, helping the child know life went on. It was Rachel's special gift to children. "Rough."

"Yes. But she'll make it. How are you doing after Tuesday's excitement?"

"A few bad dreams."

"You got off relatively light then."

"I did."

"Hey, Rachel, you've got to come see my new pet," Lisa called. "I got him this last week."

"Does it slither?" Rachel whispered.

Kate grinned, having had the exact same concern when Lisa mentioned the pet to her. With Lisa it was best not to make assumptions. "A sable ferret. He's adorable."

"The fact it has fur is itself a relief. I want to hear about this bank thing later, in all its detail."

"You will." Kate promised, accepting the fact she would have to tell the story at least once tonight. Rachel nodded and crossed to join Lisa.

"The cuts look like they are healing well."

Kate turned to see Jennifer at her side and had to smile at the opening observation. The doctor would always be there in the forefront. "I wish you had been here. I had Stephen doing the needle bit and offering a lollipop."

"I heard. We were chatting on the phone while you were still in the ER. You'll be happy to know I brought him another case of lollipops since he was running short of cherry."

"I'm never going to live this one down, am I?"

Something flickered in Jennifer's eyes. "Not until someone else in the family creates better news to talk about."

Kate searched Jennifer's expression. That flicker, had it been for good news or bad? "Would that by any chance be you?"

Jennifer flashed a knowing smile. "You'll find out after dinner."

"Leaving me the hot seat for a while?"

"You're good cover. I think I'll hide behind you for another hour."

Kate hugged her. "In that case, I think I should hurry along dinner."

Marcus was leaning against the archway to the kitchen. Kate smiled at his quiet scrutiny. His arm came out to encompass her. "I'm glad you're okay."

She drew in a deep breath and let it out with a sigh, safe in the shelter of his arms. She would have to reassure them all, and it felt nice. "I honestly didn't get hurt that badly."

"I talked to your doctors. You weren't a pretty sight."

"It's relative. I nearly had a busted nose, but Dave got in the way of that blow."

"Richman?"

She nodded. "I'd say the fight was interesting for about forty seconds."

"I talked to him on the phone briefly at the hospital. He didn't mention it."

"As it split his lip, probably not." She leaned back and grinned. "Thanks for the roses."

"My pleasure."

"They were extravagant."

"Someone has to spoil you."

"I've really missed you."

"It's mutual." He rubbed her arms. "What else has been happening in your life? Been hiding any good secrets?" She was hiding so many at the moment it made her face tinge pink. One eyebrow raised. "I think you should explain that blush."

"Maybe later. We've got steaks for the grill, as well as Polish and brats. Would you take them out to Stephen and Jack?"

"The longer you duck the question, the more interested I'm going to be in the answer."

"Curiosity is good for you."

He nodded toward the kitchen. "Get the food."

Laughter erupted from the back patio where Lisa and Jennifer had joined Stephen and Jack. Kate grinned, loving the sound. "Try to corral the kids while you are out there."

"This is your jurisdiction, not mine."

"You're the adult here. I'm going to join the fun."

"Thanks a lot."

Kate slipped her arm around his waist and grinned. "Admit it; you like being the one in charge."

"In this family, that means I get all the grief."

"Exactly." It wasn't just the fact that they were the two oldest; it was the past. She and Marcus had been at the group home over two years before the others had begun to arrive. Their history together went deeper, and unlike the others, they had never had a chance to be kids. "I'm going to hate this answer, but when is your flight back?"

"First thing tomorrow morning."

"I was afraid of that."

"Have something in mind?"

"I was looking forward to a basketball game."

He smiled. "You could use a couple more days to recover."

"I'm a little stiff, but I'm ready to play. I figured you could use the handicap."

"Been beating Stephen recently?"

"Frequently. My fadeaway jumper is red hot."

"Let me see what Jack and Stephen are doing. Maybe we can fit in an early morning game."

"Hey, Kate! We're ready for food out here."

Kate gave Marcus an amused look. "Coming, Jack."

Dinner was a riot. Kate ended up seated between Marcus and Lisa. It had been six weeks since the last full gathering. The stories were numerous and hilarious. Kate sat back and enjoyed the shared laughter. There was something about having the whole family together that made everything more meaningful.

As plates were collected so dessert could be brought to the table, Lisa leaned over to whisper, "Are you going to mention seeing Dave?"

Kate hesitated, glancing around at the group. "Do you think I should?"

"What do you think?"

Why not? It was a night for surprises. Kate picked up her fork and tapped on her water glass. "May I have your attention please?"

The family quieted down. "Knowing the grapevine that cements this family together," she smiled at the main culprit sitting beside her as laughter echoed around the room, "allow me to dispel a rumor that I'm sure will soon be making the rounds. Yes, I have seen Dave Richman since Tuesday; it was not a date. I have not changed my policy on dating cops. Now who wants chocolate or raspberry ice cream for dessert?" She got to her feet to bring out dessert. She loved the looks of surprise around the table.

"Kate is seeing someone." Jennifer was delighted. "This is wonderful."

"Absolutely," Rachel joined in. "Come on, Kate. Details!"

"I've only known him a couple days. I think he'll make a good friend."

"We can tell. Nice blush, Kate." Marcus commented. "When do we get to meet him?"

"Check him out you mean?"

"Of course. Invite him to the basketball game tomorrow morning."

"You guys would have him for breakfast."

"Only if we didn't like him," Jack chimed in from the other end of the table.

Kate grinned, knowing it was true. She might as well find out if Dave was going to survive the scrutiny. No one could read a guy better than her brothers.

"I would want an honest opinion," she said softly to Marcus.

"That serious?"

No. And yet…"Maybe someday."

His hand grasped hers. "Bring him around."

Kate helped Lisa bring out dessert.

"Since Kate has broken the ice, I guess it's time for my announcement, too." Jennifer looked…nervous…Kate decided as she resumed her seat. She glanced around the table and saw the same anxiety just under the surface with everyone at the table. To a person, they were braced for bad news.

"I appreciate you all changing your plans and flying here on such short notice. I didn't want to do this over the phone."

Rachel reached over and grasped Jennifer's hand.

"I met someone a few months ago. Tom Peterson is a doctor in my medical office building. I haven't mentioned him because, well, a lot of reasons, but mainly because it was just a really good friendship. It's gotten serious in the last few weeks." She took a deep breath, her smile tremendous. "I'm engaged."

Engaged? And she had never mentioned him? Kate tried to absorb the news, to understand. This was quick, and Jennifer was not impulsive in her actions.

The first engagement in the family. There was a quietness around the room.

"Congratulations, Jen." The first words came from Marcus. Kate glanced over and saw not only a smile, but…relief? Yes. His worry for Jennifer would have been intense. He was the guardian of the family.

"I didn't mean to worry everybody. The engagement just sort of happened."

Kate grinned. Even Jennifer was having a hard time explaining the situation. It had to be love.

"Where's the ring?"

"When's the wedding?"

"Did you at least bring a picture?"

The questions came in a flurry as they crowded around Jennifer to celebrate, to share the joy.

Jennifer took the engagement ring off her necklace and slipped it on her finger. "I want to bring him to the Fourth of July gathering so you can all meet him. Just showing up with Tom didn't sound like a good idea."

"Now, Jen, you know if you said to like him, we automatically would," Jack protested.

"You had better!"

Kate gave Jennifer a hug. "You love him." She needed to hear that reassurance, for this was her baby sister.

"More than I can put into words."

Kate could see the joy. She could also see something she didn't understand. Jennifer glanced at the others and squeezed her hand. "You'll like him, Kate." Whatever else she wanted to say, it was something she wanted to say privately. Kate returned the pressure. Later.

Stepping back and watching Jennifer, Kate felt uneasy beneath her smile—not for Jennifer, but for the rest of them. Within a few months, the family would expand, become different. She tried to imagine it and could not. It had been just the seven of them for over two decades. She felt the unexpected sensation of threatening tears and blinked rapidly not to let them form.

A hand slipped around her waist and she turned. Marcus. "This day was destined to come. It will be different, Kate, but better."

"Reading my mind again?"

"Feeling the same thing."

She leaned her head on his shoulder. "An O'Malley wedding." She chuckled, finding laughter better than tears. "Can you imagine the surprises that will be dreamed up for the big day?"

"Life is not going to be boring." Marcus reassuringly rubbed her back. "Just think, we'll finally be able to play four on four, girls versus guys, with an expanded family."

She elbowed him. "You guys won't have any more excuses when you lose."

He grinned. "There is that."

The party began to break up shortly after 9 P.M. Rachel and Jennifer were staying with Lisa. Kate didn't doubt that they would be up most of the night talking. Marcus was heading out with Jack.

"Six A.M. game time?" Marcus confirmed, giving her a hug good-bye.

"Yes. With Dave if he's interested." How she was going to word that invitation, she had no idea.

"Good."

Jennifer had stepped into the kitchen. It was the first time Kate had been able to catch her alone. "Jen, congratulations again on your good news."

"Thanks." The smile was real, but so were the subtle signs of strain.

There was more news; Kate was sure of it now. She rested her arm around Jennifer's shoulders. "This is not the only reason you came."

"No. Can we meet tomorrow after you get off work?"

"I can get away for lunch."

Jennifer hesitated. "Evening would be better."

"Okay." The swirling reality of bad news was still in the air. "I'll call when I get off, come by and pick you up?"

Jennifer's hug was tight. "Thanks."

"Anytime. You'll call before then if you need me?"

Jennifer nodded.

"Don't let Lisa and Rachel keep you up half the night. They'll have you in Tahiti for your honeymoon if you're not careful."

Jennifer smiled. "They are debating Paris or Rome at the moment."

"The travel hounds have been let loose."

"I forgot how much fun it was to watch them together."

"It is that. Enjoy tonight. And call Tom."

"It's late."

"Trust me; he'll be waiting by the phone, afraid the family talked you into changing your mind."

"True." Jennifer glanced at the clock and grinned. "I think I'll give it another half hour before I call."

Kate laughed.

"Ready to go, Kate?"

"On my way, Stephen." She squeezed Jennifer's hand. "I'll see you tomorrow."

Stephen's car was blocking hers. "Stephen."

He paused halfway down the driveway. "Yes?"

She leaned against her open car door. "Would you mind coming to the gym a few minutes early?"

"Want to shake the rust off before Marcus arrives?"

"I would hate to get embarrassed on the court."

He tossed and caught his keys, considering it. "Will you go shopping with me to find Rachel's birthday present?"

Kate knew a good deal when she heard it. Stephen could carry the packages. "Deal."

She drove home without the radio on, content with her own thoughts. The fatigue that accompanied a day of emotions was beginning to set in. What else did Jennifer have to say? It was private. She had no idea what that meant. The clock on the dash read 9:48. If she waited until she got home, she could avoid a call to Dave by saying it was too late to bother him. The guys would accept that, but it was a weak excuse. She had never been a coward. If Dave said no, he said no.

She reached for the car phone.

Dave picked up his empty bowl. "Sara, you want more popcorn?"

She was stretched out on his couch using her husband Adam's lap for a pillow. "Sure." She handed him her bowl from the floor. "We can pause the movie."

"I've seen this part." Besides, he didn't want to give her a reason to move. He liked seeing her relaxed and content with Adam. They had come out to his house for the afternoon so Sara could look through old family picture albums, then had stayed for dinner and a movie. "I'll be back in a minute."

Dave found himself a cold soda while he waited for the popcorn to finish. When the phone rang, he grabbed it before the second ring.

"Richman."

"Sorry to call so late."

He smiled. "Didn't I say you could wake me up if you wanted to?" Pulling out a chair at the kitchen table, he sat down and stretched his legs out, making himself comfortable.

"It's not that urgent."

"It doesn't have to be." From the background noise he could tell Kate was on the road somewhere. The fatigue in her voice bothered him. "Where are you?"

"I think I'm lost." There was amusement in her voice.

"Want me to come to the rescue? You can send up flares or something."

"One wrong turn in construction, and I can't tell north from south."

"Well, that's easy. Go toward the tall buildings, and you'll eventually hit the lake. It's large. Very hard to miss."

Her chuckle was better than the fatigue he had been hearing. "This is better. I just found Yorkshire." He heard a car horn in the background. "Sorry for the tangent. Why did I call you?"

He laughed softly. "I don't care. I'm just glad you did."

"Tell me what you've been doing today while I try to remember."

"I had a quiet Sunday. Church with Sara and Adam. Shish kebabs for dinner. There are leftovers if you're interested. There's nothing new on Bobby Tersh."

"It's been seventy-two hours; relax, Dave."

"Just be careful when you get home, or I'll come camp out on your doorstep again."

He was expecting a comeback not a quiet sigh. "You can shoot me anytime."

"What did you forget?"

"My sister got engaged."

"Ouch. Okay, you got more than a little distracted. Which sister?"

"Jennifer."

"You must be thrilled."

"I think I am."

"Not sure yet?"

"It will be a big change for the O'Malley clan."

Adam came into the kitchen, and Dave smiled. "Speaking from personal experience, in-laws aren't too bad."

Adam raised an eyebrow. "Kate," Dave whispered. Adam smiled, finished fixing the popcorn, and disappeared with the full bowl.

"I haven't met Jennifer's fiancé yet. He'll be up here for the Fourth of July."

"Sounds like it will be an interesting holiday."

"We'll be nice. Jennifer has already stamped all the votes approved."

"Good for her." He heard a radio turn on. There was a comfortable moment of silence.

"I've got an offer for you."

Dave leaned forward, hearing the awkwardness in Kate's voice. "What's that?"

"We're having a basketball game tomorrow morning before Marcus has to fly out. Would you like to join us?"

"When and where?"

"Six, at the gym on Haverson Street."

He was not a morning person. "I'll be there," he replied without hesitation. The things he did for a friend. There was no way he was going to mention this to Sara.

"Thanks. I told them to be nice to you, by the way."

"Did you?"

"I don't know if this is a good idea, but I would like you to meet them."

"It's a great idea. I'll meet you there."

"Then I'll see you in about eight hours. Thanks, Dave."

"My pleasure. Good night, Kate."

He held onto the receiver for a few moments after the call disconnected before smiling and walking over to hang up the phone.

"Who was that?" Sara glanced up from the movie for a moment as he resumed his seat in the living room.

"A friend."

He was glad the movie had her too preoccupied to follow up. Adam, however, looked over at him, shook his head, and slowly smiled.

Seven

The gym echoed with the sound of a one-on-one intense basketball game. The bounce of the ball, the scuff of tennis shoes, an occasional huff of expelled air. The backboard sang with the impact of two hands on the rim.

Dave was immediately impressed with the intensity of the game being played. Kate and Stephen were the two on the court. They had apparently been playing for a while; her jersey was wet with sweat. Dave glanced at his watch and saw he was on time.

"So much for her being rusty."

He looked to his left and recognized from Kate's picture that he had been joined by one of the O'Malleys.

"I'm Jack. You must be Dave?" The man's smile was friendly, his handshake solid.

"Yes."

"Glad you could come." Jack glanced at the court, shook his head. "I'm getting tired of buying her breakfast."

Dave noted the protest was said with a smile. "The price of a loss?"

"Typically." Jack grinned. "But it makes the occasional wins all the sweeter."

Skirting around the game, they walked across to the bleachers and set down their gym bags.

Kate nailed a long two-point shot from the corner. "Yes!"

Stephen laughed and hugged her. "Good game." The two of them came off the court together.

Dave enjoyed the grin Kate turned toward him. "Hi, Dave." She sat down on the bench and picked up her water jug. She was breathing hard, looking pleased with herself for the win.

"You looked good out there," Dave said.

"Just warming up. You've met the other half of the dynamic duo?"

He glanced at Jack. "Yes."

Stephen accepted the second water jug Kate offered. "Jack, we're going to have to do something to earn us a different moniker."

"It would have to be something spectacular. We've been the dynamic duo since we were fourteen."

"How about the 'twin towers'?" Kate offered. Jack dropped a headlock on her, which made her giggle. "Where's Marcus?"

Jack gestured to the door where Marcus paced, talking on his cellular phone. "Washington called."

"Figures."

These were the guys who had shaped Kate's life. That she was comfortable with them was obvious.

Dave leaned over to her and whispered for her ears only, "Anything on our friend Tersh?"

She shook her head. "No word on his location; no more black roses."

Marcus joined them. "Sorry."

"Everything okay?" Kate asked.

"It will wait for another few hours." He smiled and extended his hand. "Nice to meet you in person, Dave."

Dave didn't miss the assessment being done as they shook hands. "Marcus."

"How do you want to play this?" Stephen asked.

Marcus and Kate exchanged a look. "Three on two. Kate and I will take you guys on. It should be about even."

Jack grinned. "Oooh, I think that was a challenge."

Stephen picked up the basketball. "I do believe it was."

Kate dropped her towel and grinned. "Let's talk strategy, Marcus." The two of them moved to the top of the key to huddle.

Dave watched the two of them for a moment, then looked over at Stephen. "Let me take Kate."

"She's good outside, she can jump, and she's fast," Stephen summarized. "You sure?"

Dave smiled. "I'm sure. Besides, it has to be easier than taking on Marcus."

Stephen laughed. "All right. I'll take Marcus, and Jack can cover."

The game was more intense than Dave had expected. They were playing for fun, but they were playing to win. As the score rose, the depth of the talent on the court began to make itself clear. They were all good players, but Kate and Marcus played in a rhythm that suggested years playing together. She was a dynamo on the court, always moving.

He pulled in a deep breath, fighting to get oxygen into his muscles. He was in excellent shape. He had to be in his profession. Playing with this group reminded him why he should not take those occasional days off from his workout routine.

He coiled the speed he had left and cut right, determined to go to the basket. He cleared Kate's leaping block by mere inches and watched his shot bounce around the rim and come back off the left side. Kate grabbed the rebound with elbows out. Dave knew what trouble was. It was Kate smelling victory.

He would make her earn it.

Hands warily out, he watched her eyes. She didn't telegraph her moves. He had never met someone with her skill for concealing her intentions. She could abruptly pull up, cut, then reverse.

She made a pass without looking. He pivoted to see Marcus go to the rim with the ball. How did she do that? Three against two and they were still getting beat.

"One to go." The satisfaction in her voice was clear.

Dave took the ball Stephen tossed him and dried his hands on his shorts. "It won't be easy."

She grinned. "You're stalling."

Dave took the ball to the half court line with a half grunt, half laugh. He touched the line and cut left. Stephen broke free. Dave passed him the ball. Marcus forced Stephen to pass it back. Dave glanced at Jack and then drove for the basket.

Kate stepped in front of him.

The fear was instantaneous. He pivoted hard to avoid the collision but couldn't avoid crashing into her. She slid to a stop on her backside a few feet away.

"Charge."

To hear her, she had just won a crown rather than a bruise. He offered her a hand up. "Kate, winning is not that important!" His voice shook with anger and lingering fear.

She looked at him, puzzled.

Marcus dropped his arm across her shoulders, breathing hard. "Kate, not everyone is used to the way you throw yourself into harm's way for a simple game."

She wiped her face, then nodded. "Sorry, Dave."

He tossed the ball to Stephen, still scowling. "Sure you are. You'd do it again in a heartbeat to block my shot." From her grin, she heard his muttered comment.

"Take the ball out, Marcus."

The last few minutes of the game were played with a little less contact. Jack evened out the score before a blitz by Marcus came back to win the game.

Kate collapsed on the bench. "Who's going to carry me to breakfast?"

Jack tossed a towel over her face. "What happened to being a gracious winner?"

She laughed and tossed it back at him. "I'll let you beat me at a game of tennis."

"I could do that in my sleep."

A pager went off. Dave reached for his and was amused to see everyone else reaching for his or hers.

"It's mine." Jack grabbed his bag. "I'm gone. Nice to have met you, Dave."

"Don't eat too much smoke!" Kate called after him as he ran for the door.

"I'll be careful!"

Puzzled, Dave looked at Kate.

"Fireman."

He nodded. Fireman. Paramedic. U.S. Marshal. Her brothers had interesting careers.

She turned. "Marcus, how are you doing on time?"

Marcus was stretched out, his elbows resting on the bleachers behind him. "A fast shower and I'll need to leave for the airport."

Kate's face grew pensive. "Call me tonight."

Marcus studied her for a moment, then nodded. "Sure."

Watching Kate with her family was watching her with people she loved. She relaxed, laughed, joked, and cared. Dave was glad he had been invited to come. He was getting to see another side of her.

Marcus got to his feet and offered his hand. "I'm glad I got to meet you."

Dave felt he had passed a test. "It's mutual."

"Stephen, how about you dropping me off at the airport? We'll let Kate and Dave get a leisurely breakfast."

Kate blushed. "Marcus O'Malley—" She scrambled to grab her pager. Her look turned to one of intense frustration. "Never mind. I've got to go." She gave Marcus a quick hug.

When she paused beside him, Dave buried his worry to give her a smile. "We'll talk. Go. Be careful."

She nodded and broke for the door at a quick trot.

An hour spent talking to a woman threatening to jump from a fourth floor ledge put Kate in a quiet mood when she eventually got back to the office. In an effort to discourage conversation, she slipped on her headphones but did not touch play. It took forty minutes to complete the case notes from the incident. And when she was done, Kate felt rung out. She could summarize the woman's problem in two words: *no hope.*

She dropped her case notes on her boss's desk and left to take a tenminute walk.

There were days the job hit too close to home.

Life had never managed to break her own will to live, but it had scarred her expectations of what life would be like. She had been a wary little fighter when she was nine. With the passing years, she had gained an appreciation of life and the things that were to be treasured, but there remained part of her that listened to "there is no hope" and resonated with it.

For every bright spot, there was a shadow.

She had the O'Malleys and a past so dark it still made her flinch.

She had her job and a life expectancy that insured she would not be issued a life insurance policy.

Would Dave ever understand the somber part of her that looked at life and better understood the shadows than the light? She thought about him as she walked.

She smiled. Her brothers liked him. Even Marcus, the most protective, had signaled a qualified approval. It created a quandary for her: She didn't date cops, and her brothers were going to be asking about Dave in the future.

When she returned to the office, there was a note Dave had called. *Black Rose* was underlined. Something new? She hoped so. He was smothering her about this black rose thing. If he thought having someone leave her a rose was a problem, what was he going to be like when the threat was serious? The man was too good at his job; he didn't know how to ignore a problem around him. Why couldn't she have been stuck in the bank with a desk jock instead of a frontline agent?

She picked up the phone. When she got his voice mail, she rubbed her eyes, debated for a moment, then left a brief message that she was returning his call, was fine, and that she would be working on Henry Lott's case notes that afternoon. She scanned her calendar. "I've also got a meeting set up with Nathan Young for Wednesday, 2 P.M., if you still want to tag along. Let me know."

She hung up the phone and realized she had forgotten to say thanks for playing basketball with them this morning. Call and leave another message? She ran her hand through her hair. No, better to call back later and tell him in person.

"Hey, Kate, who's your contact over in narcotics?"

She glanced over to see Franklin, his hand covering the telephone receiver, leaning far enough back in his chair it was close to tipping over. "Christopher Atkins. Tall, lanky, looks seventeen—the one that broke up that high school track-and-field cocaine ring."

"Our Henry Lott is claiming drug money used to get laundered through Wilshire Construction."

"Why doesn't that surprise me?" She shouldn't be so cynical, but a night watchman at a construction company trying to cut a deal to get time knocked off a certain prison sentence—there were only so many things he could credibly pull out of his hat. "Want me to call over?"

Franklin spoke briefly into the phone, then shook his head. "No need. Graham's on his way over there now. He figured you would know the best person to ask." He spoke for another minute, then hung up the phone.

"Did anything else come out of the interview?"

"No. But ATF called this morning. They traced the explosives to a now defunct subcontractor that did some demolition work for Wilshire Construction ten years ago. We'll be able to put this one to bed, Kate."

She looked at the case notes on her desk. "Yes." Another couple days and the last loose ends would be wrapped up. She almost wished her pager would go off so she could avoid spending the rest of the day doing her final review of the negotiation tapes.

Kate reached over to unlock the passenger door. "Jennifer, I'm sorry to be so late." It was almost 8 P.M. She had completed her review of the Henry Lott negotiation tapes and had been ready to walk out the door when she had been put on standby for a call out that had never come. She still owed Dave a call to say thanks for coming to the game this morning. She had been away from her desk getting a late lunch when he called back to confirm Wednesday's meeting with Nathan Young.

Jennifer slipped into the passenger seat. "Quit apologizing. This is fine. If I slipped out earlier, I would feel guilty about abandoning Lisa and Rachel."

"Do they have your wedding planned?"

"They are having the time of their lives making suggestions. It is wonderful. There is no way I would have the energy to pull off what can be done with their help."

"So it's good? They are not stepping on your toes?"

"I'm enjoying sharing the joy."

Kate relaxed. Jennifer meant it. She looked at her sister, hoping to find she had misread the situation last night. She hadn't. The tension was still there. "What would you like to do?"

The lighthearted few moments changed to quiet resolve. "Let's pick up a soda at the corner store and then go for a walk."

They bought sodas, and Kate stopped at the nearby park. They set out to walk around its oval-shaped pond. It was a beautiful evening, and several people were out walking around the park.

Kate would have liked to break the silence with some light comment but forced herself to stay quiet. The longer they walked in silence, the more concerned she became.

"I didn't come with only good news."

"I know," she said quietly.

"Kate, I'm flying from here to the Mayo clinic."

She didn't make the connection immediately. "Why?"

Jennifer reached over and squeezed her hand. "I've got cancer."

"You've what?"

"The test results came back last week." Jennifer's shoulders hunched. "They were pretty bad. It's one of the reasons Tom refused to postpone his proposal."

"What did the test results say?"

"The cancer is around my spine. It's rare. And it has spread into at least my liver."

No! The emotions screamed to spill out. They turned inward instead, were stuffed deep, defensively blocked. *Keep focused.*

Breathe.

"We have to tell the family."

"No. Not yet. I'll be back for the Fourth of July. By then I will know the scope of what I'm facing. I was only going to tell Marcus, but he can't afford the distraction. Given what happened Tuesday, I couldn't afford to wait another week to tell you."

"How can you sound so calm about this?"

"Oh, Kate, the emotions roil in a thousand directions. But there is a comfort in knowing I'm okay even if the worst happens. Tom introduced me to what faith is. I *have* to talk to you about Jesus. Tuesday scared me to death."

Kate's thoughts were racing with the onslaught of unexpected news. "First Dave, now you," she murmured quietly, not realizing she spoke.

"What?"

"He said nearly the same thing the other night." She took a deep breath and slowly let it out. "What can I do to help?"

Jennifer's arm circled around her shoulders. "I know this is a shock. I know how big of a burden I'm placing on you. The news is going to affect everyone in the family, and they are going to lean heavily on you and Marcus."

"Oh, Jen, the fact it affects us is nothing compared to the reality of what you are dealing with. Is the pain bad?"

"My right side hurts. There is some numbness in my left leg. But there were few warning signs."

"What are you looking at—surgery, chemotherapy, radiation?"

"I'm being sent to Mayo to find out if there are any options. I won't kid you. Whatever they come up with is likely to be experimental."

"There have to be options."

"The doctors have advised it will be a week of long days and a lot of tests. We'll see what they come up with. As a doctor, I can cope better with the details than the speculation." Jennifer hugged Kate. "You asked what you could do. I want to talk with you when I get back about Jesus. I'm afraid for you."

Jen was afraid for *her*. There was such helplessness in being asked something so intangible. "I wish I could promise there would be no more close calls. But it comes with the job."

"I know that. But do you understand why faith has become such an important issue to me? I don't want to pressure you, but if something did happen, I would have a very hard time knowing I had never talked to you. I want you to read the book of Luke and have dinner with me, then tell me honestly what you think about Jesus."

"Jennifer, I'm afraid I'll hurt you."

"You won't. I would rather hear honest reasons for disbelief than never to have had the conversation with you." She took a slim book from her pocket. "I marked the page."

Kate looked awkwardly at the leather book Jennifer handed her. "You want me to read the book of Luke."

"It's written by a doctor. It's one of my favorite gospels." Jennifer tried to offer a reassuring smile. "Kate, if you still say you don't believe, that's okay. I simply need to talk to you about it."

She was supposed to believe in God while her sister was possibly dying? Reeling from a hit against her family she could do nothing to fight, Kate's hand clutched the book. She couldn't say no to Jennifer's request, but how could she calmly discuss something that made her feel so angry? She had no choice. She would do whatever Jennifer asked. "We'll have dinner."

The clock blinked 3:22 A.M. Kate pulled another page off the printer and skimmed the text as she drank her sixth cup of coffee since midnight. The article from the January *Oncology Journal* filled in a few more gaps in her knowledge. There were two new chemotherapy treatments showing promise, both combinations of existing drugs. Her eyes burned as she struggled to focus and read, but at least it was now fatigue and not the salt of tears. She had given up trying to sleep.

She desperately wanted to be able to talk to Marcus, but instead had listened as the answering machine took his call at 11 P.M. If he heard her voice, he would know. She couldn't come up with a convincing lie right now, even to give herself cover so she could talk with him. This was the first crisis in years where she had not been able to lean on him.

Cancer. It was hard to describe the fear the word evoked the more she read. What she had learned from the pages spread out across her desk scared her to death. According to her research, Jennifer could be facing a 2 percent survival rate beyond one year.

Premature death was part of her world, not Jennifer's. That pain seared. Jennifer didn't deserve this.

Kate had to deal with the personal risk of an early death because of her job. The power of attorney, the will, her bank accounts, financial papers, all of it was organized to make it easier on her family should something happen. She held the same documents for Marcus. There was a sense of preparation for the worst when it came to the dangers of their jobs. But she had never thought about Jennifer as being at risk. The news had struck a soft underbelly.

There was nothing she could do. That was what hurt the most.

She set down the coffee cup, pushing back the small leather book with the words *New Testament* across the front. She had promised Jennifer to read Luke, and she eventually would, but at the moment she would like nothing better than for the book to accidentally fall into the trash.

She could understand Jennifer not wanting to mix the good news and the bad Sunday night. She could understand the caution of wanting to wait until she had more details before telling the whole family. But carrying the secret was going to be the toughest thing Kate had faced in years.

Eight

K ate shifted through change for toll money, glad she didn't have to make this trip to O'Hare often. Traffic coming out of the city was a mess. Needing to get away from the office, she had offered to take Franklin's place at the monthly check-in with Bob Roberts, head of O'Hare's security. It was a beautiful day out—sunny blue skies, light breeze. She popped another two jelly beans in her mouth. After this meeting, she was going to take a few hours of personal time and get some much needed sleep.

The shock of Jennifer's news had passed. She was thinking now proactively about questions to ask the doctors. This would be a long battle that none of the O'Malleys would accept losing. If the doctors said a 2 percent chance, then Jennifer would be in that 2 percent. They were O'Malleys. They had dealt with long odds before.

She checked her voice mail messages and was relieved to hear one from Jennifer. Her early morning flight had been fine; she was getting ready to take a cab out to the Mayo Clinic. Kate hung up the phone and made a mental note to call in an hour when Jennifer should be checked in.

There was something majestic about coming into O'Hare on I-190 and realizing they had built an airport taxiway over the highway. Kate slowed her speed to match traffic and watched a huge Turkish Airline Airbus cross from the international terminal to the runway. The plane gleamed bright white, its red tail rising like a hawk. Her car passed under the shadow cast by its wing.

She glanced at her watch. 9:20 A.M. She was a few minutes early.

Kate flipped open the incident plan book and found Bob's number. She called him from her cellular phone and arranged to meet him by the United ticket counter in terminal one. She liked Bob Roberts. She had worked with the former DEA agent several times over the years. Her job today would be to listen, make note of the security changes made in the last month, and coordinate any changes he wanted to make to the incident plan book.

With one hundred flights an hour on average and over two hundred thousand passengers a day, Bob Roberts had a massive job on his hands. The security personnel at O'Hare could handle most incidents, but a constant coordination was done with the city police, fire department, bomb squad, and FBI so that when he did need to bring people in, it would happen in a seamless fashion.

Kate slipped a blank cassette into the handheld tape recorder that went everywhere with her and tucked a couple spare cassettes into her pocket. She preferred dictating notes. She walked through the airport at a leisurely pace, scanning the crowds out of habit.

"Good morning, Bob." He was a man in his late forties, perpetually in motion. Meetings with him were walking tours, the best kind of reviews in Kate's opinion. If they swung out to the general aviation terminal, she planned to make a couple inquiries regarding Dave's jet. Assuming Dave was a regular here, Bob would know what he flew.

"Kate. Glad they sent you. I always have to explain everything to Franklin."

"I'll take any excuse to get out of the office." She retrieved her bag of jelly beans and offered to share. She remembered his sweet tooth.

"Thanks." Bob gestured to terminal C. "Let's walk."

"There are a couple general changes worth noting. Customs has a new program beginning this month at Cargo City. They are adding five dogs. I expect seizures will be up over the next month.

"We have doubled the number of security personnel walking the terminals for the next month to accommodate the increase in Fourth of July passenger traffic.

"I've also got a new set of contact phone numbers for you. We've finally got the last recommendations of the review panel completed."

They walked the terminal, Kate making notes, laughing frequently as

Bob peppered his serious discussion of security changes with some of the more amusing incidents in the last month.

Bob's pager went off.

He glanced at the code. "Kate, we've got an incident. That's the air traffic control tower."

An incident could be anything from a plane in trouble to a terrorist threat. Regardless, it wasn't the kind of information people around them should hear. Bob used his access card to open a side door in the concourse. They hurried down a flight of stairs to the tarmac. The roar of planes taking off, muted inside, now reverberated across concrete. He pointed to one of the shuttle carts. "We'll take it to the tower."

Kate nodded and climbed aboard.

He tuned his radio to a private channel. "Elliot, it's Bob. We're on our way. What are the details?"

"A bomb threat was called in on the regional ATC line. Five words. 'Get ready for a bomb.' Male voice. Not enough to get a good accent. Popping on the line, possibly a cellular phone."

"Handle it Code Two, Elliot."

"Calls are already underway."

Kate knew the procedures, but since she was carrying a copy of the plan book, she flipped it open. "Is it against the tower, a plane, or a terminal?" She was thinking out loud. They didn't have enough information to know. She glanced at her watch and noted the time. 10:48 A.M. This was supposed to be a light duty morning. Two bomb incidents within a week was a toll she didn't need. Every threat was treated as real.

Passengers and flight crews in the terminals would already be seeing a noticeable shift in the intensity of the security. Unattended baggage would be cleared. Dogs would be out working the areas. The visible sweep would begin while behind the scenes the more intense work began. Fire and rescue would be on high alert. Ground crews would be paying special attention as flights were prechecked and turned around for departure. Luggage would be screened again. A search of the grounds would begin.

Kate looked at Bob. "When was the last bomb threat?"

"Sixteen days ago, called into an airline office. A hoax."

The tower handled air traffic within the tightly controlled class B airspace. Outside that zone of class B airspace, the aircraft were handled by the regional air traffic control center. "The call came in on a regional ATC phone number. How well-known is that number?" Kate asked, looking for clues.

Bob skirted around a luggage carrier. "Obviously it is posted in the regional center. Within O'Hare proper, the tower people would know it and the electrical technicians who maintain the tower. It's a restricted line, but the central phone hub for the complex would have it marked."

Kate worked on her list. "So add janitors and maintenance people in general. It's not secure information but limited."

"Yes. We can run the records, see when the phone number was last changed."

Kate nodded, looking at the words of the threat. "'Get ready for a bomb.' No clock, so he either doesn't want to give us the time it will go off, or he doesn't know the exact time it will go off. It sounds like the device is already in place."

The more she looked at the words, the more she disliked them. "Bob, it is too general to be a hoax." Hoaxes were specific. They wanted to arouse a strong reaction without showing evidence. "This is the first warning shot. Why the tower? That's the only clue we really have."

"Rule of thumb, threat calls go to the media to get attention or to the intended target to get a response," Bob replied.

It was a common convention that bombs at airports targeted planes, but it wasn't an absolute. "The tower itself?"

"Possible. At least it's a contained area to search."

The tower sat detached from other buildings, rose high above the passenger concourses, and looked out across seven runways, one of them over two miles long. Kate followed Bob inside the building and showed her badge to clear security. They headed to the observation deck.

The room was crowded with very busy people. From this location, they had a full 360 degree view of the airspace. The windows in the room had been sealed in at a slight angle with the top edge extending farther out. The glare-resistant, thick glass helped keep the controllers from squinting into the sunlight. Kate could see planes out on the taxiways, lined up ten deep to take off. Massive Boeing 747s looked small from this height. In the air, planes were stacked in defined holding patterns waiting for clearance to land. She listened to the terse chatter between air traffic controllers and pilots and understood a word here and there. ORD was the designation for O'Hare.

Elliot waved them over. "We've got three groups working the problem. Concourses, luggage and cargo, and aircraft. All the dogs are deployed."

"Let's get a team sweeping this tower," Bob requested.

Elliot nodded and reached for the radio.

"Can we route this phone line to the command center in the administration building?"

"I've got a technician taking a look. He said it might have to be a hard jumper at the punch-down block since restricted lines were not made part of the main switch."

"What about getting set up to run a trace if we get another call?"

"Working on it."

"Kate, can I borrow the tape recorder? If this is real, I hope we get more than this vague call to work with."

She already had a new tape in place. "Unfortunately, Bob, I think you will." She watched as the men worked, talking with the deployed teams, their calm efficiency reminding her of how many of these incidents they worked in a year.

It was precisely 11:00 A.M. when the regional ATC phone rang again. The mood all around the tower changed. The odds of this one being real and not a hoax had just risen dramatically. Bob took a deep breath, clicked on the recorder, and picked up the phone. "O'Hare tower."

Kate saw the anger cloud his face and caught his startled look in her direction. He apparently was not given the opportunity to ask any questions. He hung up the phone and clicked off the recorder. "Kate, what is going on?"

He rewound the cassette and pressed play.

"The bomb goes off at eleven-fifteen. The plane is talking to the tower. Tell Kate O'Malley I haven't forgotten the past."

Hearing her name was so unexpected that the detachment so necessary when working a crisis broke to show her own disbelief, and for a brief instance, fear. Who knew she was here? "I have no idea. Play it again."

She closed her eyes and listened, expecting to recognize a voice. It was badly distorted, the words understandable but altered; she could not make out any distinctive features. Probably a digital cellular phone, it didn't have static like an analog line as much as it cut in and out. The cadence of speech, the word choices, both were very deliberate. She looked over at Elliot. "Is this the same caller?"

"Yes."

"Bob, the threat sounds very real. I don't know what the reference to me implies." She had to bury the fear; there wasn't time for it. Her control slipped back in place so that only logic ruled. They would figure out the reference later; right now there were more critical decisions to make and not much time to make them. "How many planes are talking to the tower?"

He was already looking at a monitor. "There are eight departing flights still in our airspace. Fourteen incoming flights are under our control. Another sixteen flights are on taxiways queued up to depart."

"The twenty-two planes in the air. How do we get them down?"

"We can't. Not in fifteen minutes. But we can come close." Bob looked at the tower chief, Greg Nace. "Let's get everything in class *B* airspace on the ground. Take an outgoing flight over one inbound. Prioritize for souls on board."

"Agreed." The tower chief looked at the controllers, every one of them tense and awaiting directions. "Alert the pilots in the air of the threat. Tell them to set down fast. We're going to have to ignore FAA regulations for distance to get this many planes down in time. Let regional control know we will not be accepting any more aircraft into the pattern.".

Rapid, controlled chatter began around the room. The men and women talking to the pilots began orchestrating a controlled recovery of planes.

Bob turned to his second in command. "Elliot, how many open gates do we have?"

"Eighteen."

"Find us some more to use. Tell maintenance to back empty planes away from gates. Having a plane full of passengers explode on the ground isn't part of the plan. Get security to the gates to keep people calm."

The tower chief interrupted. "Bob, we've got three outbound flights reporting fuel loads above what is safe for an immediate abort. We'll have no choice but to put them to the back of the queue."

Kate picked up binoculars and watched a Boeing 747 touch down on the runway, white puffs of smoke appearing as the plane's tires touched pavement. It had been a long time since she had felt this helpless.

Tell Kate O'Malley I haven't forgotten the past.

What did that mean? The bomber knew her? How? And why a plane?

She watched the clock, counted the planes touching down, and listened to the air traffic controllers.

11:12 A.M.

There were still nine flights in the air.

11:13.

Eight flights.

11:14.

Six flights.

She heard a controller give MetroAir Flight 714 clearance to land on runway 32L.

11:15.

Nine

MetroAir Flight 714 exploded in midair.

The shock wave from the blast reverberated off the tower windows. It hit the building so hard that tables not secured moved a few inches, lights swayed, mugs rattled, and several binders fell from a nearby shelf. Kate instinctively leaned into the counter beside her to keep steady.

She couldn't tear the binoculars away from the horrific sight. Huge sections of the fuselage slammed down onto the runway and were engulfed in burning jet fuel. The rest of the plane came down west of runway 32L.

A second fireball erupted on the ground as jet fuel erupted. Cargo City—FedEx, UPS, DHL. One of the major shipping company's planes or facilities had just been hit.

Around her was shocked silence.

Bob was the first to move. His hand squeezed the tower chief's shoulder. "Divert the five flights in the air to Midway. Close the airport; helicopter transports are going to own the airspace for the immediate future."

Orders started to flow to the staff around him. "Elliot, get on the hotline. We need every ambulance, every medical helicopter they can find. Jim, send the pager codes, call everyone in. Get the command center open." He looked back at the size of the debris field already apparent. "Frank, get me the Air National Guard CO on the phone. I need his people, and I need him to enforce the closed airspace immediately."

Kate listened to the orders as she watched battalions of fire engines and rescue personnel speed onto the runway to enter a fight that appeared hopelessly one-sided. No one was walking away from the wreckage. With the binoculars she should have seen someone by now. No one was walking away.

"I want someone sitting on this phone in case he decides to remark on his handiwork. There may be a second bomb; I want nothing overlooked in the search. We need all the agencies—FBI, NTSB, ATF, and FAA."

Around the room, people were picking up the phones. "Elliot, pull together the first update meeting at 1 P.M. I'll be with the fire chief. Kate, stay with me."

She nodded, needing to be pitched into the battle for survivors. It was too late, but they had to try. There had to be hope.

In the past hour and a half, Kate had completely shut off her emotions. She was too numb to feel anything anymore. The faces around her were grim. Helicopters waited on the taxiway to take survivors to the hospitals, but there were no survivors.

It had become a massive crime scene.

This section of the fuselage had not burned, but smoke had roiled through it. The heat lingered in the metal, the seats. The plane structure had been destroyed. She crawled past mangled seats, moving aside suitcases, books, briefcases, magazines, letters. Shoes. Shopping bags. Dolls. She tried not to get caught on insulation, wires, or jagged metal.

Her hands were blistered, scraped from previous work in this section of the fuselage as she helped retrieve victims. She had discarded the borrowed fire turnout coat once the threat of the fire had been suppressed.

They had located the flight attendant who had been at the airplane door. MetroAir allowed last minute walk-ons. The passenger and electronic tickets were in the flight attendant's vest pocket. While there were copies at the terminal, knowing who had stepped through the plane door was the most important check they had; records at the terminal could potentially get tampered with. It was difficult to deal with the fact paper was her priority, a passenger list more important than the passengers were.

One of the two firemen reached toward her as soon as she was within reach. It was a tight squeeze with three of them in the collapsed galley area. "Show me."

The fireman lifted the wall.

Kate knelt down and wedged herself into the space. The name tag confirmed her identity. Cynthia Blake. Kate found it painfully hard to handle the fact the flight attendant looked like she was asleep.

Kate gently retrieved the passenger documents. She wanted to apologize to this lady, her family, her friends, all the people her death would touch. It was guilt she didn't know how to process. Because she had seen the explosion, had been unable to prevent it. Because her name had been mentioned in the threat. Somehow, in a way she did not understand, she was involved in this tragedy. The bomber probably felt no guilt. She did.

Kate turned to one of the firemen. "Have the FBI record her location, and you can move her."

She worked her way back outside.

The intensity outside was worse than that inside the fuselage. All the images blurred together. There were so many victims.

Death wasn't new.

Violent death wasn't new.

This many deaths in an instant of time was.

She did not look at the tickets she carried, did not read the names. She needed the distance for another moment.

The sick feeling in the pit of her stomach increased as she walked past the wreckage. She had been trained to put together a life from little pieces of information. The debris around her reflected so many lives. She skirted around rescue personnel working in a burned section of the fuselage where victims were just now being removed.

She had never realized how massive an Illiad 9000 wide-body plane was. The fuselage wreckage, not to mention the wings, dwarfed the vehicles nearby. Over two hundred people had been aboard this flight. None had walked away.

The smell of jet fuel would take days to clear. Most of it had burned, scorching the runway. The firefight had moved from the plane wreckage to the shipping facility where the battle still raged. Thick black smoke billowed into the air. Kate dreaded to hear news of causalities there.

Stephen was here somewhere, and Jack; she had seen both of them from a distance working with others from their units. How were they handling the disaster? Burn victims were horrible, especially for the men and women who daily risked their lives to prevent such deaths. The fuselage pieces were now smoldering remains, covered in foam and water. If only the plane had been on the ground, been on a taxiway, some might have survived.

How was Lisa going to cope with this? As one of the central staff at the state crime lab, a forensic pathologist, she would be one of those called in specifically to help identify the dead, to reconstruct what had happened. Weeks of dealing with this tragedy would haunt her. Kate felt sick just at the thought.

Who had done this?

Why?

She looked to the south. The land had been an open field of wildflowers this morning, the best of summer's beauty. Now the almost half mile square area looked like the center of a war zone, the ground marked by twisted metal, personal belongings, and shrouded white sheets covering the dead. National Guard personnel were already beginning the task of turning the field into a large grid.

The bright blue sky, the sunshine, felt like an insult.

Overhead, police and National Guard helicopters enforced the closed airspace, keeping the news media from flying directly overhead. Local stations, national affiliates would have all rushed news crews to the scene. Kate suspected that with the explosion at 11:15 A.M., the news media had been live on the air by 11:18. The satellite dishes were probably already lined up along the 294 Tollway overpass, broadcasting live pictures as they looked down on the crash site.

She could only imagine what it was like inside O'Hare's terminals. A bomb created instant panic. Not just for the families of the victims, desperate for information, but for everyone else who felt the relief and the guilt that they escaped.

She headed to the forward command center rapidly put together on the runway near the crash. It had become the nerve center for ground operations, manned by the fire chief and his support crew, Chicago police, FBI, National Transportation Safety Board, and emergency medical personnel. Radio traffic was heavy as assistants coordinated men from different districts. She handed the documents to the courier waiting for them and found a place out of the way to wait for Bob. He was talking to the National Guard commanding officer about site security.

There were hundreds of O'Hare employees standing together in clusters along the nearest taxiway, looking out at the wreckage, watching events unfold. They were spectators, but quiet ones, their faces still showing the shocked disbelief at what they were witnessing. Kate understood that shock. She ineffectively wiped at the grime on her hands and looked at jeans now ruined and wished she could close her eyes and make this nightmare go away.

She had to watch this tragedy as the others did, but at least she could do something about it. Whoever had set this bomb would pay. Somewhere in that wreckage before her, on the runway, across the field, was the evidence that would convict him. The victims would at least get justice. Someone had made a mistake when they had made this personal with her.

"Someone's targeting her!" Dave stared at the small tape recorder as he listened to the bomb threat again and felt his heart squeeze. The fear was invading. He couldn't let it overwhelm him. Black roses were one thing; this—how many different ways was Kate going to get ripped into? She couldn't go home without having her job invade her life. This threat couldn't even have been graded; it was so malicious. How did he keep her safe when he couldn't even figure out what to protect her from? Her past was a big, black, ugly hole, and it seemed to be leaping at her from every direction.

He looked over at his boss. "Where is she?" The command center outside this small conference room was packed with people, but he had not seen Kate.

"Out at the crash site. She was in the tower with Bob Roberts when this call came in."

"Oh, that's just great. She's out in the open." He pushed away from the table. "Whoever this guy is, he's out for her blood."

"Dave, we don't know. But we need to find out. You know her better than anyone else in the regional office. We need security on her, immediately. Keep her alive long enough for us to figure this out."

Dave glanced around the empty conference room. "I can't let her know I'm formally protecting her."

"Her boss knows, but she's not the type to handle a shadow very well. Keep it low key."

That was going to make his job difficult if not impossible. So much for throwing her in a safe house far from here. He sighed. She'd never accept that anyway. "I know what you mean." He thought for a moment. "There's still a reason someone targeted a plane."

"Yes. Find out why."

He nodded and picked up his jacket. "I'll go find Kate."

"Dave—"

He turned in the doorway.

"Be careful."

"Count on it," he replied grimly. "Listen—can you track down one of her brothers? He's a U.S. Marshal, Marcus O'Malley. He flew back to Washington early yesterday morning."

"I'll find him for you."

"Thanks."

Dave was not going to let anyone harm her. She was becoming too important to him. Whether she liked it or not, she now had a full-time shadow. At least now he wouldn't have to do it on his own time. He pulled on the FBI blue jacket. He had a feeling before this was over Kate was going to give him gray hair.

A helicopter lifted off from the runway tarmac, causing Kate to shade her eyes. It flew out slowly over the crash scene. Kate had seen several NTSB officials climb aboard; they must be getting a look at the debris field.

"Kate."

She turned, surprised. Dave was here. He wore a lightweight blue jacket even on this hot day, one of dozens around the area wearing the FBI colors. There were others wearing jackets from the FAA, NTSB, Red Cross, each with their own color; the visual affiliation allowing people to find each other rapidly in the crowd of investigators tasked with different assignments.

"I've been looking for you." He looked like a fighter sizing up his opponent; that was her first impression, and she went with it, instinctively shifting her weight back. She looked at him warily, not able to read what he was thinking. His hands settled firmly on her shoulders. "Are you okay?"

The depth of the emotion in his voice made her realize she had made a mistake. He wasn't hiding what he was thinking; he was trying to keep her from seeing how intense it was. She wasn't accustomed to having someone in the middle of a crisis focus on her instead of the victims. It was personal concern for her driving that emotion in him. Unexpected tears pooled in her eyes but were blinked away. Next to having an O'Malley to lean on, Dave would do. "You heard about the call."

"I did." His face was grim.

All the emotion buried from that horrifying moment when she heard her name came roiling back. To feel afraid was the worst of all emotions. It was the helpless fear a victim felt, and Kate would never let herself be a victim again. "I don't know why he used my name." She heard the slight quiver in her voice and pulled in a harsh breath to fight for control.

"We're going to find out why." His words were gentle, a promise. He brushed at her bangs. "You've been out here since it happened, crawling through the wreckage?"

She sighed, then nodded. "The debris field, some of the fuselage sections that didn't burn. We hoped for survivors, but there were none. Even in the sections I was in, the impact, the smoke was too great." She rubbed her arms. "It wasn't the fire crews' fault, they were here before the wreckage stopped tumbling."

He shook her slightly. "It wasn't your fault, either. I don't know what this guy is playing at by mentioning your name, but you are not responsible for this."

She bit her lip and nodded because he was so insistent. She knew she was not to blame but realized she was involved. "I am connected in some way I don't understand. I've been trying to remember past cases, who might have the skills to do this, but the few men I think could do this are still in jail."

"We'll find the connection."

Yes, he would feel that same certainty she did. No one could look at these victims and not proceed until the case was solved. And she already had a taste of what he was like doing his job; she felt sorry for the bomber they were after. It was difficult though, to know she would be in the middle of the investigation for the duration, that she herself would be under scrutiny by people who had never met her before this event. Her life was private and intentionally protected; to have others prying into that past would bring up old wounds she wished would stay buried. "Have you actually heard the tape, what it sounded like?"

"Yes."

"It was too distorted; I couldn't recognize the voice. If it was someone from a past case, chances are I spent hours talking to him. I should be able to recognize the voice." The call was the only known lead they had at the moment, and it galled her that she could do nothing with it.

"The tape is being sent to the forensic lab. I'm sure they will be able to clean it up." He had the luxury of distance from this, could speak calmly and objectively, a role that was normally hers. She felt an irrational irritation at that fact.

"You shouldn't be out here in the open. Come on, let's get you inside."

She gave him a blank stare. She was too tired to understand his words.

"You're a target, Kate," he said quietly. "Until we understand why, it's not a good idea to be out here."

Her jaw tightened, but she didn't protest when he turned her toward one of the O'Hare security cars. There was little more she could do here anyway, and it was about time for the first update meeting. She was about to be smothered with a blanket of protection if Dave had his way, but she didn't have the energy to fight him on it. She slid into the car without further protest.

He paused the car to give emergency vehicles the right of way. "Walk me through your itinerary for today, everything that happened."

The timeline. Yes, it was going to be critical. She took a deep breath and felt the relief of being back in a role she knew how to deal with. She thought about it carefully. "I got to the office at 6:55 A.M. I know because the news at the top of the hour was starting when I went for coffee. Franklin was fixing himself a bagel with cream cheese, and he happened to mention the O'Hare security review was on his schedule for today. I didn't want to spend the day in the office, so I cleared it with my boss and traded with Franklin. Dave, my name went on no schedule. Maybe four to six people inside the office might have known I was coming. I left the office, met Bob Roberts at the United ticket counter here at 9:40 A.M."

"Did you call Bob before you left the office to arrange the time and location? Did someone at his office have advance warning?"

"No. I called from the car when I was a few minutes out. It would have been about 9:20–9:25." She closed her eyes, thinking back. "We got word of the first phone call at 10:48 A.M. It's scrawled on the top of an envelope I was using to make notes. One hour of time in which someone could have seen I was here at the airport and made the decision to mention me. No.

It makes more sense that using my name was planned long before today. I don't think my being at the airport had anything to do with it."

"A past case? Someone who wanted you dragged in?"

"I've had several cases with men this vicious, but the problem is finding one who isn't in jail at the moment who might have the knowledge to do it. And why a plane? If someone wanted to come after me, there are much more straightforward ways to do it." She appreciated his grim expression, the fact he didn't like that reality, but it was one she had long ago accepted she would live with. She offered him the other option she had considered. "This may simply be a red herring because my name has been in the news lately."

It was obvious Dave had not thought about that. "That's possible. In fact, it would be a very good tactic. It would divert resources in the early days of the investigation, buy himself time to cover his tracks while we are busy elsewhere. It's going to take time to get through your past cases." He looked at her and frowned. "If you were named as a red herring, I wish he had used my name instead."

Kate wanted to smile at the irritation in his voice. He didn't like the fact she was in the middle of this. Neither did she. The prospect of spending days reviewing hundreds of cases was not a pleasant one.

His hands tightened on the steering wheel. "There's another problem that will have to be dealt with because of this. You had better plan to disappear before your name hits the media. They are going to chew up any tidbit of information they can find, and the tape contents will eventually leak. The information is too explosive and was heard by too many people."

"I'm already thinking about it." She could stay with anyone in the family, and she probably would to avoid the media pressure. It would be nationwide media, not just local. The last thing she needed was Floyd Tucker shadowing her every step. "Back to the timeline. The second call came in at precisely 11:00 A.M. He knew the bomb would go off at 11:15. What does that tell us? It was a device with a timer?"

"Probably. It's doubtful the device could have been remotely detonated over any great distance. The most logical scenario would be a bomb with a timer in the luggage area of the plane."

"So would the calls have been from nearby?"

"It depends on his rationale for going after this particular plane. If he wanted to see the commotion, maybe."

She absently worried at a blister on her hand that had broken while she tried to build a profile in her mind. "The words of the call were very precise, carefully chosen. 'The bomb goes off at 11:15. The plane is talking to the tower.' That's precise, specific. He likes control. That reference to the plane talking to the tower—you're the pilot; could that be literal?"

"You can listen to the radio traffic with the right equipment. But radio traffic is very concise. A normal exchange with the tower is a dozen words. It's not what you would consider a dialogue. If that statement was itself not another red herring, it meant he was referring to having heard an exchange with the plane."

"Is it possible the reference to me *and* the reference to the tower were both extraneous?" Kate considered that, then realized immediately how looking at it that way cut out the complexity. "The simple truth—he set a bomb to go off at eleven-fifteen. The plane's location was irrelevant. If it had been stuck at the terminal gate if the flight was running late, the plane would have blown up there."

"Exactly. As red herrings, those two statements are brilliant. By adding the reference to the tower, he creates churn in the initial moments before the bomb goes off. By mentioning your name, he complicates the initial investigation."

"And at the other extreme, he meant both of them."

"Yes. To speculate they are red herrings, even to believe it is likely, won't change the reality. They have to be ruled out."

Her past. What would Dave think when he learned what that really meant? She backed away from the thought, not willing to borrow trouble. *"Tell Kate O'Malley I haven't forgotten the past"* told her at least one comforting thing. Her name had not always been Kate O'Malley. She wouldn't be dealing with ancient past. "I'm glad you're here." The words were stark, but they were meant from the heart.

Dave's hand covered hers. "So am I."

The quiet interlude lasted only a moment for they had reached the administration building.

The command center swarmed with people. Leaving Dave talking with one of the other FBI investigators, she went to wash up, doing what she could with soap, hot water, and a towel. The soap stung her hands. She considered the pain a useful thing, confirming to herself that she was getting past the shock.

A table had been set up with cold drinks, and she headed there. The ice water helped ease the burning in her throat from the smoke she had inhaled. She looked around the room, assessing the mood here. It was not unlike the mood among those working out on the runway. Intense, focused on tasks, faces grim.

Bob Roberts had arrived back from the crash site. He looked at her and gestured to the east conference room. She nodded and headed that direction. People were assembling for the first update meeting.

Dave joined her and held out a chair for her at the large oval table. Out of habit, she reached for a pad of paper and a pen, jotting down the date and time. She recognized about a third of the people at the table.

Bob called the meeting to order. "This is the T+2 hour update. Elliot, what's the time frame for the folks out of Washington?"

Kate idly turned the pen in her hand while she listened to the discussion.

"The full NTSB team will be on site by 3 P.M. FAA thirty minutes after that. ATF and FBI will be bringing in people throughout the next twenty-four hours."

"Have there been any further calls?"

"No. Not to us or the media."

"Where are we with the second bomb sweeps?"

"The terminals have been checked, airplanes and luggage/cargo are going to take at least another three hours to complete. Nothing so far."

Bob looked at the airline representative. "Passenger list?"

The young man looked pale and nervous. "Still temporary. At least another couple hours to confirm."

Kate thought that was an optimistic estimate. Someone who was single, older, with no immediate family, would create an identification problem— it could take days to confirm they were actually on the plane. Beat cops loved getting sent out on the 'we think they're dead' assignments. And there was another complication, a bigger one: *MetroAir allows walk-ons.* Kate wrote it on the notepad in front of her and slanted it to Dave.

He wrote below her note—*How many on this flight?*

Gate attendant thinks a dozen. There would be less paperwork available, less information for those passengers. Walk-ons tended to be travelers who had missed their connecting flight with another airline. They were not expected to be on the flight, and so it would take time for people to realize a loved one might have been aboard.

Bob turned to the Red Cross representative. "Who do we have working information with the victims' families?"

"Jenson with the FAA. He's coordinating the Red Cross, the airline, and the media. The eight hundred number for families has been given out to the media."

"Are there enough qualified people on the phones?"

"We've three tiered it. Information, counselors, and travel support. We've established half hour status updates for the families and assigned them a primary contact person. We have arranged media-free space in the terminal and the airport hotel for the families."

"Tell Jenson to arrange for a couple floors at the Chesterfield hotel as well. Let's give family members an option of where to stay. Make sure flight arrangements are into Midway or Milwaukee. We don't need relatives flying over the crash scene once this airport reopens."

Bob looked over at Elliot. "Recovery and identification?"

"A temporary morgue has been set up in hangar fourteen. We've got hangar fifteen being cleared as a contingency if they need more room."

"Has Jenson talked to the families about what will help with identification? Jewelry, clothing, dental charts, X rays?"

"He's got Red Cross trauma counselors working with them."

Bob scanned his notes, then looked back at the airline representative. "Tell me about the flight."

"MetroAir Flight 714, departing O'Hare at 10:55 A.M. bound for New York. An Illiad 9000 Series A wide-body, the first crash for this type of aircraft. It was a connecting flight that originated in L.A."

New plane? Dave scrawled.

Kate tried to remember back to Bob's remarks during past security reviews. He commented on new planes, pointing them out like a proud papa. *Put in service last year?*

Possible mechanic failure, not a bomb?

Doubtful. The explosion ripped the plane apart.

"Any threats to the airline recently?" Bob asked.

"No."

"Labor disputes, problems with the carrier management?"

"Nothing known."

The door opened, and Kate's boss entered the room and took a seat against the far wall. She was glad to see him.

"Who worked the flight?"

Elliot scanned his notes, then answered. "The FBI is interviewing the maintenance crew and terminal reps now. We're working on identifying the baggage handlers and the ticket counter personnel."

"What about the previous flight crew?"

"On their way back from St. Louis."

"How are we doing on the phone call?"

"There is a team on it. The tape is with the police forensic lab now. Phone company technicians are pulling the switch logs to try and locate a billing record."

Dave touched her arm, drawing her attention back to the pad of paper. *Tell Kate I haven't forgotten the past.* Exact words?

Kate O'Malley. It was significant because her legal name had not changed until she was nineteen.

Bob looked at Elliot. "Security camera tapes?"

"All pulled and under seal. The last two weeks of tapes are being pulled as we speak."

"Card key access logs?"

"Being printed now. We've got the handwritten security guard logs together."

"For now, all information goes into the evidence room. I want two guards on the door and only people on the list allowed access," Bob ordered. "We need to know who was on that plane, where the bomb was located, what it was made of, and how it got onto the plane. Let's meet again at 4 P.M."

Simple questions, none of them easy to answer. Chairs pushed back from the table, and the noise level rose. Kate maneuvered through the crowd to join her boss. "You heard the tape?"

"Yes. For whatever reason, he wanted you dragged in. He accomplished it. I've got staff pulling cases you've worked. We need a lead that will help us sort through them. That's now your primary focus. Spend time going through the passenger list. Find us something we can work with, Kate."

She nodded, taking a deep breath, dreading that look into the details of two hundred lives. "Once I get through the passenger list, I'll start looking on past cases. Can you spare Debbie? Having transcribed my tapes and filed cases for the last five years, she knows how they are going to be indexed on-line."

"I'll get her cut free for as long as you need her. Anything you need, ask."

"Thanks, Jim."

"Have a cop pick up whatever you need from your apartment. The media storm has already begun, and you'll eventually be at the center of it when that phone call becomes known. I don't want you back there until I know what we are dealing with."

It was a request, but it could be made an order. She nodded rather than protest. She would be working here through the night, so it made little immediate difference. "I'll do that."

Jim nodded and moved to join Bob.

Kate rubbed her arms, momentarily unsure who in this room to talk to first. Dave touched her hand. "Stick with me. I'll be working the passenger list with you. Even if the bomber knows you, there is still a reason he chose this plane. Someone on board was likely a target. That's my immediate job, so we'll make better progress working together."

She was grateful and not sure how to say that. "Where do you want to set up?"

"Elliot has a conference room upstairs for us. Susan and Ben from my office are already working on the list."

As soon as they reached the hallway, they saw the line by the elevator. Dave gestured to the left. "Come on, let's take the stairs."

They had to wander the halls for a few minutes to find where Susan and Ben had set up shop. The two of them had appropriated a conference room off an unused office. Kate carefully stepped over the power cords and cables strung across the floor to the two computer terminals and printer that had been brought in. The room looked like one she was accustomed to seeing at the precinct. The table was strewn with printouts and hand-written pages of notes. The white board had accumulated a list of names written in different colors. On the right side of the white board was a list of questions they had considered when looking at the names. Kate already felt at home.

Dave pulled out two chairs and introduced her to Susan and Ben. Kate saw their curiosity and wondered if it was from the bank incident last week or if they had heard about the specifics of the phone call. Either way, she had a reputation before she arrived. Dave settled back in his chair. "Where are we?"

"The lists are still tentative." Susan slid across two copies. "We're patched in with the airline group working on the problem, getting real-time updates."

Kate looked at the data, sixteen pages of it. Her face grim, she read the names, the ages. So many families. "Do we have a seating layout for the plane?"

Ben cleared the center of the table to spread out the blown-up diagram. It was the chart the airline used when booking tickets. "Whether someone was in their assigned seat is an open question, but this will correlate to the ticket information listed on the printouts."

"Three sections—first class, business, and coach?"

"Yes."

Kate nodded, checking the seating chart occasionally as she reviewed names. The chance she would find a name she recognized was slim, but it was the obvious place to start. She turned page after page without success.

Dave set down his list and looked at the white board. "You've already researched some interesting questions. Let's start at the top. How many people had tickets, but did not show?"

Susan scanned her notes. "Preliminary, four. We've cleared one. Tim Verrio, a reporter for a New York paper, who took a later flight. He had tickets issued the same day for two carriers. The others, a Glen and Marla Pearse, Chicago address, no information, and a Bobby York, Virginia address, no information."

"Who is working that problem?"

"Travis."

Kate started to write her list on the pad of paper, then realized to bring the names up for discussion it would be better to have the list on the board. "May I?" Susan handed her the marker and eraser. Kate took them to the board along with the printout. "What about the variation—how many people checked baggage but did not board?"

"The checked tags appear to match, but we've got two problems. This was a connecting flight, and most of the luggage is reported to be damaged and or burned; it is going to take time to physically confirm bags and see if an extra one made the trip."

Kate thought about that debris field, how much of the aircraft had burned, and doubted they would ever be able to totally account for the baggage.

"Anyone cancel reservations for the flight?" Dave offered.

"Another open question. The airline is still working the list." Ben searched through the faxes. "Susan, did we get an answer on who bought their tickets for cash?"

"It just came in. There were two. Assuming these are real names, a Mark Wallace, Colorado address, no information; and a Lisa Shelby, Milwaukee address, no information. Travis has the names."

"We need to find out if they were actually on the flight," Dave noted, adding them to his work list.

Kate double-checked the list she had. "Has the airline confirmed how many walk-ons there were?"

Susan checked the terminal screen. "Tentatively, eleven. We're getting updates on those as they confirm the electronic tickets and the matching credit card charges."

Dave leaned back in his chair. "Does anyone on this flight look like a target? Maybe someone in law enforcement? A judge, mayor, city councilman, state representative? What about someone with a criminal record?"

"I'm about a quarter of the way through the list, and I've found a couple possibilities." Ben scrolled back through the names on his terminal screen. He tapped the screen with the cap of his pen. "The most interesting is a retired federal judge. We've also got a VP for an oil company."

"Can we get bio information on them?"

"We should be getting a fax on the oil company VP soon. But I'm having problems getting anything on the retired federal judge. His name is flagging a U.S. Marshal code."

Dave leaned forward in his chair. "Really?"

"What does that mean?" Kate asked as she saw Dave lock in on the news.

"It means his security was unusually high. They are not releasing any data through normal channels." He looked at Ben. "Was he traveling with someone?"

"No."

"Raise the urgency with Washington; we need to know why he had that kind of security."

The terminal Susan was using beeped. She read the latest update.

"We've got another confirmation. A late walk-on. Nathan Young. No checked baggage."

Kate looked at Dave.

"Say that again," Dave asked quietly.

"Nathan Young."

Kate closed her eyes. The world had just become a much smaller place. She looked back at Dave and felt as if she had fallen down a spiraling hole. "So much for our Wednesday meeting with him."

Ten

I f we are looking for a connection between me and a passenger, that is an immediate one," Kate commented, "but who would want to kill a bank owner?"

"Good question." Dave looked at her, puzzled. "The only thing I found was an indication he was raising cash. Did anything else show in your search?"

Kate shook her head, but she was running through all kinds of possible connections in her mind. "Henry Lott?"

"He used dynamite, which is not typical for an airline bombing; he didn't expect to be alive past Tuesday, and now he's in jail—but it's a very interesting question." Dave turned to Ben. "We need a list of people who have seen him since he was arrested Tuesday."

Ben reached for the phone. "I'll have it faxed here."

"Dave," Susan flipped to the back of the passenger list, "we've got another Young on the flight. A Mr. Ashcroft Young."

Kate rapidly found the page. "Related?"

"Hold on."

Susan worked rapidly, then nodded. "Brothers."

"Nathan was a walk-on?" Kate leaned across the table to view the seating diagram again. "Where were they seated?"

"Nathan is in the last row of first class, and Ashcroft—coach, seat 22E."

"They weren't traveling together?" Kate looked at Susan. "When and how did Ashcroft purchase his ticket?"

"May 24, credit card."

"So he was planning to fly coach." Kate glanced over at Dave. "Not as wealthy as his brother?"

"From the flowers Nathan sent, I doubt he would volunteer to upgrade his brother's seat. It would be useful to know why they were both heading to New York. Ben, does anything show on Ashcroft Young?"

"Searching. Whoa! Ten years in jail for cocaine distribution. Released eleven months ago."

"Our bank president was related to a drug dealer?" Kate tried to connect the implications of that but couldn't; it was too incredible to believe. "You're sure?"

Susan was already double-checking. "Yes. They're brothers. What an interesting family. I wonder if they were even speaking to each other."

"Somehow I doubt it." Dave replied, running his hand through his hair. "What a mess. We need full profiles on these two. Susan, send the information to Karen and ask her to put a rush on it. A bank president and a drug dealer certainly raise interesting questions of money laundering. Nothing appeared on the surface with the banks Nathan owned, but it's time to check that out in detail."

Kate looked at the two names, now written on the white board, and shook her head. "This would be a perfect lead if they weren't both dead."

Dave chuckled at the irony. "We solved the case. *He's dead.*"

Kate set down the marker. "Exactly."

"Run with it a minute. Suppose Ashcroft got out of jail and began pressuring Nathan to look the other way while he laundered money. Nathan resisted, and that put Ashcroft in a squeeze with his employers. Drug runners don't like failure. What about someone setting a bomb to kill them both?"

Kate wished she could find a scenario that made that work but finally had to shake her head. "No matter how you look at it, Nathan was a last minute walk-on. Until the last moment, it wasn't clear he would be taking this particular flight. You don't pull off something this complex without a lot of planning."

"You're right. But they get my early votes." The fax began to hum. Dave reached back for the page. "The oil company VP bio. Interesting. He was responsible for the company's environmental programs, among other things."

Kate smiled. "Would it be against their ethics for an environmentalist to blow up a plane?"

"I guess we're going to find out. Let's add him to the list as well."

Kate picked up the red marker. "That gives us four passengers on the possible list. A retired federal judge, an oil company VP, our Nathan Young, and his brother Ashcroft Young. One of them with an obvious tie to me. What other surprises are buried in this passenger list?"

She needed to call her family. Kate leaned against the wall of the conference room and momentarily tuned out the discussion going on. How was Jennifer doing? It was coming up on the 4 P.M. meeting, and this was the first time Jennifer had crossed her mind, a fact that bothered her. She had no illusions that this disaster could be kept from her sister. By now everyone in the nation had probably heard a plane had blown up. But there was no reason to tell her about the phone call, to add that kind of stress. The others in the family, however, did need to know.

"Kate."

She blinked and looked over at Dave.

"Ready to head downstairs to the update meeting?"

She pushed away from the wall. "Yes."

They had made good progress on the names, and though they were far from done, they had carefully selected a list of seventeen people to check out in more detail. Nathan was the only apparent passenger linked to her, but with the fax from the city jail confirming Henry Lott had spoken only to his lawyer, the obvious connection to last Thursday's incident dwindled.

The east conference room was crowded with the influx of people from Washington. Kate settled into a chair next to Dave at the back of the room as Bob called the meeting to order. Others were running the investigation now, but Bob remained the information coordinator. "This is the T+5 hour update. Where are we on the passenger list?"

The airline representative was better prepared to be the focus of attention now. "It has been 90 percent confirmed; working copies are in front of you. Two hundred and fourteen, nine of them crew."

"Released to the media, when?"

"Tomorrow noon, assuming full confirmation and the notification of the victims' families."

Who is being notified of Nathan and Ashcroft Young's death?

Dave's written question made Kate realize they had missed an interesting avenue of speculation. *Good question. Nathan's wife, obviously. Who else?*

We need to find out.

"What's the status with the victim recovery?"

Elliot leaned back to confer with the pathologist behind him, then answered. "It should be complete by sunset."

"Are we set up to work through the night?"

"Flood lights are being brought in now."

"Good. Have the black boxes been found?"

The National Transportation Safety Board coordinator nodded. "Voice and data recorders from the cockpit have been recovered. Four of the fifteen airframe data boxes have been located."

"Do we have physical evidence to confirm a bomb or its location?"

"From the debris damage pulled into the engines we are focusing on the forward section of the aircraft. We may have the first structural evidence when the cranes are able to lift sections of the fuselage."

Does the luggage area go the length of the plane? Kate wrote down the question, not certain of the answer. Dave was the pilot.

Typically.

Could the bomb have been inside the passenger cabin, not in the luggage compartment?

Suicidal passenger? Dave wrote. *Doubtful. Maybe an airline employee would plant a bomb inside.*

"When will we be able to begin moving wreckage?" Bob asked.

"Another couple hours. Hangars sixteen and seventeen have been set aside for the physical reconstruction."

"Where are we with the phone call?"

"We've confirmed two facts. It was made from a cellular phone, and whoever placed the call clicked on and played a prerecorded tape. That's how they got the voice distortion."

Why? Kate scrawled. *Hide his voice, or allow someone else to place the call?*

He accomplished both. But we're now looking for two people.

Or one trying to confuse the issue. This was another indication he wanted control. Taping what he wanted to say meant he didn't want any unintended words or noise to be heard. He had likely taped the message several times until it was exactly what he wanted. That meant the reference to her had been deliberate, not a spur of the moment opportunity.

Her past cases. When this meeting broke up, that would be their next focus. Debbie and Graham were on their way with the files.

The meeting lasted over an hour, and when it was done, the next meeting was set for 9 P.M. Kate closed the pad in front of her, feeling the weight of everything that had happened. "Dave, give me a few minutes. I need to call the family. I'll meet you back at the conference room."

He hesitated beside her, looking like he wanted to object, then nodded. "Sure. I'll see you upstairs."

Kate watched him leave, relieved. If Dave thought he was hanging around while she made private phone calls, they were going to have an angry heart-to-heart. If this kept up, she was going to be tossing a few figurative elbows. She had to search to find a quiet place in the administration building. She found an empty employee break room and settled at the table with her cellular phone. She hoped Jennifer had been too busy to see a television but suspected that was unlikely. She dialed the hospital. "Jennifer, it's Kate."

"I've been following the news. Where are you?"

She didn't want to give her the full story. "At the airport. I was doing a security review here when the incident happened."

"You've been at the crash site."

"All day. Stephen and Jack are here somewhere. And Lisa."

"It must be horrible."

"There are no survivors. I just wanted to let you know I would be working here the next few days."

"Thanks. I know it must be intense there. Don't forget to get some sleep."

"I'll manage. How did the tests go today?"

"They have run several, but they haven't told me many results yet."

"You're comfortable? They are treating you okay?"

"They are making this as pleasant as they can. Is there anything I can do for you, Kate? Call others in the family? Anything?"

"Give Stephen and Jack a call later and make sure they're okay. Lisa if you can track her down. They have really seen a horrific sight. I'm okay for now; I'm working with Dave."

"I'll call them. I'm glad Dave is there for you."

"He's stuck like glue at the moment." Jennifer laughed, and Kate forced herself to relax. "Do you know what time the tests start tomorrow?"

"Eight o'clock."

"I'll call you first thing in the morning to see how your evening went."

"Thanks. Take care, Kate."

Kate hesitated before making the next call. Marcus. What did she want to tell him? Ask him? She paged him and did something she rarely did. She added her personal emergency code.

He returned the call within a minute. She could hear muffled noise and realized with some surprise that he was calling from an aircraft. "Kate? Are you at the airport?"

"Yes."

"I'm twenty minutes out of Midway."

"You heard about the tape?"

"I heard a plane went down with a federal judge I once protected. And I've got a page I've been trying to return to Dave. What tape?"

"Hold it. You protected retired judge Michael Succalta?"

"Three years ago. A drug money case out of New York."

Marcus O'Malley had a connection to this flight as well.

"Kate, what tape?"

"There were two bomb threats called in. The first one was five words. 'Get ready for a bomb.' The second came at 11 A.M.; we've got it on tape. Marcus, the exact words of that second phone call were: 'The bomb goes off at eleven-fifteen. The plane is talking to the tower. Tell Kate O'Malley I haven't forgotten the past.'"

"Your *name?* Why didn't you page me immediately?"

Kate took his anger for what it was, fear. "I was crawling inside the wreckage for the first couple hours. I've been in meetings and deep in researching the passenger list since then."

"I'll be there as soon as I can. Where are you working in O'Hare?"

"Second floor of the administration building. Bob Roberts in the command center can give you directions. Dave and I are working on the passenger list."

"Stay with him."

She was puzzled at the intensity in the order. "Why? What are you assuming?"

"The politics of the situation are going to be dicey. There are reasons Judge Succalta might have been the target, classified reasons. You don't want to be in the middle of this any more than you already are."

"Wonderful. That gives us two real problems. That bank incident last Thursday? The owner, Nathan Young, sent me flowers at the hospital; I had an appointment with him for Wednesday. He was on the plane, as was his brother."

"The gunman—Henry Lott?"

"He's only spoken with his lawyer since Tuesday." She had a full-blown headache setting in. She so desperately wanted to tell him about Jennifer and couldn't—she had given her word, but it was all coming down on her like a tidal wave. "Hurry, Marcus. I'm in over my head."

"As soon as I can."

She got no answer at Rachel's. Rather than leave a message, she decided to call back later. She wasn't up to another surprise.

Kate took her time walking back to the conference room, trying to sort out this latest wrinkle. Marcus had a tie to a retired judge on the flight. She had a tie to a bank president on the flight. *Tell Kate O'Malley I haven't forgotten the past.* Could it mean a tie to the O'Malley family past? How many threads were they going to have to chase?

It felt like everything in her life was coming apart at the same time: Jennifer's cancer, her black rose suitor coming back, and now someone determined to drag her through a nightmare. She either needed half a day on a basketball court or somewhere private to cry.

She reached the conference room and took a deep breath before stepping inside. "Dave, we've got another wrinkle."

"Kate, I thought I taught you to duck." Marcus tossed another case file onto the stack of suspects, his annoyance clear.

She looked at the case number and winced. She hadn't told him about that one. At his insistence, they were going through her old cases while others dug into his link with the retired judge. As he had put it quietly when she protested—if someone was targeting her, he wanted to know it sooner versus later. It was classic Marcus, determined to protect her. Dave could give him lessons. She hadn't been able to move today without Dave shadowing her. She let Marcus get away with it because peace in the family often meant accepting a bit of smothering. Dave was a different matter entirely.

It was almost 10 P.M. They had sent Ben to attend the evening update meeting so they could stay here and work. Debbie and Graham from her office had joined them. Even with the extra help, it was slow going. The first pass through her cases had turned up almost sixty of interest. Twenty-three men with violent pasts released in the last two years. Three cases involving airlines. Thirty-two cases where explosives had been used. It felt like they were being dragged into a quagmire with no end in sight.

"Holding up?"

She looked up at Dave's quiet question, then nodded. He obviously didn't agree because he closed the file he was reading and dropped it back on the stack. "Let's take a short break and see about getting something to eat. Ben may have something from the update meeting that will help us focus this search."

When no one objected, Kate accepted the suggestion gratefully. She walked downstairs with Dave and Marcus. After arranging for dinner to take back, they found a corner of the break room where cold drinks had been set up. Leaning against the counter, Kate opened a soda, needing the sugar and caffeine. Just walking away from the problem was giving her a different perspective on it. "Why didn't he call back?"

Dave looked over. "What?"

"He blew up a plane, and he doesn't want to comment on it? Why not a call back to the tower, the media? Somebody?"

"It may not be a true terrorist incident," Dave replied.

Kate nodded. "That's my point. We have been assuming one person was the target. But if one person was the target, this was overkill."

Marcus frowned. "Enormous overkill."

"Is your retired judge worth this kind of collateral damage?"

Marcus thought about it. "He has some intense enemies, but I would have expected them to hire a hit man, not a bomber."

"Exactly. The same with our bank president. If someone wanted him out of the way, why not take a shot at him? The bomber has put himself at the top of every most wanted list."

"He's into looking for glory."

"Or power," Dave offered. "This is quite a statement of capability."

Kate crinkled the can in her hand and watched the metal flex. The leads were fragmenting in too many directions—the passengers on board, ties to Marcus, her past cases. Which was the right direction? Soon they were going to have to list all the leads, prioritize them, and hope they didn't go after the wrong one. Facts would be nice. She hated working with only speculation.

She changed the subject. "What's happening with your case in Washington, Marcus?"

"We're close to an arrest, maybe another ten days. It's formality now, waiting for sign off by the deputy attorney general."

"You won't be needed back there?"

Marcus shook his head. "Quinn's got it covered."

"How is your partner? Will he be coming out for the Fourth of July festivities next month?"

Marcus shared a private smile. "Now why would he want to do that?" Kate smiled back. They both knew Quinn had a habit of tracking where Lisa O'Malley was and what she was doing. "Someday Lisa will notice him."

"Maybe," Marcus replied, noncommittal. "I managed to catch her for a few minutes on my way in. She's going to be working in the temporary morgue tonight, then will be downtown tomorrow if you need her."

"How's she coping?"

"Worried about you."

Kate grimaced at that. She was now safely behind the distance of papers; Lisa was still in the middle of the tragedy. "Someone needs to worry about her."

"I paged Rachel and asked her to touch base later tonight."

"Thanks."

"Lisa will be okay. She's strong and angry that somebody did this. It will get her through the next few days."

"Sometimes I wish she wasn't so good at her job; then she wouldn't constantly get the tough assignments."

"I imagine she wishes the same about you at times."

Dinner arrived, and they took it upstairs for the group. The conference room had acquired more equipment during their absence. Kate set the food on the credenza. "What do we have, Ben?"

"Copies of the security camera video from the gate terminal. And from a variety of sources—driver's licenses, passports, family photos—pictures of the passengers."

"Facts. I love them."

Susan sorted through the pictures. "Here are the two brothers."

Kate studied the driver's license photographs. They didn't look alike, but then one man had been leading a very hard life, while the other had been living in comfort. "Do we have a photo of the retired judge or the oil executive?"

"Here."

Kate laid the four photos side by side on the table and studied them. Was one of these four pictures the intended victim?

"Let's see the video, Ben."

It was two hours of tape, and they paused it frequently, linking pictures to the video. The retired judge and Ashcroft Young arrived early and took seats in the waiting area. Both had brought newspapers to read. The plane arrived from L.A., several passengers got off with Chicago as their final stop. Over time, the area filled with passengers crowding around the check-in counter. There was no audio, but it was clear when the flight attendant began with preboarding announcements. People gathered together carry-on luggage, threw away coffee cups, and businessmen shut down laptops and closed briefcases. The area cleared in an orderly fashion as the plane began to load.

"There's our late walk-on, Nathan Young," Graham pointed him out. A tall man, wearing a suit and tie, carrying a briefcase. Two more passengers entered the walkway after him, and the door closed.

Ben stopped the tape. The room was quiet. So many people, gone forever.

"Did anyone see anything that looked suspicious?" Dave finally asked.

No one had.

Ben removed the tape. "I'll go through it again, Dave, pull stills of faces we haven't identified."

"Thanks, Ben. As you do it, pull the time each passenger arrived for the flight as well as what time they boarded the plane; the information may be useful later."

"No problem."

Dave glanced at his watch. "It's past midnight. Do we keep working, or do we resume tomorrow morning?"

Kate looked at the case files, the names on the white board, then sighed. "Time is not on our side. Let's work another hour."

"No." Marcus interjected quietly. "We'll start missing information. They are setting up cots in a couple of the business lounges. Let's get six hours of sleep and begin again at dawn."

She knew he was right, but it felt wrong to consider ending the day with so little progress. "Is there a safe place we can lock these files for the night?"

Debbie picked up the lid of the nearest box. "Elliot made arrangements for the boxes to be sealed and stored in the evidence room. Graham, you, or I will be the only ones authorized to retrieve them."

Kate nodded. They efficiently packed the boxes and moved them to the cart. Dave retrieved the overnight bag that had been brought from her apartment and his own gym bag. He turned out the conference room lights.

Marcus stopped her downstairs by the command center for a brief hug. "I'm going to see what has turned up on the judge. Let Dave walk you over to the terminal."

"Don't stay too long."

"I won't."

She squeezed his hand. "Good night, Marcus."

Dave held the door for her. The night had turned cool. She took a deep breath and tried to purge the memory of so many cases briefly relived.

"We can take one of the shuttles," Dave said.

"I would rather walk."

Dave nodded and reached for her hand. She was weary to her soul, and it helped at this moment knowing she was not alone. His hand was firm, strong, and she had to stop herself from leaning into him. It was depressing, looking over the airstrip and seeing the debris highlighted in the bright lights. Activity had not slacked off with the coming of night; the men in orange and white jumpsuits were busy moving around the wreckage. The airport would reopen tomorrow if work tonight went as planned.

"Are Stephen and Jack still out there?"

"I hope not, but it's possible. I've seen the disaster plans. The fire crews are the ones given the grim reality of removing the fire victims; they've got the extraction equipment. I saw both of them out there earlier today. It depends on which crews were released." Over two hundred deaths, most of them by fire or smoke; it would haunt her brothers. And Lisa having to deal with the victims' remains…She wanted to cry. There was no other way to describe the emotion as she looked at the burned-out wreckage. "So many children died."

"I know."

"There can't be mercy in this case. Whoever did this deserves to die."

"He'll face the courts and whatever the law decides."

"How can you sound so calm about it?" Her emotions had been stuck between shock and horror the entire day.

"There's a verse in the Bible where the Lord says, 'vengeance is mine.' I have to believe God can deal with this. It's too big an atrocity otherwise."

"Your God let this happen," she replied bitterly.

He squeezed her hand but didn't say anything.

She sighed. "I'm sorry. I didn't mean to attack you."

"It's okay, Kate. I understand the emotion," he said gently.

"Will the bomber be found?"

"You know he will be, Kate."

She needed to explain. "I'm scared that it really is someone who knows me."

"One of these cases you have worked?"

"I don't like the idea of someone who just killed 214 people focusing on me."

"I would say that is a healthy fear. Would it help to know you'd have a hard time getting more than a few steps away from either Marcus or me?"

She smiled, too tired at the moment to register more than a token protest. "Gee, I would have never guessed. I've got bodyguards, huh?"

He shrugged, but she saw the fire in his eyes and had a healthy respect for what that intensity meant. "Someone miscalculated. By going after you, they tweaked the tail of a tiger."

"Marcus?"

"Actually, I was referring to me." He shot her a wry grin. "Marcus is more like a silent black panther. He's even a little more protective of you than I am."

She stopped walking for a moment, let the words sink in. She squeezed his hand. "Thanks. I needed that image. Because of the circumstances, I'll let you tread on my independence for a few days. Please note the word *few*." She started walking again. "We're assuming the past refers to my days as a cop. What if the reference is older than that?"

"You've got enemies that far back in time?"

Her father, but he was dead.

"Kate?"

She shrugged her shoulder. "I don't like making assumptions. 'I haven't forgotten the past' could be anything. What past is he remembering? It may not be significant to me while being very significant to him. Something he considers a slight might be enough to create a fixation."

"Someone who takes a grudge out of proportion would probably not have the skill to pull off this kind of blast," Dave reassured.

"He put a bomb on board the plane—why?"

"To kill someone."

Kate shook her head. "We're back to that problem of overkill. It doesn't make sense to kill 214 people in order to kill one. Buy a gun."

"To kill more than one person?"

"Possibly, there were families traveling together. But what's the motive? Insurance? Inheritance?"

"Money is always a big motivator," Dave pointed out.

"It's still a problem with overkill. And most cases that target relatives occur at the home or office. Comfortable ground for the killer as well as the victims."

"It would still be worth looking at who inherits what as a result of this crash."

Kate was quiet for a while, then speculated, "If Nathan Young and Ashcroft Young had not both been killed, I could see that kind of animosity in their family. Bad brother kills good brother for having all the money."

"Or good brother kills bad brother for ruining the family reputation."

Kate sighed. "What other reasons could lead to a bomb?"

"It's a strike against the airline. It could put the company out of business."

"Do you think there might be someone who hates the company that much?"

Dave reached around her to open the door. "I know there is a team of agents at the airline headquarters digging to find that out."

They cleared security and entered the terminal, found it was quiet and almost deserted, with police walking the corridor. One of the airport employees quietly gave them directions. The area was roped off from the media, and general passengers had been turned into a Red Cross support area. The business club they were directed to had become a sea of cots. Kate chose an open one and sank down, weary beyond words.

Dave pulled off her shoes. "I'll wake you at six o'clock."

"Unfortunately, yes. When this is over, I'm going to need a month of sleep." She buried her face in the pillow. "Thanks."

"For what?"

"Not telling me not to dream."

"Today qualifies for a bad dream or two. I'll be over there." He pointed to an open cot.

"Okay."

He hesitated. She saw something in his changing expression, as the work focus slipped away and she got a glimpse of his thoughts, which made her catch her breath.

"What?" She struggled to get her eyes open again. She saw him start to say something and suddenly felt afraid. *Dave, not now. I can barely think straight. If you say something nice, I'm going to cry.*

He brushed his hand across her hair as his face softened in a half smile. "It will keep. Good night, Kate."

Dave shifted the small pillow again. There was no way to get comfortable on one of these cots. Kate must have really been exhausted to fall asleep as soon as she was down. He stared at the ceiling, listening to the quiet sounds around him as people slipped in and out of the room, taking turns catching a few hours of sleep.

Hearing that tape had changed things. He couldn't deny the truth any longer. He cared about Kate. More than as a friend. More than as a woman in trouble. He wanted to protect her, keep her safe, to see her laugh and smile…to free her from the shadows he saw behind her eyes. Kate tried to hide the intense emotions trapped inside her, to show only logic and unshakable control, but the emotions showed through on occasion in breathtaking fashion. She so easily pulled the oxygen in a room toward her, having the confidence, the presence, to make a lasting impression on the people she met. Unfortunately, in her job, she had been making that impression on both the good and the bad guys.

He was finally beginning to understand her. Reading the cases she had worked had been informative, tense reading, but informative. Most of the files had partial negotiation transcripts attached. Kate's ability to deal calmly with violent men surprised him, even though he'd seen her do it. It was as though she became someone else in those moments of time. He had read the cases and seen a remarkable similarity. Nothing seemed to ruffle her. There was an extra terseness in her case notes when it was a domestic violence incident, but it was the only change he had been able to find.

Her unflinching ability not to step away made it possible for her to resolve situations no one else would go near. He saw in those case notes a cop whose compassion made her long for justice.

He closed his eyes, fighting the emotion stirring within him. If he had intentionally defined the traits he hoped to find in a woman—in the woman he would love—he could not have done better.

But she didn't believe. Might never believe after this.

Lord, why this? How do I explain to Kate a plane blowing up? I saw it in her eyes, the image of every victim. How does she ever believe when this is what You ask her to accept?

He'd thought often about her comments about God, trying to find the right words to deal with her questions. Kate had a *reasoned* disbelief, and he felt helpless to overcome it, especially now. Her own statements showed more careful thought than most people gave to God: *"Does it seem logical to pray for God to stop a crisis that, if He existed, He never should have let begin?*

"My job is to restore justice to an unjust situation. If your God existed, my job should not.

"I see too much evil. I don't want a God that lets that kind of destruction go on."

They were good questions.

It took a strong faith to face the violence and still believe the sovereign hand of God had allowed it for a reason—a reason the human mind might never comprehend—not as a capricious act of fate.

Lord, couldn't You have stopped this? So many families are grieving tonight. How am I to understand this? How am I to explain it to Kate? It's as though You're pushing her away rather than drawing her closer to You. It makes no sense. She may close the door to considering the gospel because of this, and I don't know what to do. This situation has become a turning point.

Words flowed through his mind then, but not what he'd expected.

"O the depth of the riches and wisdom and knowledge of God! How

unsearchable are his judgments and how inscrutable his ways! 'For who has known the mind of the Lord, or who has been his counselor?'"

Being reminded God didn't often explain himself didn't help. Dave sighed and punched the pillow into a ball. He was drawn to Kate, and it was an uncomfortable reality. He did not want this kind of complication in his life. He simply wanted a chance to be her friend, present the gospel, and keep his heart intact in the process; instead, he had someone threatening her, his protective instincts humming, and his emotions entering a freefall.

Lord, if someone gets to her before she believes...

Eleven

S leep well?" Dave was leaning against a support post when she came back from washing her face. Kate looked at his alert face and sighed. She borrowed his cup of coffee.

"That bad?" He dug sugar packets out of his pocket and smiled. "Finish that and I'll get you its cousin."

"You better find its double cousin. I need a transfusion of caffeine."

"Bad dream?"

She shook her head. "My couch is more comfortable." The bad dreams had been there in full force last night. It had been the bomb in her hands exploding, becoming the plane exploding—then a scramble to pull out victims at the bank, pull victims out of the wreckage.

Dave turned her around and set about rubbing the kinks out of her neck. She leaned into the warmth of his hands, sighing with relief. "Better?"

She rolled her neck and for once it didn't pop. "Much."

"They've moved the update meeting in the east conference room to 7 A.M.; Marcus said he would meet us there."

"They made progress last night."

"Sounds that way."

They walked to the administration building. Kate stared across the tarmac. The water used the day before had created an area of low rising fog that shrouded the wreckage. It was an eerie white cloud given what she knew was behind it.

"I'm sorry you had to see it happen."

"It's hard to brace for something like that. I was watching the clock, knew something might happen, but I never imagined it would be the plane landing." She worked on the coffee. "It was a bright orange flash in front of the wing, and then it seemed to walk back to the engine and the big explosion hit; the plane ripped apart. It shook the tower."

"Are you going to be able to forget it?"

"You know, I probably will. It's too hard to retain an image that shocking. The image of the kid that gets shot is harder to erase."

"How are you holding up?"

"No better or worse than anyone else here. What about you?"

"A bit terrified when I heard you were mentioned on the tape."

"Why?"

"My experience with situations like that means someone has you in his crosshairs for a rifle shot."

"You've protected people like Marcus does?"

"Occasionally. Any of that coffee left?"

She slowly offered his coffee back.

Dave grinned at her reluctance, then tasted the brew. He promptly grimaced. "You like it *really* sweet."

She chuckled. "Sugar helps the caffeine."

"Remind me to buy you some gum so the sugar doesn't rot your teeth."

"If it's not sweet coffee, it's candy. Sorry, I live on sugar."

"And you're not hyper?"

"Not that anyone has been willing to tell me."

"This explains why you never stop on the basketball court."

"Are you going to make excuses for losing like the rest of the guys?"

An easy smile played at the corners of his mouth at her mock outrage. "They do, huh?"

"They don't want to beat a girl.... I was born a jumping bean.... I have home court advantage—they get more creative as time passes."

"Did you play in high school?"

She went cold. "No, I never did."

He rubbed her arm. "Touch a nerve?"

"Yeah." She shook her head. "I played some in college though."

"How many times did you foul out?" A soft laugh underscored his words.

She knew her look was defensive and couldn't help it. "I was used to playing with the guys."

"Uh-huh."

"Listen, buddy, don't knock my game."

"It's a compliment. The way you can take a charge I'm surprised you haven't busted that pretty nose." He quirked an eyebrow. "You have?"

"Jack. Then Stephen had to pack it while he was doing his best not to laugh. It wasn't amusing."

"Who won the game?"

"It's one of the few we've suspended."

"I like that about your family. They can put up with you."

"Hey!" She shoved his chest for that remark, even as she grinned.

He caught her hand and tugged her back. "Face it, you would terrify most guys."

"Why?"

"You like to play on their turf."

"Does it bother you?"

He looked at her, amusement making his blue eyes sparkle. "Why should it?"

"Someone needs to deflate that ego a bit."

"You can try," he offered, his look daring her to accept.

She wasn't going to give him the satisfaction of a laugh but it bubbled inside. "You're worse than an O'Malley."

"I'll take that as a compliment."

"It probably was, but I didn't intend it to be."

"Indian giver."

"Give me back the coffee."

"Greedy, too."

"No, just not awake."

He gave the coffee back. "I think I like you when you haven't had enough sleep."

"Gee, thanks."

"Don't mention it." He held open the glass door to the administration building. "After you."

She sighed and pushed aside their banter to face the work of the day. They were a few minutes early, but the conference room was filling up fast. Dave went to get them two Danishes and more coffee for breakfast.

"Food. Maybe it will help you wake up."

She took the coffee he held instead. "Where's the sugar?" He chuckled and tossed her several packets. "Thanks. Now I'll take the food."

He held out the Danish. "Apple or cherry?"

She lowered the coffee cup long enough to consider the options. "Apple."

Bob called the meeting to order. "This is the T+20 hour update. I understand there is now physical evidence it was a bomb. What do we know?"

"We know it went off inside the first class cabin, not the baggage storage. That it went off under a seat, probably in row three or four; that's still being worked on," the NTSB representative replied.

She scrambled for a pen. *Nathan Young. Row four.*

The judge was in row two.

"Components?"

"Not yet. The airframe metal gave us the first class area and the seats the blast pattern."

Bob looked over to Elliot. "Have we identified everyone who worked this plane?"

"The people inside—maintenance, food service, preflight, mechanics—we're at thirty-nine. The interviews will be complete by midafternoon. Baggage handlers, fuel, et cetera, give us seventeen more."

"Do we know if the device was brought on board the plane here?"

"It may have been taped under the seat during the flight from L.A.; one theory is the bomber arms it just before he gets off the plane here."

Dave frowned. *Big hole. We didn't look at who got off the plane.*

Ben will have their pictures. We saw them get off in that video clip we watched.

Bob glanced around the table. "Anything on how it could have gotten through security?"

Elliot shook his head. "We're working on it."

"What about the phone call?"

The FBI representative spoke up. "Three cellular towers in this vicinity picked up the call at different levels of power. The cloverleaf of coverage extends about two miles. A series of tests this afternoon to duplicate the power levels should give us the precise location."

Kate started playing with scenarios. They had a call made from this area at 11 A.M. It was a small fact, but a useful one. If they could pin it down to inside a terminal at O'Hare, they would be able to focus on the security tapes.

The meeting was brief, with the next one set for 7 P.M., pending additional news. Kate stayed seated as she finished her list. "Dave, if the bomb is inside the cabin, that puts at the top of the list—airport personnel with access to the plane, passengers that got off the plane, and possible targets in first class, two of them being Nathan Young and the retired judge."

"Agreed."

"I vote we take a hard look at the people who got off the plane, then we focus on background checks of everyone in first class."

Marcus leaned against the table beside her. "What are you thinking?"

"A bomb inside the plane, under a seat, small enough not to be noticed by passengers as they settled in, suggests it might not have been designed to bring down the plane. The fact the plane was landing at 11:15 could not have been planned. Maybe the bomb was only intended for someone in first class. That implies the bomber knew where his target would be sitting. Nathan Young was a last minute walk-on. His seat assignment was not known until minutes before the flight."

"So of the two on the list in first class, the judge becomes the more likely target, and we lose the connection to you."

"Which is why we had better take another look at who was seated in first class."

Marcus nodded. "Run with it."

Kate handed Dave back his pen. He accepted it and tilted his head toward the door. "Why don't you head on up to the workroom? I'll meet you there in a few minutes."

Kate glanced at Dave, then Marcus, and got to her feet. "Don't be long." They were conferring without her, which meant she was the likely topic of conversation. If she didn't know the details, she could avoid having to get mad at them. It was an amusing reality, but it had kept the peace in the family for decades. Marcus squeezed her hand and let her slip past.

The workroom looked much as it had the day before. Case files surrounded Susan, Ben, Graham, and Debbie. They were deep in a debate over the list of names on the board. Graham smiled when he saw her and pulled out a chair. "Welcome to the war room."

"Making progress?"

"We've been able to eliminate about a third of the suspicious cases so far. What's the latest?"

"Evidence suggests the bomb went off under a seat in the first class cabin, possibly row three or four." That news got everyone's attention.

"Interesting." Ben reached for the seating chart. "Only twenty-four people in first class. Susan, where's the latest updated list of passengers?"

"Here." She handed over the printout. "They've confirmed another nine names."

"Who was around Nathan Young?"

Susan penciled in names on the chart. "He was here, in seat 4C. Across the aisle to his left was the oil company VP. Directly in front of him, two sales reps from a pharmaceutical company—Vicki Marstone and Peter Alton. Judge Succalta is here, in 2D."

Kate frowned. "A nice cluster. Put the bomb under seat 3C and they are all possible targets."

"Do they know anything else?"

"Not yet. Can we set up that videotape again? I want to look at who got off the plane."

"Sure, it will just take a couple seconds to rewind." Ben handed over a red folder. "These are the still photos you can use as a reference. I counted nineteen people who got off the plane, three of them crew."

"Is there any way to find out which of them might have been seated in first class?"

Susan found a faxed printout. "This is the L.A. seat assignments."

"Thanks. Any chance we could get a copy of the security tape from L.A.? I would love to know if someone had carry-on luggage there and left the plane here with nothing in his hands."

"I'll put a call through to the agent working the L.A. connection."

"This is briefing T+32 hour update." Bob called the evening meeting to order. "What do we know about the bomb?"

Kate hoped they had something. It had been a long, grueling day with little forward progress given how promising the day had begun. A look at the people getting off the plane, the first class passengers, had revealed nothing new. They had spent hours in the old case files, and it felt like she had been reliving them all. It was frustrating to know they were this close and not have someone to focus on.

The NTSB coordinator got to his feet and turned on the overhead projector. "It was under seat 4C in first class. That makes it under the seat of a Mr. Nathan Young."

Kate let out the breath she had been holding. They were going to be able to explain the reference to her name, not have to dig through her ancient past.

"We'll come back to Mr. Young," Bob decided. "Tell me about the bomb. Components?"

A transparency went down the overhead. "We've got a seared briefcase that appears to have been punched from the inside out; a laptop appears to have been carrying the device."

A briefcase? Dave scrawled. *Someone would notice if a briefcase were left on the plane.*

Nathan was carrying a briefcase. She hesitated. *Suicide?*

No. Someone wanted him to carry the bomb that would kill him.

Revenge with malice.

Yes. Someone consumed with anger. Dave paused. *And he's angry with you, too.*

Thanks for the reminder.

Another slide. "The bomb appears to have been inside the battery pack. Note the way it blew. There were metal plates at the back of the battery pack to send the explosion out through the briefcase instead of into the laptop. The machine itself is remarkably intact for the nature of the blast, considering it was found embedded in the airframe."

"What type of explosive was used?" Bob asked.

"Chemical analysis has just begun. Based on the size of the device, it was probably C-4, not quite a quarter of a brick."

"How was it triggered? Was it set to go off at a specific time, or did someone have to arm it?"

"We're still looking for components to determine that."

Bob nodded. "Tell me about Mr. Nathan Young."

Dave referred to the bio they had assembled to answer that question. "Forty-seven. Caucasian. Married eight years, no children. His second, her first. MBA Harvard. He owns four banks in Chicago, six in New York, and recently bought one in Denver."

"The obvious question: Did Mr. Nathan Young know there was a bomb in his briefcase? Was the laptop his? If it was, who had access to it recently? Who would have reason to target him? We'll meet again tomorrow, 9 A.M."

The meeting broke up into smaller clusters of people.

"A bank president killed by a bomb he may have unknowingly carried on board, a brother who was a drug dealer killed on the same plane. Henry Lott angry enough last week that he planned to blow up one of Nathan's banks," Kate summarized. "We've got a lot of questions to answer."

Dave exchanged a glance with Marcus, then looked back at her. "I'll have Ben follow up on Henry Lott again. Why don't we focus on Nathan's schedule and appointments?"

Kate was well aware the two of them were arranging what she did, keeping her away from the one person they knew was dangerous, Henry Lott, but she let it go. She had enough to worry about without trying to figure out how to get around the protective net they were throwing up around her. She'd ignore it unless it got in the way of what she wanted to do. And she wanted to go after those bomb components. Answers could be found there. "His secretary should also be able to help us confirm it was his briefcase and laptop. How early tomorrow morning do you think we can hit their office?"

"The bank headquarters open at 8 A.M. if I remember correctly. We'll be the first ones in the door," Dave assured.

Kate nodded. It would give them a couple hours tonight to plan their questions. "We've got the primary interviews tracking down information on Nathan Young?"

"They're ours," Dave confirmed. "We generate the questions. We can pull in as many people as we need to get the interviews done."

Marcus leaned back against the table. "I'll put someone on the security tapes to track Nathan's movements through O'Hare, see if we can find out how the device got inside the airport. And I'll get the last full audits of the various banks released to see if any accounts were considered suspicious. Anything else you want me to expedite?"

"The brother, Ashcroft Young, can you get his full trial transcript and prison record? The bio we have is pretty thin on details."

Marcus made a note. "Sure."

"Oh, and when you go after the bank records, would you also put someone digging into just how much cash Nathan Young had on hand?

Dave noticed his mortgage foreclosure rate was about three times higher than last year, like he was building up cash for some reason. It was one of the reasons we had an appointment with him today."

"Anything else?" Marcus asked.

Dave reached over and closed Kate's folder. "Yes. Dinner. It's almost nine o'clock and I'm starved. This can wait an hour."

Kate leaned back in her chair, twirled her pen, shot Marcus a private glance, and then looked back at Dave to give him a wicked grin. "Are you always like this in the middle of a hunt? Ready to take a break when things get on a roll?"

Dave's eyes narrowed. "Taunting a tiger when he's hungry is a dangerous thing to do, Kate."

She blinked, startled at the comeback. "You mean I've got to find you red meat for dinner, too?"

Marcus stepped back out of the line of fire, stifling a laugh.

Kate giggled as Dave propelled her out of the chair, and it spun around behind her. "Okay, uncle! We'll go eat."

"Good." He knuckled her head. "We'll start with you eating crow."

Her giggles blossomed into laughter. "Your puns are awful when you're tired."

"You ought to hear yours."

The three of them ended up walking down to the airport employee cafeteria, appropriating a table near the dessert bar, and for the next hour left behind the work upstairs.

After two nights on a cot, Kate felt like a pretzel. If Dave didn't let her move back to her own bed for tonight, she was going to be tempted to think about murder. She propped her elbows on the cafeteria table, cradled her cup of coffee in her hands, and did her best to ignore the commotion around her. Dave was finishing an omelette, and she wondered how he could eat breakfast with such apparent enjoyment. Her system wasn't even sure what day it was anymore, let alone what time it was.

Marcus reached over to check the number on her pager. "New York said they would have the bank audit information here sometime this morning. I'll page you as it comes in."

Kate nodded and finished her coffee. She should be looking forward to getting out of the airport and hitting the road, finding some answers. She was, but it was buried under the fatigue. She had dreamed about the passengers last night. They had never said this job would be easy, but how many people was she expected to see die in her lifetime?

Dave reached over and gripped her arm. "Are you okay?"

Startled, she wiped her expression clear of emotion. "Fine."

He scowled at her. "I wish you wouldn't do that."

"What?"

"Pretend you don't feel anything."

She wanted to swear at him for going under her guard. "I'm sorry I don't bleed to your ideal specification," she bit out tersely, pushing back her chair, knowing she had better step back before the anger she felt flared toward him because he was handy.

Dave looked shocked; that made her feel like a heel.

Marcus gripped her wrist, stopping her movement. "Don't go far."

She looked at him, holding back a flare of anger at him as well. She wasn't going to have free movement again until this case was solved and the use of her name during that bomb threat had been explained. "I'll find a phone and check my messages," she finally replied.

Marcus released her wrist. "Thank you."

"Sure." She glanced at Dave, offered an oblique apology. "I won't be long."

Dave was waiting for her by the stairway when she got off the phone, his attention focused on a coin he was turning over in his hand. She could read his frustration in the way he stood, his concentration on a coin. "Ready to go?" she asked.

He glanced at her, then pushed the coin back in his pocket as he straightened. "Sure."

His abrupt answer made her sigh. "I apologize for that."

Dave gestured to the stairs. "You're predictable. You don't like someone to get in your way. Where do you want to start?"

So much for restoring the peace between them. Kate turned her attention to work. "Let's go pay a visit to Nathan's office, then visit his wife."

"We'll take my car." They headed toward the secure back parking lot.

Kate had expected the press to be out in numbers. She did not anticipate that the police would have to open a corridor on the other side of the security gate for them to be able to get past. "There are almost sixty people here, and it's only a parking lot gate."

"Welcome to the age of instant news."

Kate sighed, looking back at the reporters. "I've been intentionally avoiding the television monitors."

"Probably a wise idea. You don't need any more bad news."

He didn't even know of the worst of it for her—Jennifer's cancer. "It's been a horrible week."

"You're holding up pretty well."

"Only because I'm not stopping to think about it." She looked down at her notes. "Let's run through this from the top."

"Start with the bank."

She nodded. "A week ago last Tuesday, Henry Lott shows up at the bank with dynamite and a gun, in a tirade at First Union for foreclosing on his house. He is arrested, denied bail, and has apparently only talked with his lawyer since that time. Tuesday this week, at 9:40 A.M., I meet Bob Richards for a walking security review. At 10:48, the first bomb threat is called in. 10:52, Nathan Young boards Flight 714 as a late walk-on; he is carrying a briefcase. At 11 A.M., the second bomb threat is called in. The message is prerecorded and mentions my name. The bomb goes off at 11:15."

"How does Henry Lott pull it off?"

"Clearly, he can't. Not alone."

"Does he have any family?"

"No. That was what made him so difficult to deal with at the bank. He had no reason not to die."

"Could he have paid someone to kill Nathan Young?"

Kate tried to image that scenario. "Three problems. It would have had to be arranged before he walked into the bank. Once Henry was dead or arrested, the guy hired to do it would simply walk away. Second, no money. That was why the foreclosure occurred. Third, it's the overkill problem again. A gun would have done the job. If Henry had been out of jail, maybe his personal motivation would be intense enough to make it a bomb, but a third party would have gone for expediency."

Dave nodded. "Then who else might want to kill Nathan Young?"

"Probably his brother. But he's dead."

"What about his wife?"

"Maybe. We need to see if she inherits everything. But if she did it herself, a woman rarely uses explosives. And if she had help, why use a bomb that had to be smuggled past O'Hare security?"

"Okay. Someone at his office?"

"Interesting." Kate jotted down that possibility. "They would have access to Nathan's itinerary and to his briefcase. But what's the gain?"

"Promotion?"

"It's probably governed by an outside board, but if enough ground-work had already been laid to guarantee confirmation, it's worth looking at. Promotion…what else?"

"Employee rage? Someone decides to kill the boss?"

"Why not a bomb in his car? Or a package bomb?" She sighed. "Dave, why put a bomb on a plane? There has to be a reason."

They pulled into the parking lot of the bank corporate offices. Kate released her seat belt. "Let's go prove Nathan carried that bomb on board the plane."

Twelve

The corporate offices for First Union Bank left an impression of old wealth with the classic elegance, marble, and turn-of-the-century paintings. A brief check with the receptionist and Dave and Kate were invited to the executive floor.

Kate hung back a step and intentionally let Dave do the talking. The office doors behind the secretary opened just as he established the lady was merely a temp for the day, taking the place of Nathan Young's secretary. The man who emerged came forward with the stride of someone accustomed to power. Kate caught a glimpse of a very large room with large glass windows before the door closed. "May I be of help? I'm Peter Devlon, the vice president of Union Group."

The VP who had answered Henry's letter.

Dave brought out his badge again. "Could we speak with you privately?"

"Certainly. Please, come into my office." He gestured to an office on the other side of the hallway. Curious, Kate glanced back at the office he had been in. The discrete gold nameplate said Mr. Nathan Young.

She took a seat as Dave smoothly dealt with the pleasantries. "I'm sorry for your loss."

"It's been a very emotional day here. How can I help you?"

"We have a few questions regarding Mr. Young's itinerary," Dave replied, setting the tone for the interview. They had agreed last night Dave would pursue the questions while Kate waited, ready to step in on inconsistencies she heard.

"Of course." Mr. Devlon leaned against his desk rather than walk around to sit behind it.

"He was traveling to New York on business?"

Mr. Devlon nodded. "He was going out for a 5 P.M. meeting, planning to fly back this morning."

"He was a walk-on for the MetroAir flight. Was it an unexpected meeting?"

"No, it had been on the calendar for about a month. Nathan would have normally taken the company jet." Mr. Devlon grimaced. "His decision to take MetroAir was truly a fluke. We had just concluded a meeting in the business lounge by the MetroAir gate; the flight was boarding, and it would cut an hour off his travel time. He needed to work during the flight, and frankly, that would have been difficult to do on the company plane. His wife Emily had decided at the last minute to fly out with him and stay at their New York penthouse through the weekend. Nathan asked me to fly to New York on the company jet with her as originally planned, get her settled at the penthouse, and then meet him at the office."

Dave waited a moment before asking the next question. "Whom did he meet with at the airport?"

"There were two meetings actually. One with Mr. William Phillips, the prior owner of First Federal Bank of Denver, and the other with the owner of Wilshire Construction."

Kate remained still even though her heart raced as the company name registered. *Wilshire Construction. Henry Lott's former employer.* It couldn't be coincidence that all the threads were running back together: Henry Lott, Nathan Young, Wilshire Construction.

"Why at the airport?"

Mr. Devlon spread his hands. "Mr. Phillips was on a layover, flying on to Washington; this was the only time in their schedules they could meet. Nathan has been looking at who to put in charge of the Denver bank, and he wanted to speak with Mr. Phillips before making that decision."

"Isn't that a little unusual?"

"Not when one of the candidates was Mr. Phillips's son."

"Was he offered the position?" Dave asked.

"No. The meeting was to smooth ruffled feathers only, let him know his son would be considered for the position in a few years if he proved capable."

"Why was the bank sold if the son wanted to run it?"

Mr. Devlon smiled. "Mr. Phillips had nearly run it into insolvency. It was sell or face a lot of bad press if news got out as to the bank's real condition." Kate narrowed her eyes as she heard the satisfaction in Mr. Devlon's voice. He liked that, the misfortune of others. No wonder Henry Lott had felt like he was getting squeezed. Mr. Devlon had written that letter refusing to stop the mortgage foreclosure.

"The second meeting?" Dave's voice had cooled Kate noted; he had read the same thing in Mr. Devlon's reply.

"Wilshire Construction. It was fit in because there were a few minutes in Nathan's schedule and there was some urgency to the problem."

"What type of problem?"

"The company was having some cash flow problems and wanted to extend their loans, but we had floated them too much as it was."

"What's the status of Wilshire Construction now?" Dave asked, probing.

"We are in the process of terminating their line of credit. They have another ten days to restore enough liquidity to make payroll and buy another thirty days with us, but I doubt they'll survive. Construction can be a ruthless business."

Money trouble. Kate could feel that new thread tying the others together. Henry Lott was having money troubles; his former employer was having money troubles.

"Have they been customers for a while?" Dave asked.

Mr. Devlon folded his arms. "Actually, yes. Almost twenty years. But the son runs the business now, and he's young, inexperienced."

"His name?"

"Tony Emerson."

Kate absorbed the shock as she would a sudden act of violence, not letting the emotions register. *Emerson.* She stopped following the conversation as her thoughts began to race. This was the link to her past. Her distant past.

How many Emersons could there be in this area? Surely enough to give her some cover, at least until she knew the truth. She forced her breathing to go calm. Yes. Deal with the facts. It was a name. One she had reason to hate, to fear, but it still was just a name. There didn't necessarily have to be a connection between it and the bomb threat.

They are connected. You know it. What are you going to do when you have proof?

She wasn't some helpless kid anymore. Even if this pulled her deeper into the crisis, left her vulnerable to people who didn't know her speculating on what it meant. Tony Emerson Sr. was dead. She knew that, had once tossed a rock at his gravestone. She knew he was buried under six feet of ground.

Get through this interview. Get back to the airport. Get the facts. Then do whatever you have to…. She tuned back in to the conversation.

"Were you present for both meetings?" Dave asked.

"I was in the business lounge, yes. I was making a few calls, following up on some business we had discussed on the drive to the airport. I sat in on the second meeting to take notes," Mr. Devlon replied.

"Did anyone else attend these meetings? Associates of Mr. Phillips? Mr. Emerson?"

"I believe Mr. Phillips had his lawyer and his secretary traveling with him. They were working at one of the tables across the room."

Dave turned the page in his notepad. "Do you remember their names?"

"Sorry, no."

"Mr. Emerson?"

"He was alone," Mr. Devlon replied.

"How long did the meetings last?"

Mr. Devlon thought about it for a few moments. "We got to the airport about 9:15 A.M., and I called in a few minutes late for a 10:45 conference call after I left Nathan at the MetroAir gate, so, I'd guess about an hour."

"You said you made notes of the second meeting?"

"Yes."

"Would you mind if I see them?" Dave asked it idly, but Kate heard his interest. He had latched on to that money trouble theory as well.

"They were on Nathan's laptop, I'm afraid. I did e-mail a copy to the branch manager if you would like me to have them forwarded to you."

"The business lounge has power outlets and phone lines for laptops?" Kate broke in to ask.

Peter Devlon was surprised by the question, but answered it. "It's fully equipped as an office away from home."

"You didn't need to use a battery pack?" Kate pushed.

Now he looked puzzled. "No. It was fully charged for his trip to New York."

Kate wondered how this bit of news was going to go over back at the airport. The investigators, having reached the conclusion the bomb was in Nathan's laptop, were going to love being told the laptop had been used just before the flight, and inside terminal security at that.

"Do you have an inventory system for insurance purposes that would allow us to identify that laptop? Its serial numbers or the like?" Dave asked.

"Sure, if you need it."

"It would help."

Mr. Devlon nodded, picked up the phone, and called someone in the bank, passing along the request. "Scott will leave the printout at the main desk for you to pick up."

"What about his briefcase? Anything that might help identify it?"

"That is simple. It was handmade for him last year as a gift from the board. Scrolled leather tooling, a custom-designed handle with, how would you describe it, a form-fit grip?"

"Molded?" Dave asked.

"Yes."

Dave changed the subject. "Would it be possible to get a copy of his calendar for the last few weeks?"

"The secretary can copy whatever you need."

"Thanks, I appreciate that. Do you happen to know why Ashcroft Young was traveling to New York?"

"I'm sorry, no. I was as surprised as everyone else to find he was on the flight," Mr. Devlon replied.

"How would you characterize the relationship between the two brothers?" Kate asked, wondering how much he knew about the brothers. They were going to have to find a handle into the reality they had brothers, a bank president and a drug dealer, both killed on the same flight.

"Strained would be a safe characterization. I assume you know about Ashcroft's past record?"

She nodded. "Yes."

"It caused Nathan some grief during the audit before his purchase of the Denver bank. To the best of my knowledge, they were not on speaking terms."

Kate wasn't surprised at that news, but she was disappointed. If Nathan hadn't told his second in command much about his brother, they were going to have a hard time getting a handle on the relationship.

"I understand Nathan had no children?" Dave asked.

"That's correct."

"So his wife inherits everything?"

"I have no direct knowledge of his will, but yes; it was always assumed controlling interest would pass to Emily should something happen to Nathan. She is already a minority owner, occasionally sitting in on board meetings," Mr. Devlon replied.

Kate was surprised at that news, and from her glance at Dave, he was, too.

"Will she be active in running the banks?" Dave asked.

"I hope so," Mr. Devlon replied. "She's got the talent for it. She headed one of the small New York community banks Nathan acquired—that's how they met. If not, the banks have strong managers, and I can deal with the day-to-day management of the corporate group. We'll adjust to whatever she wants."

Dave nodded and got to his feet. "Thank you for your time, Mr. Devlon."

Kate saw the movement and closed her notepad, glad to have this interview done. Nothing had prepared her for having this case go to the heart of her past. *Tony Emerson.* She had thought she would never have to hear that name again during her lifetime.

She forced herself to wait patiently beside Dave as the secretary copied Nathan's calendar for them going back four weeks. Dave handed the pages to her, and Kate glanced at the pages briefly before indicating it was what they needed. They paused in the lobby to get the inventory list.

Stepping from the chill of air-conditioning to the dry heat of outdoors was a shock.

Dave pulled out his car keys. "Three new players on the table, all with access. Mr. Peter Devlon, the VP orchestrating things; Mr. William Phillips, former bank owner whose bank got gobbled up and his son shafted; and Tony Emerson of Wilshire Construction, about to go out of business." He held open the passenger door. "Kate."

"Sorry."

"What are you thinking about so intently?"

"I'm not sure yet."

He shot her a curious glance as he started the car. "Give me a hint?"

She forced a smile, then shook her head. "We need to see the security videotapes from the business lounge. Do we head back to the airport?" She desperately needed access to a terminal to check out a name.

"Let's see if Nathan's widow is available first, while we are still downtown."

Kate had no choice but to nod. There was no way she could mention her fear.

Thirteen

According to the maid that answered Dave's call, Emily Young was sleeping under doctor prescribed sedation. With that stop delayed, Kate got her wish, and they headed back to the airport. Dave's pager went off fifteen minutes into their trip. He looked at the number, then reached for the car phone. "Richman. I got a page."

He glanced over at her. "Hi, Marcus."

Surprise jolted Kate out of her thoughts.

"Are you sure you want to handle it that way?" He nodded. "All right. We'll be expecting you." He hung up the phone.

"What?" Kate already knew she wasn't going to like it. The fact Marcus had called Dave and her was a pretty big clue.

"The bomb threat phone call contents just leaked to the press."

"Wonderful." She squeezed the bridge of her nose. "That guarantees a fun afternoon."

"Kate, the passenger list was released an hour ago."

When she didn't immediately connect the dots, he did it for her. "Nathan Young was listed. The media is already running with the connection to the bank incident last week. Your boss wants you to lay low, doesn't want you back at the airport. To quote Marcus, it's become a firestorm."

She had to get to a computer terminal. This was atrocious timing. Why couldn't it have held another few hours? "I can't exactly step back from this investigation; I'm in the middle of it." She rubbed at her headache. "Take me to the office then, I guess. I'll work from there and stay with Lisa tonight since my apartment has already been ruled out." She saw the expression on his face. "What?"

"Marcus suggested a more secure place was in order, both for you to work and to stay."

"Why? The press is aggravating and to be avoided but hardly dangerous."

"Because you are a target. Someone who killed 214 people wanted to see you squirm under this media onslaught."

"What's his suggestion?"

"You stay at my place."

Stay with Dave. Of course. It was just like Marcus. Protect her twenty-four hours a day. And Dave had probably been the one to plant the suggestion with him on the assumption this situation might develop; the two of them had been thick as thieves the last couple days. *Stephen, where are you? They are smothering me. I need to be rescued from all these good intentions!* "That is a little overblown." There was a niggling doubt that it might not be, but she was not letting ghosts chase her until she had her hands around the evidence.

"No, it's not. Right now the media is your enemy, not just a nuisance. If they tell where you are, this guy can come knock on your door. Do you want that to be Lisa's door?"

That thought was chilling. "No."

"There is room to work at my place; the security is good, and I won't have to wonder where you are."

"You have access to the files from home?"

"Basically anything I can do at the office downtown, I can do from home."

It wasn't worth the fight. She was losing precious time. "Fine. Let's go to your place."

Dave watched for a moment from the doorway as Kate read through a fax. She had been holed up here in his office for the last half hour. "Finding anything useful?" The fact she about jumped out of the seat made Dave strongly suspect his guess was right. When she reached to blank the computer screen even as she swiveled in his office chair toward him, she confirmed it. Whatever lead she was puzzling over, it worried her.

Something from her past.

He had put that much together. It concerned the case, and she didn't want to talk about it. He set down the cold drink on a coaster by the keyboard. "Sorry I startled you. Are you okay?"

She swallowed hard. "Yes."

He could feel her nervousness, worse, could see almost panic in her eyes. The mask she so easily wore was in shreds. "Susan called," he said quietly, choosing his words carefully so as to give her room to settle down, "the briefcase and laptop both match the information Peter provided."

"Oh...good."

He frowned. Very distracted. What information had her coiled tense like this? He had seen her calmly face down a man with a bomb. This change was alarming.

She had been distracted when they left the bank. What had he missed? He thought back through the information Peter Devlon had provided. It was useful, but nothing to result in this kind of response.

He was not going to crowd her, not when he needed her above all else to trust him. He settled his hand on her shoulder. "Can I get you something to eat?"

"Maybe later."

He squeezed her shoulder gently and stepped away. "I'm going to check security for the house. If you hear the door, it's me."

She nodded. "Thanks."

He closed the door to the office to give her the privacy she clearly wanted.

Whether she realized it or not, this house had just become a formal safe house again. There were already 214 victims. There would not be 215. She was spooked. That was sufficient warning for him.

He would have to explain the security grid to her soon, show her how the grids inside the house turned off and on in zones, but for now he would get the overall security tightened. He called Ben from his cellular phone as he circled the estate grounds, not needing Kate to hear the call just yet. A few minutes later, he closed the phone, satisfied. Travis and Susan were both on their way.

On the drive out here he had wondered what Kate would think of his home. The estate had been in his family a long time, and one person got lost in its spaciousness; it needed a family. Sara had shared the place with him until she married Adam. Kate had simply looked across the well-kept grounds and shown her cop's priorities by asking first about security, then commenting that the landscaped grounds were beautiful.

Satisfied eventually that everything was in order, he reentered the house, reset the security grid for the grounds. It beeped as he was turning away. Thinking he had made an error, he turned and saw a car had pulled to the gate. Surprised, he lowered the grid and cleared the car past the gates.

He was waiting at the door when Marcus got out of the car. "I didn't expect you this soon. Come on in."

"I asked Ben to cover the afternoon update meeting." Marcus offered the sealed box he was carrying. "Those should be copies of all the security tapes of the business lounge." He looked around, curious. "Nice place. Where's Kate?"

"She's working in my office." Dave hesitated. "Marcus, something is wrong."

"Oh?"

"She's been distracted ever since we left the bank."

"Where's your office?"

"Down the hall, second door on your left."

Marcus nodded. "Sort those tapes into some sort of order, and I'll be back to watch them with you." He moved down the hall toward Dave's office.

Dave could see the wall Kate still had up with him—her family could get answers where he could not. How long was it going to be before she trusted him? He hated being left on the periphery of her life, and that realization troubled him. This friendship had been subtly morphing into a relationship even though he knew how dangerous that was for him.

Lord, Kate is invading my heart. She's so determined not to be dependent on others. I want to be in that circle of people she trusts and turns to when life is tough. I want her safe—physically, emotionally—and it's becoming intensely personal with me.

Hearing the knock, Kate instinctively moved her hand over the keyboard, prepared to clear the screen. "Kate."

Marcus. The relief was incredible. "Come in."

Her brother pushed open the door. He looked at her, turned, and made sure the door was closed.

"Did you say anything to Dave?"

"No. He thinks I came to bring the security tapes." He took the second seat and wrapped his arm around her shoulders. "Twenty-two years, and you've never sent a drop everything page before. What's wrong?"

She took a deep breath, not sure how to prepare him for what she had found. It terrified her. "Mr. Nathan Young had a meeting at the airport with his VP Peter Devlon and the owner of Wilshire Construction." She turned the screen toward him. "Check out the incorporation papers for the company."

Moments later, Marcus stilled. "When was this filed?"

"A change of registered agent to this name and address was made four years ago."

His hand started rubbing her arm even as he continued to read. "Who has this information?"

"I'm not volunteering anything, but it's only a matter of time."

"Is your name change part of your personnel file?"

She shook her head. It was the only faint piece of good news there was. "No. But neither were the court records sealed. If it's not on a piece of paper in the stacks of data being looked through, it will be soon."

"What about the address?"

"That is sealed as is all information regarding the case filed by the DA against my parents. My past goes back to Trevor House, and there it ends. But with my real name and my real birthdate, they will eventually match the address. Two Emersons in a bomb case, one of whom changed her last name? Instant conflagration."

He tightened his arm. "How do you want to play this?"

"I want to know if I've really got a brother, first of all. Then I want to know if he blew up a plane with 214 people on board. If he did, I may just kill him myself."

Marcus winced. "Have you pulled his birth certificate? He's not a cousin, another relative?"

"Tony Emerson Jr., named for Dad no doubt," she said bitterly. She flipped back a screen to show him the birth certificate. "He's twenty-six. It fits. He would have been born the year after I was removed from the home." Her hand shook as she blanked that screen. The pain she had been forced to endure because she was not a son…the courts called it child abuse, but that was too polite a word for what had happened. The shaking was anger, rage, and pure fear.

Marcus's hand grasped her chin and turned her to look at him. "Let it go. Come on, Ladybug. Let it go." He tore her out of the memories by the force of his will.

The cop she was pushed the rage back, the rage at feeling helpless and defenseless. "I have to know."

"Yes." His hand brushed down her cheek. "Stay here. Let me check it out."

"I need to go with you."

He looked at her for a long moment. "No."

"Marcus—"

"You'll kill him," he said simply. "His name is Tony Emerson; he probably resembles your father, and you will kill him. It wouldn't have anything to do with this case."

She closed her eyes. She didn't dare wonder if it were true.

He buried her head into his shoulder. "You don't need the memories. Stay here. If you think you can handle seeing him, go through the security tapes with Dave and make your first look a distant one."

She took a deep breath and nodded. "What do I tell Dave?"

"As little or as much as you want. It's going to take me some time, Kate. I'll call as soon as I can, but you need to keep yourself occupied."

"Be careful."

"You have my promise."

With a final hug, he was on his feet and moving.

Kate watched the door close and slowly uncurled her fist. The O'Malleys were her family. Not someone named Tony Emerson Jr. Not someone born to the man who had nearly destroyed her life. She wanted to run; it was the strongest emotion of all the conflicting ones. Hide. Get away from this reality. She had a brother. How was she going to deal with that if it were true?

She would have given anything in her life to have a real brother when she was young. Now, she could only hope it wasn't true.

Fourteen

K ate, come sit down," Dave asked. She was pacing the living room, arms crossed, looking once again like she felt caged in. Whatever had her worried, it had been sufficient for Marcus to leave immediately after talking with her. The only thing Marcus had told him was an absolutely firm "don't let her leave" warning.

If she heard his request, she didn't indicate it.

Dave set down the remote control. The last thing Kate was ready to do was look at security videotapes. There would be time when Travis and Susan got here. He got to his feet. She looked startled when he touched her arm. "Let's go for a walk."

She blinked, then nodded.

He changed the security grid so they could walk the grounds. They walked the path around the flower gardens in silence. Dave knew she wasn't seeing the beautiful day around them.

"I never said thanks for offering me a place to stay."

She was thanking him for something a few hours ago she had been protesting? Dave felt a cold sensation brush across his spine. He reached over for Kate's hand. "I don't mind the company, and the security fits what you need. This place served as a safe house for my sister. No one will get on the grounds easily."

"What do you mean, it was a safe house for your sister?"

"Maybe you know her as Sara Walsh."

She stopped walking. "Oh." Obviously, she remembered when the case had made news. "You were part of her detail?"

"Head of security for a good part of her life. She was an endearing little brat when she chose to be." He tried to distract her. "You remind me a lot of her."

"How? She's rich and beautiful and…" She sputtered to a stop.

"She has a whimsical sense of humor like you."

"I've seen her children's books." She shook her head and frowned at him. "This is just great. Can't you have a normal family?"

Laughter felt good. "Me? What about the O'Malleys? Sara wants to meet you, by the way."

"You've told her about me?"

"You've been all over the news, remember?"

They had reached the back of the grounds where a small bench was tucked beside a reflecting pool. Dave steered her toward it.

"Do you think we will find out who did this?"

"I think the answer is on the security tapes in the living room."

He was surprised that she looked distressed at the thought. The first inkling of understanding came. "Do you know one of the people Peter Devlon mentioned?"

"No!" It was so sharp, her face so pale, that his hand caught hers to keep her from bolting. Fear. It flashed across her face and then blanked away as she took a breath, buried behind the curtain that dropped across her expression. "No, I've never met either one of them."

That was the truth, he was certain of it, but she had heard of at least one of them. How? She was not someone who gave in to fear easily.

"Did you ever get another call like that one the night we had pizza?" He asked the first thing that came to mind as something to distract her again, and then he realized what he had said. He blinked. *The call.*

"Sounds like you have trouble coming your way. Soon it will be more than you can handle." He distinctly remembered the laugh.

Whoever had made that call knew what was coming.

Kate's eyes were wide, bright. "Dave, I *need* those answering machine tapes. They are in my briefcase at the office."

"How many calls were there?"

"Three. No, four." She shook her head. "I don't know if the third one was the same person. But the others definitely were. The last one was Monday morning."

"They are all on tape?"

"Yes."

He wanted to sweep out an arm and hug her, for he shared the sense of relief; instead he held out his hand and pulled her to her feet. "Come on. We can be to your office and back in a little over an hour."

She started with him toward the house, then stopped. "No. I have to wait for Marcus. That's more important."

Dave watched her bite her lip, obviously torn as to what to do. "Who else can access your briefcase for us?"

"Anyone on the team could get the tapes. And we would need a similar model answering machine."

"Call your boss; ask him to send someone to bring what you need out here. I'll see about getting us a cleaned up copy of the call to the tower."

She nodded, and once in the house, went immediately to pick up her cellular phone.

"Kate," she paused her dialing, "have him send an officer to your apartment to retrieve that answering machine tape, and make sure the officer puts in a new one. You haven't been home since this blast occurred. What if that follow-up call we expected was made to your home?"

Nodding, she punched in numbers and was soon in a detailed conversation with her boss.

Dave left her to make his own call. He was relieved to find the lab had been able to remove most of the distortion from the voice. A copy of the cleaned up tape was on the way. His call finished, he went to join her.

"Do you really think there's a chance my harassing caller is the bomber?"

"I've never been one to believe in coincidences." She looked... pleased...at the idea someone who knew her phone number might be the bomber. He wondered if her need for justice made her blind to the risks she accepted. She scared him; she really scared him. "It will be a while before the tapes arrive. How about dinner?"

"Food?"

"Unless you would like to look at the security tapes first."

"Tell me what I can help fix." She followed him into the kitchen.

Watching Dave sort through cupboards was an interesting distraction. Kate settled against the counter and worked on a piece of celery as she watched.

"Spaghetti?" Dave asked.

"Can we have garlic bread?"

"Do you treat garlic the same way you do sugar?"

"Wimp."

"Hey, if I ever did want to risk an emotional firestorm and kiss you good night, I would prefer that one kiss not taste like garlic."

She moved away from the counter and leaned past him to pluck a glass jar of homemade sauce from the shelf, realizing he had apparently decided to break his own rules about this friendship. "If, huh? Of course, you're assuming I would let you."

His hands spanned her waist and lifted her back slowly. She couldn't explain why, but she could sense there was a struggle going on behind his teasing words. "It's called self-preservation. If we were...involved—" He paused, then cleared his throat and went on. "Then *one* kiss good night would go a long way to insuring I keep my hands to myself the rest of the day."

She blinked at the impact of that smile and knew she would be a goner if he ever intentionally turned that charm her way. This was just the moment, pure and simple, he'd be back to keeping his distance soon, but still...she grinned. "Hands."

He dropped her to her feet, and the emotion—the regret—in his eyes troubled her. "I didn't mean it literally."

She patted his arm, forcing a light tone to her words. "Fine. But I still want garlic bread if I'm eating Italian."

"Then I'll fix it."

"Under the broiler? Nicely toasted, not dark?"

"Whatever happened to the benefit of the doubt? I can cook."

"O'Malley men. They say the same thing."

He grinned. "They can't cook?"

"Not if it involves fire."

He found her a pan for the sauce. "I feel duty bound to defend them as they are not here to defend themselves."

"Don't bother. Once you've eaten one of Jack's charred delights, you'll learn that the best defense is a good offense."

"So who's cooking for the Fourth of July?"

"Jack."

"Really?"

She smiled at his amusement. "We give him the matches. He's happy. Then Stephen guards the food like a pit bull. When it's time to come off, there's this little signal that goes to Lisa, and she distracts Jack while I go steal the food. We've got it down to a science." His laughter made her grin. "I know. But it's Jack. We wouldn't want to hurt his feelings."

"Can I come watch this adventure?"

She blinked. "I guess so, if you want to."

"Trust me, Kate. I do. Hand me the bread knife."

Dinner made it to the table in a companionable fashion.

"Pretty decent," Kate allowed as she bit into the hot garlic bread.

"It's great and you know it," Dave countered. "What did you do to this salad?"

"I'm not telling."

"My sister will kill for a good recipe. I owe her. Come on, give."

"You'll have to ask Lisa. She has sworn me to secrecy."

"Over a recipe?"

"Hey, we know what is valuable in life."

He ate another bite and sighed. "How much to bribe it out of you?"

She grinned. "It would be cheaper to beg it off Lisa."

"Really?"

"Really."

"Now you've piqued my interest. What would it cost?"

"A chance to read that first edition Mark Twain you have in your living room."

"The frog story?"

"That's the one."

"Good taste."

"I know good literature."

He chuckled. "I knew your sense of humor came from a master."

"Twain was a step above comic books."

"You were a reader as a kid?"

Her laughter disappeared. "I don't think I was ever a kid."

The silence drifted a few moments. "I step across that line before I realize I'm even near it. I'm sorry."

She tried to make the shrug casual. "You get too far under my guard. Normally a comment like that wouldn't hit me by surprise."

"I gather the orphanage was rough."

"I had Marcus."

"I wondered. You two appear to almost read each other's minds."

"Considering I knocked him flat the first half dozen times we met, we were destined to be either friends or enemies for life." She smiled at the memory.

"He let you?"

"Hardly. I was a fierce little fighter when I was nine. He didn't think he was supposed to hit girls back, so I sat him in the mud a few times to make my point."

"What did he call you?"

"Nothing. He was the one trying to be nice."

"Oh."

She looked at him. "Don't give me that painfully understanding look. I was an angry little kid, and he wanted to butt into my business. I didn't like it."

"So you hit him."

"It seemed like the thing to do at the time."

Dave leaned back in his chair with his coffee. "What changed your mind?"

"He gave me a puppy."

He choked on his coffee.

She looked at him, daring him to say a word. His eyes narrowed, but he kept silent. "It was this black fuzz ball that had sharp teeth and an attitude, and it tried to bite me every time I tried to pet it, feed it, or work the tangles out of its mangy fur. Marcus just walked by, dumped it in my lap, and said *here*. I was too busy trying to keep the thing hidden from the staff to wonder why Marcus was so determined to pick on me. Every time that dog would get away, Marcus would have to go canvas the neighborhood and bring him back in a box."

"How long did this go on?"

"Probably six months. Then the dog got hit by a car, and I think I nearly pulverized Marcus for not finding him alive. That sort of ended the hostilities on my side."

"I'm sorry about your dog."

"You know, I never called him *my dog* until after he was dead? I always dumped him back on Marcus with all this 'you know what your dog did today' outrage."

"How old was Marcus?"

Kate pulled herself back from the memories. "What?"

"How old was Marcus?"

"Oh," she thought about it a moment. "Eleven."

"That qualifies as a friend for life."

"Probably." She grinned. "I'm going to have to repay him for that dog bit one of these days though. Maybe I'll get him one of those yappy terriers."

"You are dangerous, lady."

"I've got a long memory. Did I hear you say something about dessert?"

"Want something for that sweet tooth?"

"Got the fixings for a sundae?"

"Sure."

"That would be perfect."

He went to the freezer to find their options. "Ice cream appears to be your favorite."

It took her three drawers to find the ice cream scoop. "I'm a creature of habit."

"That's good to know."

"Why?"

"I'll only have to learn everything about you once."

"Dream on." She pulled open the refrigerator. "Do you want caramel or hot fudge?"

"Fudge."

She pulled out the glass jar and put it into the microwave to warm. "Does this qualify as having dinner together?"

He looked over at her, surprised. "I would think so. Why?"

"That's what I was afraid of. Lisa will be expecting a verbatim rundown on the conversation."

He grinned. "Will she?"

"She also wants to know if you've got a cousin or something."

"Lisa doesn't need help in the dating department. Trust me."

"Oh? What have you heard that I haven't?"

"You didn't see that ER doc hanging around her when you were at the hospital?"

"Kevin?"

"I think that's his name."

"She dumped him six months ago."

"Well, he wants another chance."

"Not with my sister. I'll flatten him first."

"What did he do?"

"Made her cry."

"Over what?"

"How should I know? She won't tell anyone. But she was crying, and he's a creep."

Dave passed her a spoon to lick. "Make an O'Malley cry, and you're in mortal danger?"

"Exactly."

"Nice to know you are all such diplomats."

"Simple rules work best."

"That one is simple enough. What's another one?"

She looked at the jar he was holding. "Don't hog the chocolate."

He passed it over with a chuckle. "You're predictable."

"Thank you. I'll take that as a compliment."

They settled at the kitchen table to eat dessert.

Kate worked through half of the ice cream in silence. It was almost time to face those security tapes. The thought made her light mood turn dark again.

"Kate, what's wrong?"

She looked over at him for a moment, then back at the ice cream. "Stuff I can't talk about." She would love to tell him all of it—Jennifer's cancer, the fear the name Emerson generated, but couldn't do it. It was more than just her at this point, it was others in the O'Malley family, and they had to be protected whatever the cost. She didn't need reporters digging into the story of their family history.

"You're sure?"

He sounded disappointed, and she regretted that. "Yes." She caught the red flash from the security grid out of the corner of her eye and turned.

Dave got up to check and looked frustrated at the interruption. "It's Susan and Travis."

She picked up their two bowls and stacked them. "Go meet them."

He looked at her and hesitated.

She smiled, touching his arm. "Dave, I'm not trying to shut you out. I'm just not at liberty to talk about some issues yet. I'm sorry. I may be able to tell you later."

He squeezed her hand. "Just don't keep secrets that are going to affect your safety, okay?"

She couldn't answer that; she wasn't going to lie to him.

He went to meet Susan and Travis.

The patrol officer arrived with the tapes as Travis and Susan walked the grounds with Dave. Kate set up the answering machine on the coffee table in the living room. Why Dave felt the need to have two agents on the grounds tonight she didn't understand, but trying to change his mind about something he had settled on was a hopeless cause.

She heard the front door close and glanced up as Dave came back into the living room. "Which one do we start with?"

He settled in the chair across from the couch. "The one that just came from your machine. I want to know if he called back after the bomb went off."

Nodding, she found the tape. It was a full tape of calls; the point in time that her name was leaked to the media was obvious by the immediate bombardment of the media. Nothing useful.

Kate put in the first tape with the call from Wednesday afternoon and picked up a pad of paper and pen to make sure she transcribed it word for word.

"Hello, Kate O'Malley. I've been looking for you, and what do I see—you made the news last night. We'll have to meet soon."

"Have to meet soon? The guy is stalking you!"

She had heard too many of them over the years to give it that kind of weight. She had known they were going to disagree on this; she tried to placate Dave's concern. "The call talks about the bank holdup. Yes, it sounds like a convict from a case I've worked, but that doesn't mean he has me located yet." She ignored his frown. "Here's the one you heard."

"Hello, Kate. I taped the news tonight. Sounds like you have trouble coming your way. Soon it will be more than you can handle."

The laugh made her shiver. "If that is the bomber, the words could be interpreted as a reference to the plane."

She looked at the jotted notes on the cassettes. "This one would have been—Saturday afternoon."

"I think you've given up trying to catch me. Does that mean I win?"

"Different voice," Dave said immediately.

"Yes. We've already got an idea who this guy is. There's an outstanding warrant for his arrest on an unrelated matter." Kate drew a line through the words she had written. She changed the tapes. "Last one. Monday morning."

"Did you enjoy your weekend? It will be the last one for a while."

"That sounds like another reference to the plane."

She frowned, looking at the words. "Maybe."

"Let's hear the cleaned up tape from the tower."

She found her pocket recorder, inserted the tape, and pressed the play button.

"The bomb goes off at eleven-fifteen. The plane is talking to the tower. Tell Kate O'Malley I haven't forgotten the past."

"The same voice," Dave said grimly.

Her hand shaking slightly, Kate rewound the tape to play it again. It was the same voice. "Call Jim, tell him to pull my phone records." *The bomber had been calling her.* The fear was overwhelming. Could she have prevented all of this? The crash? Her stomach roiled at the thought.

Dave was already dialing. "You are not going back to your apartment till we find this guy, Kate." For once she totally agreed with him; changing cities sounded like a good option right now. Someone wanted her dead. He was toying with her, mocking her, and warning her he was coming. *The black rose of death.* She had probably totally misjudged that "gift" as well as the calls.

Dave got her boss on the line and explained what they had found and arranged to send the tapes to the lab. He hung up the phone.

"Kate!" Dave's hand closed around the back of her neck and pushed her head down. "Don't you dare pass out."

She needed that stinging voice to pull her back from the brink. "Sorry," she mumbled, feeling the rush of blood returning to her face.

He briskly rubbed her back. "Don't do that! You scared me," he complained.

She pushed his hands away, sitting back up. She took a deep breath to push away the tremors. "The rose, Dave. It's not Tersh, it's the bomber. It's a black rose of death."

Dave paled. "He was at your apartment?"

"Yeah. I think so. It's too coincidental that Bobby Tersh would appear within days of that call and the message 'we'll have to meet soon.'"

"Did the black roses make the papers five years ago?"

"They were mentioned when Tersh was arrested, then committed."

She looked at him, hoping he would contradict her interpretation. He didn't. "Bobby's car was never seen in Illinois."

"The bomber borrowed his MO," she agreed, feeling cold.

Set it aside, she demanded of herself. *There was more information about this guy available now that they knew he was making the calls. Don't you dare overreact to this threat! You've vowed never to let someone else dictate, control your life by fear. You're letting him win!*

The reminder settled the emotions, shoved them aside, and calmed her inside. *That's better. Control the situation; don't let it control you.*

She got up to pace. "They were running the tests this afternoon to find out where the bomb threat call originated. What did they find out?"

"Hold on." He called Bob Roberts and asked the question. "How certain are they about that?" He scrawled something on the pad of paper. "Okay. Thanks." He hung up the phone.

"Bob says they've determined the call was not made from inside any of the terminals. The power levels drop way off inside the building. Outside, the area is harder to pinpoint. The power levels were consistent along a strip of ground that goes from the general aviation terminal to the long-term parking lot. They found one area of elevated ground by the parking area that would let you look down onto the runways. If you wanted to watch what happened, that would be a good location."

Kate nodded at the news, but her focus had already shifted. Had she ever heard this voice before? When? Where? The bomb threat was as clear as the lab would be able to get it. She closed her eyes as she listened to it, again, and then again.

Come on. She could nail this guy if she could just remember the voice....

She paced over to the window, holding the recorder to her ear as she played it again. Likely a bomb case...one by one she went through the list of names they had focused on from her past cases, and one by one she eliminated them. They would do it officially at the lab with the tapes on file, but she didn't forget faces or voices.

She felt like throwing the recorder but instead dropped herself down on the couch. "I don't know the voice."

"It was a long shot that you would."

She shook her head. "I don't forget voices, and if I haven't met him, then we've got real trouble." She got up to pace back to the window. "How are we going to catch a ghost?" She saw a car pull up to the distant security gate and heard Dave move to check the monitor.

"Marcus is here."

Kate rather numbly gathered up the evidence that would need to go to the police lab. She sealed the tapes and marked the evidence bag. Marcus was back. He hadn't called. There were several ways to interpret that, and she didn't know which one to prepare for.

Marcus paused just inside the doorway. She had never seen that look before on her brother's face. He held out his hand. "Kate, let's take a walk."

She set down the pad of paper without a word and joined him. The sun was low in the sky now, and the breeze from earlier in the day had died down. She had been through so much with Marcus. He didn't want to hurt her; she could see it in his face. She was braced for the bad news long before he spoke.

"No one has seen him since the blast. He's gone underground."

He had run. If there had been doubts about Tony Jr.'s involvement, hope that somehow she was wrong, they crumbled in the dust. "There was no one at his home?"

"His wife, Marla. Clearly frightened, nervous, but I think telling the truth. She hasn't seen him since Tuesday morning."

Tony was married. She hadn't considered that possibility. If he had a good life, why destroy it? Did he hate Nathan so much? Was losing the business so impossible to live with that he took it out on innocent people?

"There are men watching his house. This is being kept very close to the vest as the facts are checked out—it's high priority, getting a lot of resources, but need-to-know for now."

She nodded, knowing they had to move quickly.

"We should have a good bio on him in the next couple hours. But I've already learned one fact you need to know. He worked as a baggage handler at O'Hare several years ago. He was dismissed under suspicious circumstances. There wasn't enough to charge him, but eight others in his section went to jail for moving drugs."

"So he knows both security procedures and people who still work there."

"That's a safe assumption."

She shuddered at the pieces of this puzzle. "You're saying he did it."

"I don't know. Marla went pale as a ghost at the suggestion. She clearly believes he had nothing to do with it. I asked if she knew anything about the meeting with Nathan, and while she didn't know specifics, she surprised me by offering us access to the company books. It's possible the threat of losing the company was sufficient motive. He probably had access to the explosives. We'll have to find out."

There wasn't much doubt really. He had the means and the motive; he had the opportunity. "He's disappeared."

"Not a good reality, but if he thought there was enough circumstantial evidence to make him look guilty? Maybe he panicked. It wouldn't be the first time we've seen that."

"Did Marla know Tony had a sister?"

"No. He's never mentioned you."

They walked in silence. She tried to absorb the news he had given her but was too tired now to do more than nod. "Get me another place to stay."

"What? Why?"

"I don't want to be here when the word gets out. You know what the media is going to be like. 'Cop's Brother Prime Suspect in Bombing.' I don't want Dave pulled into the middle of this." She didn't want to be near him twenty-four hours a day when the doubts, the suspicions, tore apart what might have become a good friendship.

"Kate, I wish you would reconsider. I think you need Dave's help. He's good at his job."

"I know he is, but I don't want him in the middle of this. Please."

Marcus sighed. "Think about it, in light of what we now know. If Tony is the man responsible, look at what he has done. He killed Nathan not caring how many others he killed. He pulled you directly into it by putting your name in the bomb threat. He's striking out at those who he thinks are responsible for his problems."

"He doesn't know me."

"He probably thinks he does. I'm sure your father had you as the person responsible for all his problems. I'm sure Tony Jr. thinks all the grief he endured in that household was because of you. When he snaps, he goes after Nathan and he goes after you."

"How did he find out who I am?"

"Can you imagine how the bank incident played in the old neighborhood? Some of those folks have lived there forty years. Someone would have remembered what happened to little Kate Emerson."

"I haven't thought about the name Emerson for a decade, and now it's back to ruin my life."

"Kate—"

"Okay, maybe during domestic violence cases. But I closed it off and left it behind." She sighed. "Find me somewhere else to stay. I need some space, and Dave is already beginning to subtly push. He knows something is wrong."

"The news will hold for the night. Give me a day."

She reluctantly agreed.

"Stephen, Jack, Lisa—they will be by later."

"You've already told them?" At his look, she gave an apologetic smile. "Sorry." Tony was her embarrassment, but Marcus was right; it was a family problem.

His arm around her shoulders tightened. "You should be. We stick together, Kate. It will help to have real family around you."

"Marcus, thanks for the thought, but not tonight. Let me get some sleep. Come pick me up tomorrow morning."

"You're sure?"

She forced a smile. "I'm sure."

They walked back to the house in silence. He gave her a long hug before he let go. "I'll see you first thing in the morning."

She nodded and watched until he had made the turn in the drive before closing the door and walking back to the living room. Dave was fast-forwarding through the security tapes. He looked up, got to his feet, and came to meet her. She could only imagine what she looked like to put that expression on his face. "Kate—"

She simply couldn't face telling him. She wanted it all to go away. Did that make her a coward? She didn't care. "Would you mind if I looked at the security tapes tomorrow? I need a few hours sleep."

He hesitated, then nodded. "Sure. Come on. I'll show you to one of the guest rooms."

She retrieved her bag, and he showed her to the guest room at the top of the stairs, gave her a fast review of the security panel if she was up during the night, then laid out fresh towels and got her a new toothbrush.

"Thanks."

The back of his hand brushed down her cheek. "Get some sleep."

When he left, she looked at the wide bed and didn't even bother to pull back all the covers. She collapsed on them, caught a corner of the quilt, and brought it up around her shoulders. The way life was going, she wanted simply to shut it out for a few hours.

Fifteen

The page woke her up. It was dark outside, and she came awake, momentarily confused before locating her pager on the nightstand. She pushed back the blanket draped over her; Dave must have tucked her in at some point in the night. She looked at the numbers, saw the area code, and let her heart rate settle. It wasn't the dispatcher. The area code made it Jennifer.

She looked around for her phone, then remembered she had called her boss last. She had probably left the phone in the living room. Moving quietly, she left the bedroom, changed the security grid as Dave had shown her, and went downstairs. She didn't turn on the lights; the cast of moonlight was enough light to move around by. She curled up in a corner of the couch, drew up her knees, then stared at the glowing numbers on the phone. She had to pull in a deep breath before she began to dial. If this was more bad news, she was going to shatter.

"Hi, Jennifer."

"Kate, I just got the message Marcus left with my answering service. I've got reservations for the first flight out in the morning. I should be there by six."

Kate leaned her head down against her knees and started crying. "Jennifer—"

"I can come sit in a hospital and be poked anytime. I'd rather come hang out with you."

She laughed around the tears. "You guys are priceless, you know that?"

"We're family."

"Yes." It felt so good to hear that reassurance. She drew a deep breath and smiled. "We'll talk about your coming back early in a minute. First, tell me how the tests you've had are going."

Dave heard Kate moving around shortly before eleven, heard the stairs creak as she went downstairs. Restless? Dealing with bad dreams? Either case, he didn't like it. He frowned and pulled a pillow over to ease the strain on his neck. She had looked almost deathly gray when she had come back from talking with Marcus, and he had been hoping she would sleep through the night. He hated the strain he didn't understand, the fact she didn't trust him enough to tell him what was wrong even more. He waited, wondering if she had slipped downstairs to the kitchen to get a drink, but he heard nothing. And when she didn't return, he quietly got up and got dressed.

He kept a hand on the banister as he walked downstairs, wondering what he would find.

Kate was curled up on the couch, knees drawn up, her phone dangling in one hand. He could hear the muted tone of an off-hook signal. She had apparently finished a call but had not yet moved to close the phone.

He crossed the room to join her, clicked on the table lamp, and sank into the couch cushions beside her. She was silently crying. He took the phone from her limp hand. "Who were you talking to?"

"Jennifer. She paged me."

He wanted so badly to wipe away her tears. He let himself wipe at two, which drew a shaky smile from her. She backhanded her sleeve across her face.

"What's wrong, Kate?"

She closed her eyes, then looked over at him. "She's at the Mayo Clinic."

Understanding flickered across his face, and when he pulled her to him, she went willingly. He didn't let go of the hug. He didn't have words to heal the pain he saw.

"She's got cancer. Probably terminal."

She kept her head buried against his shoulder, hiding. He rubbed her back, wishing she would show more than silent tears. It made sense now.

It was family, and with Kate that would strike at her very heart.

She pulled back after a few moments, scrubbed a hand across her face. "She hasn't told the others in the family. It makes it hard. There is no one to talk to."

"There's me."

She touched the wet stain on his shirt and gave a rueful smile. "I wish she had let me go with her. I would have been far away from the crash."

"They are running tests?"

"Trying to determine a treatment plan." She bit her bottom lip. "It's around her spine, into her liver. Mortality rates are horrible."

"The engagement?"

"Tom didn't want to wait."

"I can understand that." He looked at the tired circles under her eyes and thought back to the basketball game. "When did she tell you?"

"Monday night."

He rubbed the bridge of his nose. "And the plane exploded Tuesday morning."

She half laughed. "It's been a *really* bad week." She rubbed her arms. "Jennifer wanted to come back early. I told her no."

He hesitated. "Is she a Christian?"

"Yes." She looked over at him, and under the weariness, he saw something approaching defeat. It troubled him more than anything else he had ever seen. "She gave me her Bible; she wants me to read the book of Luke."

He stilled, praying for the right words. "Kate—"

"I don't want to hurt her Dave, not Jennifer."

There were fresh tears appearing, and he understood better than she could comprehend. "You can't believe just because Jennifer wants you to." It would break her heart to hurt someone in her family. He smiled and gently brushed away one of the tears. She was past the hard part and didn't even realize it—she *wanted* to be able to believe. "Have you read Luke yet?"

"No."

"Set aside your preconceived notions and just read it. I'm sure that's all Jennifer is asking."

He hated the fragileness he saw. She was coming apart at the seams; she was so tired, worried, and given the black rose and phone calls—rightfully scared. And he still didn't think he knew everything she was hiding; he still didn't understand what about the bank interview had troubled her. "Come here." He didn't give her a choice. He simply wrapped her into his arms and tucked her head back against his shoulder. "You'll get through this, Kate."

She sighed. "Sometimes I envy you."

He brushed back her hair. "Why?"

"You can still hope."

She went silent, and he waited, hoping for another glimmer into what she was thinking. After a few minutes passed, he rubbed her arm. "Want some hot chocolate?" She needed a distraction, and it was the only thing he could think of.

"In June?"

He heard the amusement. "Yes, in June. Come on; it will do you some good. You're cold."

She eased herself away from him. "Got marshmallows?"

"Somewhere."

"You need lots of them."

He settled his arm comfortably around her shoulders as she swayed a bit on her feet. "Do you?"

"Of course, but if you don't have many, you can put the mug into the microwave, and they puff up really big so you can make a few seem like a lot."

He buried a smile. Definitely exhausted. "Now why does that sound like an O'Malley guy solution?"

"They never remember to go shopping."

"So you help them out."

"Someone has to."

He turned on the kitchen light, and she winced. "Ouch. Headache coming."

"I'll find you some aspirin."

He settled her onto the kitchen chair and frowned at her bare feet. He disappeared for a moment to come back with clean socks. "Careful you don't go sliding with them on, but at least they're warm."

"Thanks."

"Don't mention it." He found aspirin for her headache, then went to look through the cupboard. "Do you want milk chocolate or dark chocolate?"

"You're making it from scratch?"

"I actually surprised you." He grinned. "Is this a first?"

"Probably. But only because it's late. Dark chocolate."

"Coming up."

He was relieved to see a little life coming back into her eyes.

She idly ate a pretzel from the dish. "I forgot to tell you company would be over early."

"O'Malleys?"

"Marcus, if not the full clan."

"I like your family."

She rested her chin on her hand. "I wish you had met Jennifer."

"Did she always want to be a doctor?"

"As far back as I can remember. You should have seen her playing doctor at Trevor House. It was annoying. She would turn our bedroom into a waiting room for her patients."

"She had a lot of them?"

"Anybody younger than her with a sniffle. I'd have to play the receptionist to protect my stuff."

"Sounds like a rough time."

"I especially liked it when the boys would come to have their scrapes patched over. If you went to the house mom, you got grounded for fighting, so there was an underground black market for Band-Aids."

"Did Jennifer know?"

"I didn't tell her." She shrugged. "Hey, it was free enterprise. They were the ones who got into the fights."

"How many did you get into?"

"With a budding doctor as a roommate? If I showed up with a scraped knuckle from a fight, she would take a strip off my hide. Why do you think I became a negotiator? It was pure self-preservation."

He brought over two mugs of hot chocolate. "Enough marshmallows?"

"Yes. Thanks."

He sank into the chair beside her. "My pleasure."

"Are you always this mellow?"

He quirked an eyebrow, amused. "I don't think I've ever been called that before."

"You're like one of those cuddle bears, kind of soft and spongy."

"Kate, you need some more sleep."

"Are you blushing?" She pushed herself up in her seat. "You are!"

"I'm opinionated and stubborn, and I have that on good authority."

"Whose?"

"Sara's."

"What were you playing heavy-handed brother about when she told you that?"

He frowned at her. "Why do you assume I was at fault?"

"Three brothers. I have experience."

"I'm not heavy-handed."

"You admitted someone could tweak your tiger tail, so fess up."

He scowled. "I am not tattling. And don't try to pester it out of me, either. You and Sara are cut from the same cloth. It won't work."

She grinned and dunked a marshmallow with her spoon. "Your roar is really cute with that British accent."

He closed his eyes. "Drink your chocolate."

"Tired?"

"Are you sure you weren't raiding the sugar stash before I came down?"

"When I'm tired, I talk. It's how you stay awake during a long negotiation."

He looked over at her and felt something remarkably like love. Every one of her defenses was down. This was the real Kate under all the layers, and he was falling in love with her. The problems of that reality he would deal with in the light of day. "Then keep talking," he said gently.

She nibbled on a pretzel. "Believe it or not, I'm running out of subjects."

He grinned. "You?"

"I didn't figure you would want any Aunt Gladys stories."

"Have a repertoire, do you?"

"She's a spunky lady. She's done everything from skiing to skydiving."

"Of course. She was created by an O'Malley."

"You've got it." She tipped her mug and frowned. "Got any more hot chocolate? I've hit empty."

"Of course." Her aim was a little off when she handed him the mug. He looked at her more sharply. Past exhausted, getting punchy. Convincing her to go back to bed soon moved up a notch on his priority list. He brought the bag of marshmallows with him back to the table.

She speared one with a pretzel and spun it like a top. "We used to feed these to the squirrels."

He grinned. "Quit playing with your food."

She grinned back. "Have you ever seen a squirrel try to eat one of these? They're sticky inside, and they have to sit and clean their paws forever."

"We get raccoons around here occasionally. They like them."

"I watched a snake eat one once. Lisa came in and shrieked."

"You smuggled a snake into her room?"

She frowned at him. "It was her snake. She thought he had eaten Rachel's hamster."

"Let me get this right—Trevor House, which does not allow pets, had you hiding a dog, Lisa hiding a snake, and Rachel hiding a hamster?"

"Well, kind of. There were the other pets we hid in the garden shed, but that didn't really count because the groundskeeper smuggled in the food. Besides, Lisa arrived at Trevor House with a lizard in her backpack. It wasn't fair not to let her keep it. And once we hid the lizard, it just kind of got easier to, well, *add* things."

"Why do I get the feeling you were the chief instigator of this endeavor?"

Her smile was touched with seriousness. "It was important that the place feel something like home. Everyone should have a pet."

He cradled his mug, liking her all the more. "Marcus protected the O'Malleys, and you watched out for them." She shrugged, not admitting to it. She didn't have to. It was in practically every story she told. From protecting Jack's feelings about his cooking, to guarding Jennifer's dream of becoming a doctor. "I think I like you, Kate."

She grinned. "You're not sure?"

"Pushing for a compliment?"

She laughed and ate the marshmallow.

"Come on. You need to go back to bed."

"I'm too tired to go to sleep."

"Then let's at least move you away from the sugar."

She wrinkled her nose at him but finished the hot chocolate. "That really was good. You didn't scorch it like I sometimes do."

He took her mug to the sink. "Nothing is worse than scorched milk in the middle of the night."

"Tell me about it."

"Buy instant. It will make your life easier." His hands on her shoulders, he turned her back to the living room. "You're going to have a rat's tail to brush out tomorrow."

"Thanks for noticing."

"Don't mention it." He tugged her down on the couch beside him. "Feet."

She frowned at him but picked up her feet. He tucked the throw cover firmly around them, then made her comfortable against his shoulder. "If you're not going to sleep, at least close your eyes."

"What are you planning to watch?"

He flipped the remote over a couple channels. "The replay of the Cubs game."

"They lose."

"How do you know?"

She tilted her head back. "Because they were playing Milwaukee."

"That insures they were going to lose?"

She sighed and gave him a long-suffering look that said he didn't understand baseball. "They were going to lose. Check the scores showing on ESPN News if you don't believe me."

She was so certain she was right he flipped the channels to prove her wrong. She was right. The Cubs lost by three runs.

"See. I told you."

He turned back to the Cubs game, scoreless in the first inning, set down the remote, and slouched down on the couch to get comfortable.

"We're still going to watch it?"

"It's even better when you know the outcome. You don't have to waste all that energy wondering who wins."

"You and Stephen will get along great. He always has to watch from first pitch to last."

"You can either go to sleep or watch it with me. Take your pick."

"Give me the pillow." He reached for the throw pillow to give her. She mashed it into a lump before settling back against his shoulder, her feet tucked up on the couch. He smiled at her. "Comfortable?"

A yawn popped her jaw. "Not entirely, but you're better than that cot last night."

"You're welcome to go back to bed."

"I'll watch a while."

She made it until the third inning. She didn't snore, but she went limp as a dishrag. Her shoulder dug into his arm. Afraid both of them were going to end up feeling bruised, he woke her up. "You need to go to bed."

"Yeah."

She got up but nearly fell over. He grabbed her arm. "Okay?"

She rubbed blurry eyes and nodded. "Good night."

He smiled as he watched her head for the stairs.

Lord, what am I going to do? You know my heart, and it just landed somewhere at that lady's feet. Come tomorrow I'm going to have to scramble like mad to get some distance back so that every time she smiles my heart doesn't stop. But for the record—she's got beautiful eyes, a grin I adore, and I could see myself flirting with her for about the next fifty years.

Wooing someone to faith is what You do best. Please, I'd rather not get my heart broken.

Sixteen

Dawn was still an hour away, but the sky was beginning to tinge pink. Kate lay back against the pillows and watched the colors change. Today was irreversibly going to change her life. She knew it. The news about Tony Emerson Jr., if it all checked out, could not be contained more than a day. By nightfall the press would be looking for her.

She picked up the small book she had found in the side pocket of her gym bag and gave a rueful smile. Jennifer's New Testament. The officer who had packed for her must have thought it was important.

She needed to do this, for Jennifer would be here soon, and there was no predicting when the next calm moment would appear in her schedule. *"Just read it without preconceived notions."* That was so easy for Dave to say.

She retrieved the notepad and pen from her bag and opened the book to the bookmark. If Jennifer wanted to talk about the book of Luke, then they would talk about the book of Luke. Her sister was more important than her own unease with the choice of subject. The notepad was habit. Writing questions, notes, and observations would keep her focused. She started reading.

It was a struggle to get through the first three chapters. History had never been one of her better subjects. She was glad reading documents without having the full context was part of her job. Floundering a bit but determined to get through it, she kept reading.

Finally, she wrote on the pad of paper—3:38. Son of God.

Over an hour later she turned the last page in the book of Luke and clicked her pen. It was a relief to close burning eyes for a moment.

She read the four pages of concise notes.

Setting aside the questions, she focused on summarizing what she had read, consolidating the observations. The sketch she drew of Jesus made her hesitate because it was so unlike any other sketch of a man she had ever done.

He was not an ambitious man seeking power. He had power in Himself. People around Him, both supporters and enemies, acknowledged that He spoke as one having authority. He was a man that attracted crowds, but did not seek them out. Departing for a lonely place seemed to be His preference.

He was a man of compassion, gentle, kind, and liked children. He spent Sabbaths teaching. He traveled. There was never a question or hesitation on His part. No doubt. One insight in Gethsemane of a man facing an enormous coming burden.

He healed. The accounts were astounding. They were accounts of immediate, complete healing. A high fever seemed the most minor. Lepers. Paralytics. He raised the dead.

He claimed to have the ability to forgive sins, was personally a forgiving man.

She brought her summary to a conclusion with a stark observation— *Jesus did not receive justice.* He was the Son of God. He was innocent. And He was crucified. She had turned the last pages in Luke and read of the Resurrection on the third day, hard to believe, but at least it gave some justice. Jesus should be alive; He had done nothing to deserve death.

He said the Father was merciful.

Why had He not said the Father was just?

The book she had just read showed within it a culture divided over the issue of Jesus. Betrayal. Plots. Conspiracies. Adoring crowds. Power brokers. Politics.

People had died because they believed this book.

If someone had written Luke as a hoax, they had done a compelling piece of work. She had spent a lifetime studying people. People by nature wanted to lie in a way they would be believed. As a hoax, the book would have been written less grandiose, so that it would be accepted, not scoffed at. To dismiss this as a lie, she had to accept someone had written such a masterful forgery. It was harder to imagine that than it was to at least wonder if it could actually be true.

Jennifer believed, as did Dave. That was also not easy to dismiss.

Troubled, wanting to ignore the topic but unable now to do so, she stared at the ceiling and wondered.

If Jesus were real, the Bible were true, why doesn't He heal Jennifer?

Great. Telling Jennifer that would be just wonderful.

She had to get out of here, do something. Dave would protest, but Marcus would understand. If nothing else, she would go shoot hoops at the gym for an hour. She reached for her phone and paged Marcus. He could tell her the news from overnight while he drove her to the gym.

Any more body blows like she had taken lately, and she didn't think her composure would hold. She really didn't want Dave to see that. The tears last night had been embarrassing enough. She was glad she had told him about Jennifer, but it was hard to envision what it was going to be like when he found out Tony Jr. was her brother. Hopefully, Marcus had been able to make other arrangements for where she could stay. She was realistic enough to know the news would hit like a lead balloon, and she wanted to be far away from here before the fallout hit.

Dave bounced a tennis ball with one hand while he watched the second hand sweep around the face of the hall clock. Kate had barely said hello this morning before she had made a hurried excuse and left with Marcus. If he didn't know better, he would say she was running. She had refused to meet his eyes, mumbled something about needing to shoot some baskets, and swept Marcus out the door. He glanced at his watch to make sure the hall clock was right and knew that if she didn't get back soon, he would have to leave for the morning update meeting without her.

His hand clenched around the tennis ball, then he sighed and tossed it back into his gym bag. He had wanted to wrap his arms around her and give her a hug, nudge her chin up and get her to smile at him; instead, he'd shoved his hands in his pockets and watched her leave.

He was falling in love with her, and it was one of the scariest propositions he had ever faced. He was desperately afraid he was going to end up in a situation where the one thing he wanted most, he couldn't have.

"I envy you. You can still hope."

Remembering her words from the night before, he half smiled. Did hope born out of desperation count?

He was taking every grain of evidence that she was inching toward considering faith and hoping it would actually mean something. And yet, he knew he was blowing the evidence he had out of proportion. Kate was moving toward a decision, but she was still far from it. And his hands were tied until she did. *"You can't believe just because Jennifer wants you to."* He would give anything to be able to take back those words from last night. He wanted desperately to be able to say, *"Believe because I want you to."*

It didn't help that he had no idea what she was thinking—if she even thought about having a relationship that was more than a friendship. He'd deflected her early comments, and she had taken the hint. She was treating him like one of her brothers. Well, almost—she didn't trust him enough to tell him why she was scared.

And she *was* scared. That fact haunted him. He'd already asked Ben to look into it, to see if he could uncover why. There was little he could do about the pressures hitting her, but at least he could look into that. Maybe if he could simply make her feel safe, she would finally begin to trust....

The alert from the front gate security pushed him to his feet. She was back.

He checked the monitor and his disappointment was acute. "Come on up, Ben." He met him at the door.

"I've got some information I think you need to see."

"Sure." Dave glanced at the folder in Ben's hand and gestured to the formal dining room table where there was room to work. "Can I get you some coffee?"

"I'm fine."

Dave looked over at Ben, and something in his voice warned him. "What have you found?" he asked quietly.

There was a rare hesitation from his friend before Ben opened the file folder and laid down several pieces of paper. "Tony Emerson is her brother."

Dave lowered himself into the chair he had pulled out, shocked. "Her brother."

"We had to go back into the juvenile court records to find all the pieces. She changed her name at age nineteen to Kate O'Malley. Before that it was Kate Emerson."

Dave pulled over the indicated piece of paper. "It's not a coincidence?"

"No. Once we were into the court records, we got access to birth certificates." Ben handed him the photocopies. "She was made a ward of the state when she was nine. You really don't want to read the court record," Dave raised one eyebrow at that comment. "Suffice it to say there was sufficient reason for parental rights to be terminated. She was taken from the home a year before Tony Emerson was born. Dave, I don't think she knows."

"She knows," he said wearily. "I'll lay odds she found out yesterday." He rubbed his eyes. "I think Marcus has been checking into it, so he's probably told some of the Washington guys, her boss. Who else knows?"

"Susan. It wasn't easy to find, Dave. If you hadn't told me to look for a connection between Tony Emerson Jr. and Kate O'Malley, I doubt I would have found it. I did some checking. They put a watch on Emerson's house last night; there are patrols looking for him, so the information is getting acted on. Somebody high up must have made the call to keep this close to the vest."

Tony Emerson Jr. was her brother. "Can you cover the morning update meeting? She's at the gym with Marcus. I'm going to head over there."

"Sure. I'm sorry, Dave."

He slowly nodded, and even after Ben left, he sat motionless, staring at the folder. *Why not just rip out my heart, Kate? You could have at least trusted me.*

Marcus was alone at the gym, shooting hoops when Dave strode in. "I've been waiting for you."

Dave felt more than fear at the realization Kate was not here; he felt betrayed. "Where is she?"

"Safe."

"Marcus, don't give me that. She's a material witness to this, a target, something; she's so far into the middle of it I can't figure out which way is up."

The basketball came his way hard enough to sting his hands as he caught it. "And she's my sister."

They stared at each other, both breathing hard, emotions roiling. They were one wrong word away from a fight. "You're sure she's safe?"

"She's with Stephen."

Dave tossed the ball back without the stinging speed. "And that's shorthand for safe."

"In this case—yes. The media will have this information today; we both know it. She doesn't want it landing in your lap. She's somewhere safe, and hopefully distracted."

She didn't want it landing in his lap—great—she really was running. She had run to her brothers, at least there was some comfort in that. But having her somewhere else was only going to make it worse for him. "I want to talk to her."

Marcus considered him for a moment, then turned back to shooting baskets. "I don't think that's a good idea."

"I didn't ask for your opinion."

Marcus froze, then looked over at him. Dave almost backed down...almost. He could still remember Kate sitting at his kitchen table spinning a marshmallow on a pretzel stick, too tired to see straight. He wasn't backing down.

"She said you wouldn't take no for an answer."

The mild answer surprised him, then amused him. "Did she?"

Marcus walked over to the bench and picked up his towel. "Get your car; I'm parked in the side lot. You can follow me."

Marcus led him to a nice neighborhood north of the loop where trees shaded the streets and older homes showed the impact of new money restoration. He stopped in front of a brick, two-story home that was undergoing major reconstruction. Dave spotted two surveillance cars keeping watch on the house.

Marcus led the way up the walk. "Stephen is always restoring something. It's his escape as much as his hobby."

"What's Kate's?"

"Sports."

That made sense.

Marcus unlocked the front door and stepped inside.

The hallway was torn down to open studs and new drywall waited to be hung. The home smelled of fresh paint and new plaster. Dave looked around with interest. A couple walls had been taken down, opening up the rooms on the main floor. Empty of furniture, the potential was obvious to see.

Stephen came down the stairs, wiping his hands on a rag. "You're back soon."

"Where is she?" Marcus asked, glancing around.

"The back bedroom. I pulled the carpeting last night and found hard-wood flooring."

"Really?"

"It's in great shape, too."

Marcus moved upstairs, and Dave decided to stay put. Stephen was blocking his way, and it wasn't accidental.

They waited in silence.

Kate finally appeared, coming down the stairs. Any fragileness he had sensed yesterday was nowhere in evidence. When she got near him, the fire in her eyes cautioned him he had better be careful. She was cornered, by the situation, now by him, and she was going to come out fighting.

"Stephen."

Dave gave Marcus points for tact. He waited until Stephen disappeared up the stairs. "Why didn't you tell me yesterday? Trust me?"

"Tell you what? That I might have a brother who is possibly a murderer?" Kate swung away from him into the living room. "I've never even met this Tony Emerson. Until twenty-four hours ago, I didn't even have a suspicion that he existed."

"Kate, he's targeting you."

"Then let him find me."

"You don't mean that."

"There is no reason for him to have blown up a plane just to get at me, to get at some banker. We're never going to know the truth unless someone can grab him; and if he gets cornered by a bunch of cops, he'll either kill himself or be killed in a shootout. It would be easier all around if he did come after me."

"Stop thinking with your emotions and use your head." Dave shot back. "What we need to do is to solve this case. That's how we'll find out the answers and ultimately find him."

"Then you go tear through the piles of data. I don't want to have anything to do with it. Don't you understand that? I don't want to be the one who puts the pieces together. Yesterday was like getting stuck in the gut with a hot poker."

He understood it, could feel the pain flowing from her. "Fine. Stay here for a day, get your feet back under you. Then get back in the game and stop acting like you're the only one this is hurting. Or have you forgotten all the people that died?" He saw the sharp pain flash in her eyes before they went cold, and he regretted his words.

"That was a low blow and you know it."

"Kate—"

"I can't offer anything to the investigation, don't you understand that? I don't *know* anything. I've been trying to erase the name Emerson all my life. I don't know him."

"Well, he knows you. And if you walk away from this now, you're going to feel like a coward. Just what are you so afraid of?"

He could see it in her, a fear so deep it shimmered in her eyes and pooled them black, and he remembered Ben's comment that he probably didn't want to read the court record. His eyes narrowed and his voice softened. "Are you sure you don't remember him?"

She broke eye contact, and it felt like a blow because he knew that at this moment he was the one hurting her. "If you need to get away for twenty-four hours, do it; just don't run because you're afraid. You'll never forgive yourself."

"Marcus wouldn't let me go check out the data because he was afraid I would kill Tony."

Her words rocked him back on his heels. "What?"

"Tony Emerson Jr. If he's my father all over again, I'd probably kill him."

He closed the distance between them, and for the first time since this morning began, actually felt something like relief. He rested his hands calmly on her shoulders. "No you wouldn't. You're too good a cop."

She blinked.

"I almost died with you, remember?" He smiled. "I've seen you under pressure." His thumb rubbed along her jaw. "Come on, Kate. Come back with me to the house, and let's get back to work. The media wouldn't get near you, I promise."

Marcus and Stephen came back down the stairs, but Kate didn't look around; she just kept studying Dave. She finally turned and looked at her brother. "Marcus, I'm going back to Dave's."

"I thought you were. I repacked your bag for you."

Dave found his keys and listened with some amusement as Kate turned on Marcus for making that assumption. Marcus was a pretty good guy, all things considered. Dave dropped his hand firmly on Kate's shoulder and turned her toward the door, cutting her off in midsentence.

"Stephen, you'll bring out to the house anything Marcus missed?"

"Sure."

"Thanks. Let's go, Ladybug."

Kate swung back to Marcus. "Great, now you've got Dave calling me that. Did you even tell him what it means?" she demanded.

Marcus rocked on heels, arms folded. "That you're either a lady or a bug depending on how annoying you are? Sure, I told him. You're buzzing like a mosquito at the moment."

"Try a bee. You are about to get stung."

Marcus just grinned. "Nice to have you out of your funk. Go get back to work, Kate."

Seventeen

L et's solve this case. The answer has to be somewhere in these piles of data." Dave heard Lisa from his vantage point at the base of the stairs where he was waiting for Kate to appear and wondered with some amusement how he had managed to miss the fact Lisa was the bulldog of the O'Malley clan. It was Saturday morning; the case had become stuck, and Marcus had recommended last night that it was time they shook things up—hence the invasion.

Dave's formal dining room had become a mini war room.

Marcus apparently had some serious strings he could pull, for seven large boxes of files now sat against one of the dining room walls—copies of everything that could be found on Wilshire Construction, Tony Emerson Jr., Nathan Young, Ashcroft Young, and Henry Lott.

Lisa, Jack, and Stephen had trailed Marcus in the door, helping him carry the boxes. How Marcus had managed to get clearance for them to see the files, Dave didn't want to know and wasn't going to ask. He had thought it was a full house only to have Franklin and Graham appear next from Kate's office, and then Susan and Ben from his. He was beginning to feel like a poorly paid doorman. If the ten of them couldn't make sense of the data, it wasn't there to be found.

Dave paced at the base of the stairs, beginning to think Kate was intentionally stalling.

Grinning, Marcus leaned against the doorpost beside him. "Waiting on a woman is a very bad sign."

He had to smile. "Lay off, Marcus. If Kate figures that out, my goose is going to be royally cooked."

Marcus laughed. "Lisa sent me for Post-it notes and masking tape."

"Do I dare ask what for?"

"Probably not."

Dave thought for a moment. "Try the top left drawer of my desk."

He sipped his coffee and wondered what it took to get out of this family once you were in. It didn't take much effort to realize the crowd now plotting strategy in his dining room had adopted him. No, maybe it would be better to make this a permanent arrangement. With Jennifer getting married, the family would balance out four girls, four guys. But if he dated Kate, the numbers would tip five to four in the guys' favor. His grin widened. Kate would be ticked.

"What are you grinning at?" She stopped one step up from him.

"Nothing." He let her take his coffee. "Sleep okay?"

"Fine."

He wondered how true that was but didn't push it. "Good."

She tilted her head. "Where is everyone?"

He turned her toward the dining room. "There."

"Then I guess I had better get to work."

"I noticed you're stealing my coffee again, but I'll let you get away with it this time."

"It needs more sugar."

"Why do you think I let you have mine rather than let you fix your own?"

She disappeared into the dining room with a laugh.

"There is nothing on this security tape that shows Tony Emerson messing with that laptop." Jack set the tape on the dining room table and dropped back into a chair.

Lisa, on the other side of the table, looked up from her printouts. "You're sure?"

Dave looked up from the case file he had been reading to listen to Jack's conclusion.

"I've been through it three times. There is a total of eight minutes and fifty seconds where the laptop is not in view; six minutes of that was when it was with Peter Devlon, so I can't rule out that Tony didn't touch it. But there is nothing here that proves he did, only that he did meet with Nathan Young."

Dave watched Lisa scan the large pieces of easel paper taped to his dining room wall, find the right purple Post-it note, and remove it. A yellow Post-it note went up in its place. Lisa was playing colors. Every piece of data was labeled—red for guilty, green for innocent, and yellow for inconclusive. It was a crazy way to work a case, but he had found after an hour her visual system worked. At the moment, with half the questions eliminated, Tony looked circumstantially guilty.

"So we still don't know how the bomb got into the briefcase," Dave observed.

"It's circumstantial that it was Tony Jr. It could just as easily have been Peter Devlon," Jack replied.

Lisa looked over the unresolved Post-it notes. "Okay. What about Wilshire Construction? Do we have any leads on why Tony's company was having such serious cash flow problems?"

"Stress *serious*," Marcus added from the other end of the table. "From the bank records on the line of credit, it looks like he lost almost a quarter of a million dollars in the last year. I'm surprised the bank didn't pull the plug on him months ago."

"The records I've got make it pretty clear his suppliers were beginning to demand cash on delivery, no longer willing to extend even thirty days of credit," Susan offered.

"You ought to read the union contracts," Stephen added. "Two months ago they forced Tony to renegotiate the contracts so that medical insurance and retirement payments would be made weekly, concurrent with paychecks."

"Had he ever missed those payments?" Lisa asked.

"No."

"Then the unions either knew or suspected something," Lisa concluded.

Stephen nodded. "Looks that way."

"So what was going wrong? Lack of business? Cost overruns?"

"He's busy, and I have yet to find any particular job that is hemorrhaging red ink," Ben noted.

"But he was laying off people," Lisa interjected. "Correct?"

Franklin nodded. "Seventeen in the last three months alone. This business was running on fumes, and he was juggling every week to keep it floating."

"I think Tony was paying off someone." Kate dropped that fact into the room, and it landed like a bombshell.

Dave studied her pensive face for a moment. "What did you find?"

She set down the company books she had been paging through, looking at her notes. "I'm honestly not sure. It looks like nothing at first, just another subcontractor. But it's odd. There aren't invoices for materials on file as there are with every other subcontractor, just reimbursements. It's like the subcontractor doesn't really exist. And when I dig deeper, the payments each month keep adding together into nice round numbers. Five thousand, ten thousand, spread across a few checks. This last month for example: two checks, the first $2,046.11 for cement; the second, $2,953.89 marked lumber."

"Five thousand dollars. Pretty convenient."

"Exactly." She turned pages in the registry. "It's been going on for months."

Jack walked a nickel through his fingers, thinking. "I don't get it—if someone was bleeding Tony dry, wouldn't he get angry at the person squeezing him, not the banker holding his line of credit?"

"You would think so," Lisa agreed.

"Unless they were one and the same," Marcus said quietly. He looked over at Dave. "Can we get the canceled checks for those last payments, see how they were endorsed?"

Dave nodded and reached for the phone. "I think we had better. Kate, what are the check numbers?"

She wrote the numbers and amounts down, then slid her notebook over to him.

A red note went on the board. Blackmail was a pretty good reason for murder.

"Okay, we've got two new stickers to resolve—who was blackmailing him, and why?" Lisa commented.

"Kate, when did the payments start?" Marcus asked, reaching for the blue binder that was the last bank audit for the First Union Bank.

She hunched over the table, paging back through the check registry. It took her several minutes to find it. "Nine months ago. It looks like October 15 is the first payment for $9,500."

"And you think he paid out how much? Roughly?"

Kate did some quick calculations. "Maybe two hundred thousand, give or take."

"And all the checks below the federal notification amount of ten thousand dollars—so even if they were converted and deposited as cash, there would be no immediate trail," Marcus both stated and asked.

Her eyes narrowed. "Yes. Banker knowledge. Or someone who launders drug money."

"Exactly." Marcus started thumbing through the accounts.

Kate glanced at Graham. "Didn't Henry Lott claim in his interview that he suspected Wilshire Construction had been used in the past to launder drug money?"

"Yes, but I talked to narcotics, and it was old news. They've checked periodically, and the business has been clean ever since the kid took over."

Marcus marked a page in the printout. "I think I've found the account. The first deposit is right—$9,500, October 18. There is over a hundred fifty thousand still in the account."

"Who was Tony paying off?"

Marcus double-checked the account numbers. "Nathan. It looks like it might have been routed through another account first, but the money was definitely ending up in Nathan's account."

Stephen set aside what he was reading. "What did Nathan have on Tony to be able to blackmail him like that? And why so much blackmail he put the company out of business as a result?"

"He knew something about Wilshire Construction?" Lisa offered.

"Even if he did, why would Nathan risk it?" Jack asked. "Wasn't this guy supposed to be lily-white—head of some big banking conglomerate?"

Kate nodded. "We thought so."

Marcus tapped the printout. "We've definitely found a money trail. Who could explain the reason?"

Kate rubbed her eyes. "Nathan—he's dead. Tony—he's on the run." She sighed. "Marla."

"Yes." Marcus reached for the phone. "If there is a third person who would know, his wife Marla is a good bet. She got along well with Linda; let's see if she wants to add anything to what she said."

Jack scanned the notes and shook his head. "It's got to be drug related. Nothing else makes sense. Everywhere you look there's a tag that somehow leads back to drugs."

Lisa lined up those notes, and there were a lot of them. "I agree, it's there, but it's too nebulous."

"All we've really got so far is Nathan blackmailing Tony, and Tony killing him," Dave concluded.

Kate closed the Wilshire books and slid them back to the center of the table. "Dave, let me see that transcript from Ashcroft Young's trial."

He found the gray trial transcript binder and passed it to her. "Still think there is some link between both Nathan and Ashcroft getting killed?"

"I just can't buy the fact it was a fluke he was killed, too. Did we ever sit down and plot out a list of Ashcroft's enemies?"

"It is awfully convenient that the blackmail began a few months after Ashcroft was released from prison," Marcus agreed.

Dave glanced between the two of them. "You really think someone planned for Nathan to walk on that flight at the last minute?"

Marcus shrugged one shoulder. "I don't know what I think. It's simply…interesting…that a man who probably had a lot of enemies ended up dead."

Dave looked over at Ben, then Susan. "What do you think?"

"I agree with Marcus," Ben replied after a moment. "Ashcroft—if he came out of prison looking for trouble, he's the type that could find it in a hurry." Ben leaned forward in his chair and started turning down fingers one by one. "We know Ashcroft dealt drugs and at one time had a network operating through O'Hare. We know the blackmail started soon after he was released from prison. His brother is a banker. Even if we can't prove money laundering, the situation smells like it."

Dave thought about it. "So was Ashcroft the intended victim?"

Marcus smiled. "Good question. I bet we could find a long list of motives for killing him."

Kate tossed her pen on the table. "With Ashcroft as the target, we have known criminal activity, an unknown but probably long list of enemies, and a very big problem in the timeline. There's just no getting around the fact Nathan was a last minute walk-on for the MetroAir flight."

She then gave the other scenario. "With Tony going after Nathan, we've got means—he had access to explosives; motive—he was being blackmailed; and opportunity—he's on tape as one of the last two people to see Nathan."

"He's also disappeared," Lisa added.

Kate nodded. "He's also disappeared. But it's still an enormous amount of overkill and a big risk that doesn't make sense."

"Hold it, Kate." Dave rapidly flipped back in his notes. "Nathan wasn't supposed to take that MetroAir flight. Remember what Devlon said?" He found his notes from that meeting. "Nathan was scheduled to take the private company jet to New York. It wasn't until after the meeting with Tony that he changed his mind, decided at the last minute to take the MetroAir flight."

"So Tony never intended the overkill," Kate speculated.

"Exactly."

"And the risk of planting a bomb—play your cards right and if those security tapes don't convict you, they create reasonable doubt."

Dave nodded. "So the risk might actually have been a good gamble."

Kate finally shook her head. "I don't know. We're making this kid out to be a very well-planned, shrewd, no-nerves-showing type of guy. But he doesn't have a serious criminal record; his wife is shaking in her shoes, and Henry Lott called him *that young brat*. It still doesn't compute." She pushed back her chair with a sigh. "I need a walk and some more caffeine."

The news that Tony Jr. was her brother broke in the media just before 7 P.M. Kate watched the first five minutes of the special news report, then retreated as far as the rose garden and sat with her cold soda resting against her jeans.

They had called it a day shortly after 5 P.M. so Marcus, Ben, and Graham could get to the evening update meeting. Marcus was going to fill the other investigators in on what they had so far. Kate was relieved in a way that the family wasn't here. This was a private grief, a private pain, and it cut deep.

"Are you okay?" Dave asked quietly, settling into a seat nearby.

She didn't have words, simply shook her head. She was related to a man who had blown up a plane. She couldn't even put into words what it felt like.

"Kate, it's still speculation. We are so far from knowing everything that happened. You have to know we're barely past the beginning of this investigation."

It was nice that he was trying to offer the reassurance, but its impact was muted by the reality. The press was screaming the news: *Bombing Suspect Related to Investigating Cop*. The assumptions in the story didn't matter. "Are you sure you can keep the press away?" She asked, keeping her focus on work.

"Yes."

"It's going to get rough."

"I've dealt with worse. Kate, look at me."

She reluctantly turned her head.

"It's okay to explode. You're worrying me."

Kate fought back the desire to cry. "I can't change any of this."

"No. But you're giving up. I can see it happening."

She reached over to squeeze his hand, hearing how badly he wanted to help her; she deeply appreciated that fact. "I'm temporarily retreating, Dave. Don't worry. I'll find my sea legs again. I just *hate* having my name plastered all over the news." She didn't want to talk about it anymore, didn't want to *think* about it. Tony Emerson Jr. was going to destroy her life before this was over. She was surprised Dave was not backing away from her; she didn't have years of experience with him to generate the kind of loyalty he was showing to her.

She entwined her fingers with his. "They are going to put me on administrative leave, move me out of this job, something," she said quietly, admitting her biggest fear. "The pressure created by the media attention will demand it."

"I've met your boss. There is no way Jim will let that happen."

"He'll try to protect me. It may be taken out of his hands."

Dave squeezed her hand. "If the worst case happens, and they do? How are you going to cope?"

Kate closed her eyes, relieved he wasn't trying to pretend it couldn't happen. "I've endured worse."

"The O'Malleys will be there for you. I'll be here, too."

"I appreciate that."

Dave hesitated. "You should have more than your job at the center of your life, Kate. Put God in the center. He won't shift even if everything else gets taken away."

Dave, if your God were there, if He cared, why is He letting my life be shaken apart? She was wrestling to understand how what she had read in Luke fit with what was going on, but she wasn't ready to talk about it. She certainly wasn't ready to believe. She bit her lip, not wanting to be rude but knowing she couldn't deal with this subject tonight. She looked over at him, hoping he would understand. "Change the subject, Dave? It's not that I want to knock what you believe, but your God is already supposed to be in the center of this, and I don't like what I see. I'm just not up to a discussion about it tonight." She saw him pull back as if slapped, his expression showing his hurt before it went carefully neutral. She tightened her hand to apologize even as he released her hand.

"Sure. Better yet, I'd better go check security on the grounds for the night." He got to his feet, his voice tight. "I'll be a few minutes."

Kate watched him walk away, then raised her hand and squeezed the bridge of her nose, wanting desperately to throw something, anything, for being such a jerk. She knew how important the subject of religion was to Dave. It wasn't like she hadn't been thinking about what she had read in the book of Luke during the quiet moments of the last two days. She owed him the freedom to mention the subject without having her bite his head off. He'd been listening to all her problems since this disaster began, had been trying to help, and she'd just shown him she didn't have room for his priorities.

There were days she was a fool.

She might as well have never gone to bed. Kate lay staring at the ceiling, watching the moonlight paint shadows around the room. The depression was heavy.

Dave was a nice guy, and instead of being able to have something with him, she was in a situation where they were both getting hurt. She should have stayed with Stephen and not come back here despite the media risk and the threat it would mean to be out in the open. She didn't want to look like a coward, but she didn't have the strength to deal with this. Dave deserved better, and she'd managed knowingly to hurt him this afternoon.

She was running, mentally, emotionally. She just didn't want to deal with the past, and every time he got close, she felt it clawing back at her. The survival instinct of her childhood was back center stage—run away before she got hurt.

She rubbed her hand across her face, looked again at the clock. Two minutes had passed since she had last looked. At this rate she was going to count the seconds until dawn.

Wondering if insomnia was going to be a permanent reality, she rose and quietly dressed in jeans and a sweatshirt. It would help to get out of the closed four walls. The night looked quiet and calm; she might as well sit outside and enjoy the stars.

She turned off the alarm as Dave had shown her and descended the stairs. Two steps from the bottom, the world around her erupted. The lights snapped on, a piercing alarm sounded.

Dave was at the top of the stairs, breathing hard, before she had oriented herself in the confusion. "I didn't set it off, I swear."

He hurried down the stairs past her, pulling on his shirt. He silenced the audible alarm on the pad by the front door. "Grab your phone and get back upstairs. There's a second sidearm in the safe in my room. I left it open." He was already moving to the back of the house, keying the radio he carried. "Ben, what's on the video?"

She nodded and bolted back upstairs. She hadn't set it off, she knew she hadn't.

The picture over his dresser had been set with a hinge and was moved to the side, leaving visible an open safe. She reached for the Glock inside and fitted a clip. She felt marginally safer just carrying the weapon although it came with a sense of dread for the possibility of ever having to use it. A reporter? Please let it be something innocent. She moved to her bedroom, scanned the front grounds and saw nothing moving.

She moved downstairs to rejoin Dave. This was a big estate; even with one other agent stationed at the guardhouse, Dave would need the help doing the search.

The sliding glass doors to the back were open an inch. She stepped outside. "Dave?"

"Here, Kate." He was crossing the grounds to the south of the rose gardens. She moved to join him.

"You two can relax. I've got the culprit," Ben radioed. "Our prowler is back, Dave."

Dave visibly relaxed. He flipped on his flashlight and directed her toward his partner coming around the house.

"Who?" Kate asked, confused.

"Marvel. We thought he had found a new home; it's been a couple months since he last put in an appearance. But I should have planned for him."

Ben was carrying a fat, yellow tabby.

"He's named Marvel because it's such a marvel he's still alive. He must be the dumbest cat in the city," Dave remarked, smiling. "For some reason he likes to warm himself on top of one of the sensor posts. He has to climb a tree to get up there and dangle himself in the air to drop down on the camera perch, but he keeps doing it. The only thing we can figure is it's warm and it feels good on his old bones." Dave took the hissing cat from Ben and gave him a good-natured rub behind the ears. "You just like to cause us all kinds of trouble, don't you?"

"I'll reset the grid," Ben said, slipping his radio back on his belt.

"Thanks, Ben. And you might as well kill the camera feeds, just leave the infrared hot for the night. I'm sure he'll be back to his old habits as soon as we set him down."

"Will do."

Dave glanced speculatively at Kate. "Want to carry him? He's your typical tomcat. Bad mannered. Likes to eat."

She laughed softly, well able to see the two of them had nevertheless reached an understanding. She bet the cat set off the security alarm just so he would guarantee he got a meal out of the deal. "Sure, give him here."

She let out a small huff as the cat became hers to hold. "This isn't a cat; it's a small beast covered in fur."

"It would be nice if he got too fat to climb that tree."

"You could move the camera you know."

"He'd just get more creative."

She rubbed the cat's ears, ignoring the rumble. She somehow figured it was as close to a purr as this cat could get. "What are we going to offer him to eat?"

"There's some grilled fish left."

"That sounds like a four-star feast."

"He'll have it on the back patio. I made the mistake of letting him inside once. A house cat Marvel is not."

Already becoming attached to the heavy cat in her arms, she found the idea amusing. "Well, while you fix him some baked fish for his delight, fix me a milkshake, and Marvel and I will share some dessert."

"Deal. Now hand me that Glock. I'm more comfortable without my guests being armed."

"Gladly." She handed it over, and he removed the clip.

They walked back to the back patio. The earlier depression was gone, and in its place were a few moments on the back patio entertaining a cat with an attitude.

She fell in love.

When Dave brought out the dish with fish, the cat attacked it.

Dave handed her a tall glass. She had learned early on that milkshakes were one of his specialties. "Thank you."

"My pleasure." He settled on the chair beside her with a tall glass of his own. "Greedy little devil."

"He's hungry."

"Somehow I think he's always hungry."

When the bowl was empty, Kate filled it with a little of the milkshake. Marvel wasn't sure what to think about it, was tentative about getting his nose close to it, then began to cautiously lick it.

She was surprised when the cat stepped back from the dish and hissed.

"What?"

"He's got an ice cream headache," Dave explained.

"Oh, you poor darling." She felt horrible. She scooped the cat up to rub its head while Dave laughed.

"The cat will live. I promise you."

"You could have warned me."

"Why? You would not have given him the ice cream, and he loves it."

She shot Dave a skeptical look, but the cat was trying to get out of her hands. She let him, and he returned to the dish, showing a little more caution this time.

"What were you doing up when the alarm went off?"

She had hoped to avoid the question. "I just couldn't sleep."

"Anything you want to talk about?"

"No."

He was quiet for a moment. "Fair enough. We're taking tomorrow off."

"What?"

"We're taking a break. No case files, no notes, no interviews. We both need a break."

She thought about it. The idea felt wonderful. Maybe she'd be able to sleep again. "Deal." The cat finished licking the bowl clean and walked, tail swishing, over to the next empty chair, leaped up, and promptly began to groom his coat, pausing occasionally to stare at them.

"Think he'll stick around?"

"Probably."

"That would be nice."

Dave winced as the cat jumped across into his lap, dug in his claws, and tried to get near the tall glass he held. "It depends on your perspective."

She laughed.

"If he sticks, he's yours."

"Marcus gave me a dog with an attitude; you're giving me a beat-up tomcat. Should I see a pattern in this?"

"Absolutely." He scooped the cat from his lap and held him out. "Marvel, if you're smart, you'll be nice to her. She's the one who thinks you're adorable."

Kate had to hold him still while he thought about bolting, then he malevolently stretched out across her lap.

"Looks like you've got a cat."

Kate looked over, hearing the satisfaction in Dave's voice. "And here I don't have anything to give you," she said tongue in cheek.

"Just make very sure it's something that doesn't breathe, okay?"

"Come on, Kate, the day is wasting," Dave called from downstairs.

She hurried to get her hair brushed. "I'm coming. Hold on."

He had gone to church on his own, leaving her to sleep in, and she was grateful in a way that he had backed off what had been such a painful collision of values the day before. He'd come home, brought lunch with him, and announced they were going out for the day. He'd proceeded to inform her there was a motorcycle in back that qualified as his pride and joy, and she had ten minutes to get ready to go.

She'd scrambled. She loved the idea. She grabbed her leather jacket, knowing regardless of the temperature she would need the protection. She trusted Dave; she didn't trust the other drivers. She joined him downstairs.

"Where are we going?"

"Wisconsin, a quiet out-of-the-way lake. And if you're really good, I'll even bring you home."

She wrinkled her nose at him. "Where's this second helmet you said you had?"

He handed it over. "It's Sara's, so it should fit you."

She tried it on, slipped down the visor, and glanced in the hallway mirror. "I look dangerous."

"Anonymous at least. Come on. Let's hit the road before traffic flowing downtown to the Cubs game picks up."

He had brought the bike around to the front of the house, and it was obvious it was something he took considerable pride in—the motorcycle gleamed. He tucked water bottles in the carrying case.

"You've ridden before?"

"Jack has a bike." She saw his expression and grinned. "My brother," she pointed out. "I ride with him frequently."

"Just remember to sit straight, and let me be the one to shift my weight in a turn."

She slid on the bike and adjusted the footrests to a comfortable distance. "Drive. I want some wind in my face."

Dave slid onto the seat and kicked the ignition.

Two hours later, tired, content, and smiling, she slid off the bike at a gas and grocery corner store miles into Wisconsin.

"Enjoying yourself?"

"Immensely." She took off her jacket and draped it over the seat grateful for the chance to enjoy the breeze. "How far is the lake?"

"Five minutes. I figured if we get ice cream here, there's a chance it won't melt until we get there."

"I'll get it. What do you want?"

He handed her a twenty. "Whatever you're having."

Kate nodded and headed for the store. She felt the attention that came her way from others at the store, the kind of open curiosity natural between travelers in a new environment. She looked like a casual biker. It created a reaction she didn't normally get. When people looked twice, it was typically because she was a cop, not because they were quietly wondering why she and Dave traveled by motorcycle rather than car.

She wandered through the aisles to the back of the store and the glass door freezers and took her time considering options. She bought strawberry ice cream and added a box of plastic spoons. It was fun doing this for a day instead of working. She didn't goof off nearly enough.

"Give me the twenty."

This wasn't happening. She felt the knife tip prick her ribs from behind at the same instant her peripheral vision caught the stockroom door swinging back the other way and saw in the small pane of glass the kid who had made the threat. It was a teen, barely fifteen, sweating—she could smell the desperation. Clearly the crack problem was as bad in Wisconsin as it was in her Chicago neighborhood; she'd seen that look of desperation too many times. He'd stepped out of the stockroom and was probably planning to retreat the same way.

She shifted the twenty dollars from the palm of her hand to between her middle fingers, extending it to him without saying a word. What a mess. It wasn't even her twenty bucks. And he was going to use it to get high.

He grabbed the bill, stepped back, and she turned and rammed the open flat of her hand under his nose. If she broke his nose it was incidental, she just wanted to guarantee he dropped the knife. If he used the knife once, he would use it again, next time on someone he might hurt. The teen howled, the knife dropped, and the boy made the mistake of reaching down for it. She hooked a foot behind his and put him on his back.

Dave laid a cautious hand on her shoulder, and she about hit him, too. He had seen enough to get the drift. "I've got him, Kate."

She stepped back while he hauled the teen to his feet.

"Buy a box of plastic sandwich bags and get that knife in evidence. You ever testify in the Wisconsin courts?"

"Once."

"Fastest courts for juvenile cases I've ever seen." He looked her over. "You just couldn't take a day off, could you?"

It was said with humor, and she let herself smile in return even though what she wanted to do was hit something to get rid of the fright. "If I were working today, I would have wasted time trying to convince him he really didn't want the twenty bucks before I just took the knife away."

Dave laughed. He got a good hold of the back of the boy's collar and steered him toward the front of the store. "Okay, son. Lesson one. Next time, you really don't want to try and rob a cop."

By the time the local cops had taken statements, reports had been filed, and they were officially free to go, it was almost 5 P.M. Dave slid the paperwork into the bike satchel, glanced over at her, and straightened. "What?"

"I'm sorry about all this."

"Why? You didn't cause it."

"I was looking forward to a day off."

"The sun hasn't set yet, has it?"

"No."

"Then give me a chance to get creative here. I'd like to think I could make some of this up to you."

"Make it up to me?"

He nodded and handed her the jacket. "I chose the place to stop, remember?"

"Now that you mention it…"

"What do you think about ostentatious displays of wealth?"

"What?"

"Just answer the question."

"Tacky."

"I figured that would be your answer." A long stretch limousine tried to maneuver into the parking lot never designed for a car of its length. "So I asked for your basic black instead of your more flashy white."

"You did what—"

She had to laugh as he walked over and held open the limousine door. "Two hours on a bike when you're tired is not fun. Kevin volunteered to drive the bike home. We'll make the trip in a little more comfort."

Kate vaguely remembered Kevin when he got out of the passenger front seat as one of the men who did landscape work for Dave. "I can't believe you did this."

"Two phone calls. The second was for the order of Chinese take-out. I believe someone mentioned you like wontons?"

"I'm sold." She slid into the back seat of the limousine and felt her body sink into the plush leather. The car was huge. With the facing seat it would allow four people to travel in comfort with their legs stretched out. Dave joined her.

"This is really ridiculous. Do you know what my family will say when they hear how I got home?"

"Don't tell them." Dave made himself comfortable as the car pulled out of the parking lot. "It's got a TV, too. We've got food, entertainment, tinted windows. I'd call it a date, but you're still in jeans."

She was too amused by how pleased he looked with himself to do anything but laugh. They were stuck in traffic for an extra hour during the drive home. It was the first time she had never cared.

"Canceled checks confirmed what we suspected. Nathan was apparently blackmailing Tony. One hundred and eighty thousand was paid to the fictional subcontractor, and it all ended up in Nathan's private account. Whatever Nathan knew, Tony was willing to pay handsomely to keep it quiet. Do we have any idea what it was?" Dave asked, looking around the table. The group had reassembled early Monday morning, picking up where they had left off in the work; already the first pot of coffee was gone, and they were well into the second.

"I still think it's drug related," Jack offered, looking at the Post-it notes. "We know Tony was fired from O'Hare under the suspicion that he was moving drugs. Eight of his coworkers went to jail, but the cops didn't have enough evidence to charge Tony. What if Nathan had that evidence?"

"Assuming it exists—how would Nathan have acquired it? Do we have any indication Nathan was involved in drug activities?"

"Nathan—no, but his brother Ashcroft? According to this—" Kate tapped the Ashcroft trial transcript binder on her lap before reaching over for another doughnut—"we know Ashcroft once moved drugs through O'Hare. What if Tony worked for Ashcroft and there was proof of that, could Nathan have gotten hold of it?"

"Ashcroft went to jail for a decade. Someone had to store his stuff, settle his affairs. It would have fallen to Nathan," Graham offered. "A notebook, a tape, it's possible."

"Tony Jr. didn't start to work at O'Hare until after Ashcroft went to jail," Marcus cautioned, looking at the easel sheet with the master timeline.

"Ashcroft could have continued to run his business from inside prison," Graham offered.

"So in order to explain Nathan's blackmail, we need to find a link between Tony Jr. and Ashcroft," Dave proposed, glancing around the table.

Marcus nodded. "Yes."

"This is like looking for a needle in a sprawling haystack," Susan commented, opening a box they had yet to go through. "Dave, which do you want? Tony's O'Hare personnel records or the investigative notes for the charges that weren't filed?"

"Personnel records."

The room was quiet but for the turning of pages.

"Marcus, didn't you say Tony's wife was named Marla?" Susan asked.

"Yes."

"She also worked at O'Hare in the baggage department, the same time as Tony. They must have met there."

"Really? Anything in the cops investigation about her?"

Susan checked the records. "No."

"The background check we did showed only two parking tickets for her, nothing else, so I guess that's not surprising."

"Found it." Dave pulled out three blue pieces of paper. "Guess who wrote a recommendation for Tony to work at O'Hare? None other than Ashcroft Young."

"You're kidding." Kate reached for the pages Dave offered.

"Didn't they bother to check who his references were from?" Graham asked, astounded.

Dave tapped the top of the sheet. *"Business owner.* Isn't that novel?"

Marcus looked at the timeline. "Ashcroft made the recommendation from jail?"

"Bold fellow, isn't he?" Dave checked the dates. "He would have been three years into his ten-year sentence."

"So he was trying to run his operation from jail." Marcus said.

"Yes."

"That explains the what of the blackmail. Tony worked for Ashcroft moving drugs, and somehow Nathan learned about it," Lisa concluded.

"It's a reasonable hunch. So where's the evidence now? Nathan's dead. At Nathan's home? His office? Tucked away somewhere never to be found?" Graham wanted to know.

"It's going to be rather hard to get a search warrant for a victim's home with what we've got," Dave remarked.

"We can put cars watching both places. If the evidence exists, Tony may try to retrieve and destroy it," Susan suggested.

"Good idea." Ben reached for the phone.

Kate got up to pace the room. "Is it worth killing for? Even if convicted, Tony was looking at what—ten years in jail, out on parole in seven? A decent plea bargain, he's out in five. Why pay almost two hundred thousand and then commit murder to stop that kind of possible conviction?"

Marcus shook his head. "It doesn't add up."

"Exactly. We're missing something. Something big. We just scooped up a little minnow, and a catfish is still lurking in this muck."

"Of all the…" Kate nearly exploded out of her chair a short time later.

Everyone around the table looked up. "What?" Dave asked, speaking for all of them.

She looked at the trial binder as if it would strike out and bite her. "Ashcroft went to jail for a decade for distributing cocaine. Would you like to guess who his partner was?"

Dave could see the anger in her eyes, glowing hot.

"Tony Emerson Sr." She bit out tersely.

"Your father was dealing drugs?" Dave said slowly.

"He cut a deal with the DA; he got five years suspended time and three years probation for testifying against Ashcroft. The judge apparently tossed part of the search warrant evidence against him on a technicality, and the DA decided that his testimony against Ashcroft was worth the deal. I don't believe this. Talk about a pot calling the kettle black. They should have put him in jail and thrown away the key."

Stephen offered a slight whistle. "Ashcroft would have been out for Tony Sr.'s blood."

"Put someone in jail for ten years, yeah, he'd hold a grudge. Tony Sr. was lucky; he died in a car accident while Ashcroft was still in jail," Kate concluded.

"Anything suspicious about the accident?" Dave asked.

"He was driving drunk, and he put his car into the side of a tree."

Dave nodded. "It's an interesting link. Does it tell us anything?"

"Just personal family history," Kate replied grimly.

Dave dug his fingers into the back of his neck. Kate didn't look surprised her father had been mixed up in dealing drugs. It was a hard image of her past.

"Do you want me to finish the transcript?" he asked, not sure how to deal with the anger, justified anger, she was feeling.

"No." She pulled her chair back to the table with a sigh. "I've got it."

Twenty minutes later he saw her sit up straighter and pull the trial binder toward her. "Now this is interesting…."

"Got something?"

"Yeah. Ashcroft's bank accounts were frozen—pretty standard stuff, but the guy who originally fingered the accounts and actually triggered the entire investigation? It was Nathan."

"Nathan turned his brother in as a suspected drug dealer?" Dave asked.

Kate nodded. "He sent a letter to the DEA showing a list of suspicious deposits into one of his brother's accounts. It's what triggered the investigation that eventually sent Ashcroft to jail. Tony Sr.'s testimony was used so they could raise the charges to cocaine distribution, not just money laundering."

"So Nathan is into blackmail but won't touch drug money."

"Protecting his banks?" Lisa asked.

"Or kicking his brother where it hurts," Marcus remarked.

It was shortly after 5 P.M. when the last of the folders were closed.

"So what do we think happened?" Lisa asked finally, looking around the room. Dave could tell no one wanted to say what was clear to all of them.

Marcus looked over at Kate, his expression one of quiet sympathy. "Tony Jr. was being blackmailed, forced out of business. That's motive. He used explosives from his own company. He met Nathan at the airport and was able to plant the bomb. That's means and opportunity. Tony Jr. thought Nathan would be taking the private jet, he never intended to kill all those people. That removes the overkill. He's disappeared, not normally the act of an innocent man. That's what the evidence suggests. It may be wrong, but that's what is here. The feud between Ashcroft and his brother is also there, but I think it's unrelated to the events that happened on Tuesday—it was an ongoing family feud, and they are both dead. It's Tony."

Dave listened to him quietly summarize what would go to the DA and knew the case was there. There were still problems. How Tony Jr. knew what type of laptop Nathan carried. Why he had placed the calls to the tower if his intended target was a private jet. But the case was there. He watched Kate drop her head into her hands. She had to hate this job about now.

He kept hoping something would break in her favor, and yet every day that passed, the situation just got worse for Tony Emerson Jr. and therefore her. How long before the stress she was under broke her? She didn't have God to lean on. She was trying to get through this on her own strength, and he knew it couldn't be done.

Dave just hoped she didn't push him away before that crunch time came. He needed to be there for her. It was the one point in time her need for the gospel might overcome her resistance to it.

Lord, please, help her yield. She needs You. She's just too stubborn to real-ize it. It's breaking my heart to watch her go through this and know I haven't been able to reach her with the gospel. What am I doing wrong? Why can't I get her to listen?

Dave looked over at Kate as she wearily ran her hands through her hair and then began packing away the files in front of her, and he suddenly realized just how badly he had handled the entire problem of faith.

He had been pushing too hard.

He had seen so much emotion in Kate during the last few days he had assumed her decision about God would be an emotional one. It wouldn't be. That wasn't Kate. It would be a decision made with her heart *and* her head. Rather than give her the time she needed to ask questions at her own pace, he had been pressing for the decision. *"Put God at the center of your life."* It had been the totally wrong way to handle that moment of vulnera-bility on her part, and he had lost an opportunity to simply tell her God cared.

In wanting everything at once, he risked losing everything—that was the bottom line. It was time to back off and get his own act together. Kate needed a friend. It wasn't his job to convince her to believe. God knew best how to draw her to Him. Dave knew that.

It was painful to wait. He wanted the freedom to circle around the table, draw Kate into a hug, and let her rest against him until that strained look on her face disappeared. He could physically keep her safe despite her protests, but at the moment there was little he could do to keep her emotionally safe.

Lord, give me patience with her, please. I need more of it than I have. Her own pace, Yours, not mine, because I can't handle a failure…not on something so important to the rest of my life.

Eighteen

er family thought Tony Jr. had done it. Somewhere inside there
had still been the glimmer of hope that the O'Malley clan would
look at the data and find something to change that initial
hypothesis; instead, they had found proof to confirm it. Kate accepted it
because she had no choice.

Jennifer was due into town tomorrow afternoon. Kate was glad now
that Dave had convinced her to invite Jennifer to stay at his house. She
talked to Jennifer every day, but it wasn't the same. She wanted the excuse
to put her time and energy into Jennifer instead of this case, to be useful
to someone instead of being the focus of pity. The O'Malleys didn't mean
it, but they were drowning her trying to fix the problem. Kate needed to
hear Jennifer's perspective.

"Kate."

The back patio overlooking the rose garden had become her favorite
retreat, her spot of territory in Dave's domain that she had appropriated as
her own. Kate didn't have to think here, didn't have to consider what was
going on in the investigation. At least for a few moments she could forget.
She turned her head with some reluctance at Dave's interruption.

He took a seat beside her on the lounge chair. "You once said you
wanted a good steak, a cold drink, and a nap, not necessarily in that order.
You still interested?"

She saw something in his expression she had not seen before, a deep
sympathy, a heartfelt wish to share the pain and take it away, and she drew
a deep breath as she felt his words penetrate her sadness. He had remembered, practically word for word. She didn't think she would ever smile

again, but this one reached her eyes. "Yes."

His hand brushed down her cheek. "Close your eyes and start on that nap. I'll wake you for dinner in about an hour."

It was a quiet dinner, eaten on the back patio, finished as the stars began to shine. Kate carried their dishes into the kitchen while he closed the grill; then she slipped upstairs for a moment. She owed Dave something, owed herself something.

When she returned to the patio, he handed her a bowl of ice cream.

"Thanks."

"Sure"

She ate half of the ice cream before she opened the topic she was still uncertain about raising with him. "I read the book of Luke the other morning."

"Did you?" He sounded pleased but continued to eat his ice cream, didn't leap all over the comment as she had been slightly afraid he would do. Maybe they had both learned something from that last aborted conversation. "What did you think?"

"The crucifixion was gruesome."

He was silent for several moments. "A cop using the word *gruesome*. It helps to see that scene with fresh eyes. As time goes by, it becomes easy to say He was crucified and immediately go on."

She set aside her ice cream. "I've got some questions I need answered before I talk to Jennifer."

"Sure." He opened the top of the carafe to see how much coffee was left, refilled his, and after a nod from her, refilled hers.

"It might be a long conversation."

"Discussions about Christianity should never be sound bites. I've got as much time as you want to spend."

"When it is over, I still won't believe." She felt compelled to warn him.

"You don't now, and I still like you." He smiled over at her, and he actually sounded relieved. "Would you relax? I don't mind questions, Kate."

She realized her shoulder muscles were bunched and forced herself to let go of the tension. The fact she could talk about a crime easier than she could this subject annoyed her. "That's one thing that struck me early on about you; you're comfortable with what you believe."

"I am. Jesus encouraged honest questions. In Job, God says, 'come, let us reason together.' What do you need to ask?"

She appreciated the simplicity of what he offered. Not a lecture, not pressure. A sounding board. She so desperately needed that tonight. She flipped through her notes for a moment in the light from the kitchen, then closed the spiral pad and set it aside. "I need some context. You believe Jesus really lived."

"I do. Roman historians of the time wrote about Him. Agnostics will argue over who He was, but even they concede there was a man named Jesus."

She thought about what she had read that morning, then slowly began to think out loud. "If I accept the premise that God exists and that He created everything, it is logical to infer He would be able to do what He liked with His creation—heal someone who was sick, still a storm, raise the dead—the things I read about in Luke. The power to create grants the power to control."

"You surprise me."

"Why?"

"You easily accept the premise that God could exist and do what the Bible claims He did. Most people want to say there is a God and yet dismiss the miracles as something that didn't occur."

"The Bible has to be all true or all false. Otherwise, it would be everyone's interpretation. There is no logic to that."

"It's all true."

"If it is, then I have three initial problems with what I've read."

"What are they?"

"God should be just. Yet Jesus did not receive justice. He was innocent and God allowed Him to die. God should be consistent. Jesus healed in Scripture every time He was asked; yet Jennifer believes, prays, and is dealing with cancer. God should care. From what I've seen during my life, He does nothing to intervene and stop violence. Either God is not involved, or He has an ugly side."

"The mysterious plan of salvation, unanswered prayer, and the character of God. Not a bad threesome. Most theology students would have a hard time articulating a better list." Dave sipped at his coffee.

"To answer your first question about justice, you have to understand God's mercy. He is both just and merciful in equal measure. Why did Jesus say He came?"

She flipped through her notes. "That story with—" she hesitated on the name—"Zacchaeus? Jesus said He came to seek and save the lost."

"Part of the mystery of salvation is that to save the lost, us, Jesus had to die in our place."

"That doesn't make sense."

"The people that killed Jesus, what would justice say they deserved?"

"To die."

Dave nodded. "Yet Jesus chose to forgive them. Why?"

"He was showing mercy."

"You don't like that word."

She rolled one shoulder. "It denies justice."

"You instinctively feel the great quandary. How can justice and mercy exist in equal measure? To ignore the penalty, justice is shortchanged. To ignore mercy, people have no hope once they have done wrong—and we have all sinned."

"They can't exist together as equals."

"Kate, God didn't shortchange justice to grant mercy. He paid the full price Himself."

She thought that through. "He was innocent when He died."

"Exactly. Jesus can forgive sins; He can extend mercy because He already paid the full price justice demanded. He took our punishment."

"If He paid the price for everyone, a blanket forgiveness, then mercy is larger than justice. They aren't equal."

"Earlier in Luke, Jesus warns—unless you repent, you will perish. God's wrath against those who reject the sacrifice His Son made will be fierce. There is restraint now, to see who will accept, but on the day Jesus returns, the judgment will be final. Those that haven't accepted the mercy extended to us by Christ's sacrifice will face justice."

"Is that restraint total? God allows anything to happen now, regardless of how innocent the victim?"

"I can understand why you feel God is too hands-off. The plane is a pretty vivid example of the violence man can do to man. God really meant it when He gave man free will to do either good or evil. He allows sin because He allows our choice. But He is not standing back, uninvolved. I know prayer makes a difference."

"Then why hasn't it made a difference for Jennifer? According to Luke, Jesus healed everyone who asked Him."

"Do you remember the parable of the widow and the judge?"

"The only person who could help her was the judge, so she pestered him until he gave her justice."

"Jesus told the parable because He wanted to remind us to pray and never lose heart. He knew we would wrestle with unanswered prayer. If God decides no, or not now, does it mean He is not loving? He does not care? He is not capable? Jesus knew we would not always understand God's plans. He simply assured us not to be discouraged but to keep praying."

"Jennifer having cancer, that is supposed to have a noble end?"

"God is allowing it today for a reason. He may tomorrow decide to cure her."

"Then how do you know He is loving?"

"Because the Bible says God is love. You take Him at his word, even if you don't understand the circumstances. It's called faith."

Kate tried to wrestle through the conflicting emotions. "There is nothing easy or simple about being a Christian."

"No, there isn't." Dave ran his hand through his hair. "I believe, and I still wrestle with the questions you ask. The bank holdup, it had the effect of pushing me closer to God. Is that a sufficient reason to explain why God allowed it to happen? Probably not. Is the fact we met that day a sufficient reason? If Henry Lott had not come into the bank, would he have committed suicide instead? We don't know what God sees in a situation, why He allows something to happen. The bomb on the plane—only God can understand tragedies like that. You learn to trust Him, even when you don't understand."

"'I don't understand' describes exactly where I am."

"You ask good questions. It's the place to begin."

"You would like me to believe."

He looked over at her, and his half smile was rueful. "More than you will ever know."

"I can't believe just because you want me to or Jennifer wants me to."

"I know. Faith is the ultimate personal decision. No one else can make it for you. That is all the more reason to ask the questions."

Kate leaned her head back. The night sky was spread out as a shimmering layer of stars. So much power, so far away. Was God near or far?

She was grateful Dave didn't try to break the silence. The questions lingered, unsettled. From her perspective, belief looked like stepping off a cliff, and she didn't want to get any closer to the edge.

Nineteen

Jennifer pulled out a kitchen chair, having finished a quick phone call, leaving a message with her fiancé Tom's answering service so he would know she had arrived safely. "I like your friend Dave."

Kate smiled back at her sister, pushing the glass of lemonade toward her. "So do I."

There was an inevitability now about the case against Tony Jr., a matter of waiting for him to be found. Kate had spent today pacing, expecting at any time to hear her pager go off. Having Jennifer arrive late in the afternoon had been a relief, had changed the entire tone of the day for the better.

It wasn't apparent when she looked at Jennifer that anything was wrong. Even the strain of the long trip back was not obvious. Stephen and Jack had brought her out to the estate, and the three of them had been laughing as they came in. Kate was sure neither of her brothers suspected anything. Jennifer had explained the trip as a consult on a case. She hadn't mentioned the fact she was the patient.

"You didn't mention he was British."

"I thought you would enjoy that."

"He reminds me of that singer I had a crush on when I was...sixteen?"

"About that."

"I thought so. I still love the accent. So—" Jennifer twirled the glass; her eyes twinkled—"this is your childhood roommate talking. How serious is it between the two of you?"

Kate grinned. "Good friends, Jennifer. Just good friends." If her life ever settled down again, she might get the perspective she needed to decide if it could ever be anything more. Dave didn't fit the mold of any cop she had ever met. She was learning to her surprise that protection also felt a lot like care. She would be disappointed now if Dave didn't care enough to know where she was and what she was doing. She found she kind of liked that attention.

"Given the fact I've heard rumors on the grapevine that Marcus approves, I thought it might be more serious."

"Marcus is weighing in?" Kate was stunned. He did not normally weigh in on the family grapevine chatter.

"He decided to let Dave protect you. I guess he felt that deserved an explanation."

"This place served as a safe house in the past; it's simply a logical place to stay."

Jennifer smiled. "You don't have to explain it to me."

Kate rested her chin on her hand and looked at Jennifer. "Dave *is* good-looking."

Jennifer grinned back. "He is that."

They looked at each other with the history of two decades spent together and shared a laugh. "We always said we should get boyfriends at the same time," Jennifer reminded her.

"I'm just glad we didn't actually plan this. It was one thing when we were in high school, another when we are supposed to be adults." Kate used her spoon to fish a lemon slice from her glass. "So tell me, how is Tom? Is he still planning to come up for the Fourth?"

"He'll fly in Sunday night and stay through Wednesday. I've booked a couple of rooms downtown at the Hyatt since he's not been to Chicago beyond the occasional convention. I thought I would show him the sights, take him to the Taste of Chicago."

"How did you manage to get rooms at this time of year? They book six months in advance."

Jennifer touched the locket she wore and smiled. "I prayed. And there were two cancellations."

Kate saw the peace on Jennifer's face and wished she understood it. "Tell me about how the tests went."

"I know now why I like to be the doctor, not the patient. Blood work, CAT scans, a biopsy, more blood work, the tests were like a parade. Bottom line—I'm in great shape for someone who has cancer."

"Do they have a plan to suggest?"

"An aggressive cocktail of chemotherapy and radiation. Surgery is a nonstarter."

"When do you begin?"

"It depends if Tom wants to have a bride that has hair or not."

"Jen—"

"That was a joke, Kate. Seriously, sometime in the next three weeks. The radiation comes first, and they may send me to Johns Hopkins for the first round to try to spot target the cancer around my spine."

"Did they tell you what to expect as a prognosis?"

"Kate, it might buy me an additional year."

"That's all?"

"I pulled that guess out of them. They don't like such numbers because they're afraid patients will stop fighting."

"They haven't met an O'Malley."

"Exactly. I'll fight this cancer for every minute I can get. But I may scrap the idea of a wedding and suggest a nice elopement instead."

"The family will understand that once you tell them."

Jennifer drew a circle on the table with her glass. "I'm going to tell Marcus next."

"He needs to know; I hate keeping the secret from him."

"I'll tell him after the Fourth, then let the two of you help me tell the others."

"Okay."

"Enough about my health. What's happening regarding Tony Jr.?"

"There is an APB out on him. Officers are combing his friends and associates to find out who might have seen him. There is no indication he has left the area, but assuming he was well prepared and is traveling with cash, he's probably far away; it could be some time before they locate him."

"I'm sorry for what is happening."

"It's not the shock that I have a brother I never knew about; it's not even the fact he apparently hates me having never met me; it's the reality that he could have done something this horrific. I don't know how to deal with it." She sighed. "Jennifer, how do you deal with the fact Jesus said love your enemies?" She saw her sister's surprise. "I read Luke."

"I wasn't going to ask because I knew how chaotic your time has been." Jennifer studied her. "That is the one thing I thought might be the hardest problem for you in the book; for all the O'Malleys when it comes to that. How do you deal with *God is loving* when you consider the past horrors in each of our lives. I don't know how you are supposed to love Tony Jr., how that applies to this situation."

"I wanted to kill him when I first realized what the evidence showed."

"So many innocent people are dead."

"That, but also just the fact he was there, someone I could hate, with a name I hate, when my father has been dead so many years."

"What do you think now that it's been a couple days?"

"I just want him brought in to face the courts. I want that sense of distance that he is just another suspect in a case. But it's personal, even though I've never met him, and I can't figure out how to get that distance. I'm either angry or sad." Kate studied the water beading on the outside of her glass. "Mainly angry."

"I can understand that. I don't know how the anger changes. I know Jesus has the ability to love the just and the unjust. I guess that is where the change of heart comes from. He does it for us."

"Have you forgiven that drunk driver that killed your parents, Jennifer?"

"Yes. I'm still glad he is doing time, but the hate is gone."

Kate nodded, glad in a way her sister had been able to leave that behind. "I can't undo the fact this guy's my brother, much as I would want to."

Jennifer sighed. "Tony Jr. did a good job messing up your life."

"That he did."

"What else did you think about what you've read?"

"Do you find it easy to do what the Bible says?"

"Not easy, no. But possible. It's different than reading a how-to book and struggling to figure out how. I've found Jesus is much more personal. That prayer makes those directions real for my situation. That tough one, love your enemies, comes with names, things I am supposed to do."

"Give me an example."

"Alisha Wilks."

"You're supposed to love the nurse working pediatrics who doesn't *like* kids?"

Jennifer nodded. "Stop and chat for a few minutes when I make rounds. Smile pleasantly when she complains about their noisy play. I even got reminded to take her cookies on her birthday."

Kate winced. "I bet she complained about the crumbs."

"She did. She's still a terror for the kids, but at least she's a little nicer to mine."

"Loving her means letting her stay in the wrong job?"

"Hardly. I've practically got ordered to stop complaining about it in my prayers and do something about it."

"You've been trying for six months."

"Well, now I've been trying harder. I've met with her supervisor, the head nurse, the chief of pediatrics, and the hospital administrator himself."

"Going to the top?"

Jennifer nodded. "Rocking the boat. The other doctors are shaking their heads, hoping I succeed, but not going near it."

"What happens now that you're going to be off full-time practice for a while?"

"The partners are closing ranks to cover my patients, and Tom has a doctor friend out East who's a great pediatrician. He's agreed to come out for six months, get a feel for my patients, the practice."

Kate knew that had to be killing Jennifer. She had always wanted one thing: to be a doctor practicing medicine.

Jennifer's hand covered hers. "Don't, Kate. I'm okay with it. I'll still be able to do as much as I have energy for; there will just be someone there to help and do what I can't."

"Do you understand why God has not healed you?"

"Kate, it is a complete mystery to me—I don't know. The Bible is clear and pretty blunt: God hears and answers prayer. I don't understand why there has been no improvement. People at church give lots of confusing justifications for why I haven't been healed, but frankly they sound like excuses.

"I do believe God heals people as a result of prayer. In the years I have been a doctor, I have seen a lot of kids get well when all my scientific knowledge said it couldn't happen. I'm convinced now that I was seeing the power of prayer. Why He doesn't act in my case is a mystery to me, only He knows.

"There has been some good come out of the cancer. I'm certainly going to better understand my patients—being a patient is the pits. And you have to admit, it's changed my priorities in life."

Kate grinned. "Married. It's going to be great."

"I can't wait."

"If you elope, none of us will get to be bridesmaids."

"You do realize being a bridesmaid means wearing a dress."

She winced at the thought. "Maybe you can half elope. Just show up at an O'Malley dinner with Tom and a minister and get married right then."

Jennifer smiled. "I think Dave would prefer to see you in a dress at least once."

"He would." Kate turned to see Dave leaning against the doorjamb, smiling at her. "Does she even own anything but jeans?" he asked Jennifer.

Jennifer grinned back. "Not that you would know it."

Kate scowled at them both. "I'm on call. I can't afford to be caught wearing something I can't live in for a while if I had to."

Jennifer chuckled. "She's good at excuses."

"I bet she would look fabulous in blue."

Jennifer quirked an eyebrow at him. "Want to help pick out bridesmaid dresses?"

Dave slowly grinned. "She'd have to model them?"

"Every one of them."

"There would be worse ways to spend a few hours."

Kate, thoroughly embarrassed, slipped from her chair to get out of the line of fire. Dave took two strides over and caught her hands. "We were just teasing."

"Did I say anything?"

"Your face says it all. You look nice in jeans, especially that old pair with the heart patch on the back pocket." He grinned. "They've shrunk just about perfectly. It's just that you would look fabulous in a dress."

She let a smile slip through. "I'll have you know I look better than fabulous."

"Then how about an expensive date somewhere so you can show me?"

"Wear that teal dress you got in Paris, Kate," Jennifer suggested, smiling as she watched them.

"Paris?"

Kate smiled and nodded. Paris, Illinois, but he could live with the mistaken assumption. Rachel, Lisa, and Jennifer had ganged up on her to celebrate her last promotion and had convinced her to spend almost a month's pay on one single dress. Kate glanced at Jennifer. "Do you think Marcus would approve?"

Jennifer winced. "Dave, how's your health insurance?"

His gaze lazily appraised Kate; then he flashed Jennifer a wicked grin. "She looks that good in it?"

"Yes. Just tread lightly if Marcus sees you together. Protective big brother will have something to say."

"When?"

Kate slipped her hands free of his, then grinned. "I'll think about it."

"Kate—"

"Jennifer and I are going to watch a movie tonight. Do you want to join us?"

"Is it going to be mushy?"

Kate looked at Jennifer. "We'll compromise with a comedy. We girls get the couch, you get a chair."

Dave waved them on. "Go pick it out; I'll make the popcorn."

Kate slouched on the couch to finish the popcorn in the bowl on her lap as the movie tape rewound. Jennifer had just gone up to bed. It was still early, and Kate was toying with the idea of raiding Dave's collection for another movie. The first movie had been great. It had been good to sit with Jennifer, share laughter—be reminded that all the good times with her sister had not suddenly disappeared.

"What would you like to watch next?"

She tilted her head back to look at Dave. "You're game for another?"

"Sure." He opened the cabinet that held the movies.

She scanned his selections. "How about *Apollo 13*?"

"You like the classics."

"Love them."

Dave put in the tape. "Should I make more popcorn?"

She considered what she had left, then grinned. "This should get me to *'Houston, we have a problem.'*"

He chuckled as he took a seat on the floor, using the couch as a backrest. "Just let me know. I'll pause the movie. Is that what you remember from your favorites, the dialogue?"

She nodded. "Occupational hazard. Voices are my thing. I can pretty much give you word for word my favorite movies."

"I remember the music."

"Do you?"

"*Magnificent Seven* is the best."

"The guys wanted to make that our theme song. We shot down the idea."

"It would have been a great choice."

"But it had one flaw: It only allowed for seven."

"True."

The opening movie credits began.

Kate glanced toward Dave a few times during the movie. He was absorbed in the story even though he must have seen it numerous times. She liked that about him; he focused on what he was doing. It was a long movie, and by mutual consent they paused it halfway through.

"This was a good choice."

Kate trailed him into the kitchen with the popcorn bowls. "Very."

"Join me for some coffee?"

"Sure."

He set about fixing it. "Can I ask you a serious question?"

She tilted her head. "Sure."

"Why don't you date cops?"

"Wow, you don't mind tossing a tough one."

"It's late. I'm curious."

"Have a reason behind the question?" She laughed at his look.

"I'll take the fifth for now."

She nodded and decided he deserved a serious answer. "You haven't been around for the 2 A.M. pages; watched me walk out of back-to-back crises; seen me focused on a case to the point I forget to eat. I don't like to explain my actions, talk about me, plan for the future. All those things put together are tough on a relationship." The deeper reason, concern that she would choose the wrong man and walk into a stress-filled marriage was private. She had seen Dave under the stress, and he handled it well.

"Was there someone?"

"A few years ago, a friend of Stephen's. He's in Atlanta now."

"Were you close?"

She shrugged.

"I'm sorry."

"So was I at the time." She smiled. "It's easier now simply not to date cops."

He nodded, handed her a cup of coffee, and slid over the sugar. "Like kids?"

"Who doesn't?" She heard the wistfulness behind the amusement in her own voice. He was broaching a subject pretty dear to her heart.

"Think you will like being a mom someday?"

"Not as long as I'm a cop."

"The two can't go together?"

"No child should have to wonder if his mom is coming home from work."

"Can you imagine a kid having to deal with two cops for parents?"

She was grateful he shifted the topic slightly. "It's not the kid, it's the parents. Even the most rebellious teen would not be able to dream up what cops would wonder about."

"I can just see it—late at night, the kid out with the car, and he's past curfew. Are you the type who would pace or go look for him?"

"I'd be calling the car phone, paging him, and checking with his friends. *Then* I would get serious."

He laughed at the image. "You'd make a great mom."

"Maybe."

He smiled. "You're comfortable hanging out with me."

"Fishing for a compliment?"

"Just checking. Come on; let's finish the movie."

Kate nodded, appreciating the fact he was closing the conversation for now. She was coming to respect that about him. The things he cared the most about were the topics he was the most careful with. She had seen it when he talked about faith, and he had just shown it again. It was a rare trait for most people—patience. As a negotiator she could deeply appreciate it. While she had learned the skill, she sensed something different with Dave. He had the patience inside him.

She knew how much he wanted her to believe. It was probably the only thing stopping that date question he skirted around. There had been numerous friends who had never asked her out because of her job, a few who met her family and chose not to ask, but Dave was one of the first to do so because of principle. It said something about his priorities that she admired.

It was also frustrating her—this was one evening where she would like to be sharing the couch with him rather than have him apparently content sitting in a chair several feet away.

Kate went no farther than the patio chairs, settled down, and made herself comfortable. The movie was over. She had convinced Dave to go ahead and turn in. She would be up in a while and would set the security grid.

The stars were bright tonight. She rested her head back, studying them overhead. It had been a day of great emotional swings, and this pause, this solitude was desperately needed.

She was falling in love with him.

She was emotionally vulnerable right now. She knew it, and she tried to remind herself of that as she felt her heart softening. Jennifer's cancer, learning she had a brother.... Other than Jennifer's engagement, Dave was the only good thing that had happened recently. That's why his steady support was making a big difference in her life right now.

But no matter how hard she tried to explain away her emotions, she knew she was denying the truth. She was falling in love with him.

It was scary. She didn't want to risk getting her heart mangled again in a relationship that could go nowhere. It wasn't only the question of faith; she had only to look around Dave's home to see how different their respective backgrounds were.

The idea of sharing the depth of her past with anyone, let alone someone she wanted to think well of her, petrified her. And as much as Dave knew, he knew only the tip of what he would eventually learn if it did get serious between them. She poured herself single-mindedly into her job because she knew how risky it would be to open up the rest of her life. Would Dave understand the things that gave her nightmares? The underlying reasons the O'Malleys were so important to her?

She would love to be able to rest the weight of what was happening on Dave, curl up in the protection he offered, and find a safe haven here. It wasn't fair to him. She had to consider the reality of her family, his.

What would his family think of her? She hadn't met his sister Sara, but Kate knew how close Dave and Sara were. How would Sara feel about having her brother involved with a cop? Sara had seen enough violence in her life already; somehow Kate didn't think it would be easy for her to have another cop in the family.

She sighed and forced herself away from it. Love just wasn't a good idea. Not with the two of them. They were destined to be only friends. And there were other questions she had to decide tonight. She couldn't afford to think about it.

She turned her attention away from the emotions that confused her to the reality she had to accept and find a way to live with.

She had a brother.

Did she want justice or mercy? It was a hard decision to make, but it was time to make it. Tony Jr. was her brother. She wanted to deny the ties, keep away from the hurt, but she couldn't any longer.

The circumstantial evidence strongly suggested he was guilty.

When he was located, did she want to meet him? He was family. Yet to get to know him in these circumstances would only make the hurt go deeper.

Did she want to distance herself from the case, from him, or did she want to seek some form of mercy from the courts? Did she owe him that because he was her brother? Did she owe herself that?

She needed there to be mercy, she had to have justice. Both now strained inside in equal measure. She could feel the paradox that Dave described existed in God—justice and mercy in equal measure. God might be able to create a situation that had both, but she didn't have that ability.

She looked at the expanse of stars.

"Jesus, I'm not sure yet what I believe, but I'm trying to understand. You said You hear and answer prayer. If You do exist, I know You'd understand the struggle I'm facing. You're bigger than I am. You make decisions I will never understand. If there is a way out of this dilemma, will You show me?"

Prove he's innocent.

It was such a soft reassurance; it was the peace she felt first, then the reality of the words. Yes, that was the only way out of this problem. It would be mercy for Tony and justice for the families.

Evidence pointed to Tony being guilty. To prove he was innocent...could it be done?

She pushed out of the chair with new resolve. There was only one way to find out.

Twenty

He had called in a bomb warning. If he weren't already dead, he would have killed him just for that.

Where were the videotapes? Three hours of looking had led to nothing. He knew they were here somewhere.

If that call led back to here and they started digging into the past, his perfect alibi would be destroyed. All because that stupid fool had to go and taunt the cop.

He was glad he was dead. He had made the decision in the spur of the moment. No more than twenty seconds to see the opportunity and take it. He was glad he had taken it. But where were those videotapes?

He had thoroughly searched the apartment, a long tedious job when he had to make sure everything went back neatly in its place, and the tapes weren't here. Short of tearing out a wall, there was little else he could do. If the videotapes hadn't already been destroyed, they had to be tucked somewhere.

Probably a safe-deposit box...but he had found no key.

Maybe they were lost forever now.

Maybe.

Maybe not.

They would make no sense to just anybody glancing at them. They were simply old security tapes after all—over a decade old, and the company that made the machine required to play them didn't even exist anymore.

Even if they were found and turned into the cops, they would be of very little use unless someone actually explained where they had been taken and what they captured.

There was only one other person still alive who knew the videotapes existed and what they meant.

He could kill him, too.

He lingered on that thought, considering it, tasting it, evaluating the risk.

Yes. If he had the chance, he would kill him. Then this conspiracy would be down to one, with no witnesses left. The future he had dreamed about for years was his, and he was not going to let anyone take it from him now.

Yes. Best to kill him.

Twenty-one

D ave tucked the cordless phone tight against his shoulder as he wrestled on his shoes. Sara's call had woke him up, and he realized with some dismay that he had slept through his alarm. The house was quiet, and that had him concerned. Jennifer normally slept late, but Kate—if she was out wandering the grounds it wasn't going to be good.

"How is Kate doing?"

"I'm worried about her," he replied, understating the reality. He was afraid for her, and how she was coping. He was having to stand back and watch the situation tear her apart, and it was killing him. Several times in the last few days he had found her sitting on the back patio, staring off into space, not hearing him join her. For a cop trained to react to her environment it was a disturbing thing to see. About the only thing that drew a smile from her these days was that fat tabby cat, and Dave found it annoying to be jealous of a cat.

"I have to imagine it will take a while to get over the shock of learning she not only has a brother, but that he's probably responsible for the bombing."

"Shock I could handle. Something else is going on." What, exactly, was hard to figure out. Kate was ignoring the manhunt to find Tony Jr., something he had expected her to want to be very involved with. She had instead been going back through the files for the last several days with an intensity that had him worried. Dave had no idea what she hoped to find. She wasn't saying, and his offers to help her had been dismissed with an absentminded thanks but no.

"Would it help if I came over?"

He brightened at the idea. "Actually, yes. I would like you to meet her, and it would be a good distraction for an afternoon. And I think you'll like Jennifer; I'd like you to meet her while she is here."

"Why don't Adam and I join you for lunch after church tomorrow?"

"That would be wonderful. And I want to hear all about your trip to New York. You didn't call me nearly often enough."

"It was an adventure. I spent too much money. Adam had me walking until I thought I would collapse. Lunch with my editor went well. I'm frankly relieved to be back home."

"Shall I plan to put something on the grill? The weather should be nice."

"Please. I'll put together a salad and bring dessert."

Dave slipped on his watch as he said good-bye to Sara. He set the phone back on the night table. It would be good having them over; he had missed her the last couple weeks. And he really wanted Sara and Adam to meet Kate.

He headed downstairs to start breakfast and get himself some coffee. If he didn't strongly suggest breakfast, Kate tended to bypass the meal. Dave stopped, surprised, and backed up. Kate was in the living room, comfortably slouched in a chair, feet propped up on the coffee table, folders stacked around her on the floor, a notepad in her lap. It looked like she had been there for a considerable amount of time. "Have you been up all night?"

She looked at her watch and grimaced. "Yes."

Diverted from his plans to get coffee, he crossed the room to join her. Unable to resist, he ran his fingers lightly through her hair. "What are you doing?"

She leaned her head back against his hand. "Now I know why a cat enjoys that so much."

Her sleepy smile was adorable, and he wanted to lean down and kiss her, but wisely smiled instead and let his hands slide down to her shoulders and gently squeeze. "You're punch-drunk tired."

"Probably. I've got an idea."

Curious, he took the seat across from her. "Tell me."

"It untangles if you look at the fact Ashcroft wanted to kill Nathan."

"Ashcroft is dead."

"Ignore that for a moment."

Ignore that for a moment. Right.

The focused grim stress from the last few days had disappeared, and he wasn't about to say something to bring it back. Realizing he was humoring her, he nevertheless settled down to listen, relieved to have her at least willing to discuss what she had been doing. "Go on."

"This was more than a family feud. Ashcroft wanted to kill Nathan because he was the one who turned him in and sent him to prison for ten years. He was bitter and angry and out for revenge. Ashcroft wanted his brother to suffer.

"Next, look who cut a deal with the DA to provide evidence against Ashcroft. Tony Emerson Sr. So if you buy the fact Ashcroft would go after his brother for writing that letter to the DEA and starting the drug investigation, he would certainly like to go after the man who testified against him. But since Tony Sr. is dead, that leaves Tony Jr. and, through a twist of fate, me."

Dave stopped thinking about humoring her and started seeing the connection she was making. It was curious. "Where does that lead?"

"What if it was Ashcroft blackmailing Tony, not Nathan? Ashcroft might be able to implicate Tony as one of those who had moved drugs for him at O'Hare. So Tony was paying off Ashcroft. It makes more sense than Tony paying off Nathan. That never did feel right."

"Then how did the money get into Nathan's account?"

"Someone put it there to make Nathan look less than lily-white. I haven't figured that out entirely, but it's logical. If Ashcroft hated his brother enough to kill him, he would certainly like to destroy his reputation in the process."

"A lot of assumptions."

"It's there and plausible. Ashcroft planned to kill his brother and frame Tony. He was laughing at me when he made that Wednesday call because he could do it and drag me down at the same time."

Dave nodded. Someone had gone directly after Kate by using her name in the bomb threat, by sending the black rose, by making the calls. He could see Ashcroft doing that.

"Tony is being blackmailed, and he's running out of money. Ashcroft puts the pressure on, blackmails Tony to kill Nathan. Then Tony gets lucky when Nathan decides to take the MetroAir flight and the bomb kills Ashcroft as well."

"Tony is still guilty."

She tossed her pen across the room.

Startled, he looked at the pen buried in the dirt of a fern and thought the flash of temper was a pretty healthy sign. Her aim was good, even upset; he'd have to remember that. He looked back at her, seeing the frustration. "It's a good theory, Kate. It just doesn't clear Tony."

"Well, I hate the current theory."

"We watched Ashcroft Young on videotape. He was at the gate terminal reading a newspaper. He could not have planted the bomb. We know from the security tapes that the laptop was checked by security; the bomb was not in the laptop when Nathan arrived at the airport. So even if Ashcroft did plan to have his brother killed, he still had to have help. Tony is still a coconspirator."

She groaned and rubbed her eyes.

"You think he might be innocent?" That realization surprised him. He knew she would like him to be, but the evidence was overwhelming that Tony was involved.

"I would prefer it." She sighed and looked over at him. "I want to go to First Union Bank today."

He hesitated. "Okay. May I ask why?"

"We go back to the beginning. I want to know about that foreclosure rate increase. The bank manager might give us a straight answer."

"You're sure?"

"Yes."

He offered his hand. "The bank opens at 8 A.M. We can have breakfast before we leave."

"Good. Jennifer was going to sleep in, but I'd like to be back early."

"I'll leave her a note as to our plans."

"Okay." She walked over to retrieve the pen. "Sorry for throwing stuff."

She sounded so sheepish about it that his chest rumbled with laughter when he hugged her. "With that aim, at least I won't have to wonder if I get hit by accident."

The glass doors to the bank had been replaced. The walk across the parking lot to the doors was very much a repeat of the time weeks before, down to the asphalt sticking to her tennis shoes. Staff at the bank looked startled when they walked in and were recognized. The bank manager came to meet them, his smile profuse. "Thank you for what you did that day."

Kate remembered him. He had done pretty well for the pressure he had been under. She smiled in return, liking him. "You're welcome, Mr. Tanner. I was wondering, could you answer a couple of questions for us?"

"I would be glad to. Please, come into my office; have a seat."

Looking around the bank, the evidence of what had happened had been erased. Kate followed him to his office and took a seat.

"We noticed the mortgage foreclosure rate was unusually high this year, like Nathan was raising cash. Would you have any idea why?" Dave asked.

"Actually, I would say it's more like Peter Devlon was the one raising cash. If someone with a loan problem could get past Peter to see Nathan Young and have a reasonable case, the loan would be extended. I was getting faxes from him all the time directing action to be delayed on certain loans."

Dave glanced at his notes. "Was there any such arrangement for Wilshire Construction? I understand Tony had a meeting with Nathan, and the notes were e-mailed here."

"Let me check the business loan files." The manager moved to the file cabinets and came back a few minutes later with a thick blue file. "Yes, here are the meeting notes." He scanned them, then frowned. "They are from Peter Devlon in regards to the meeting, basically say no change is to be made, and to proceed with terminating the line of credit." He set aside the page, looked at the next one, and smiled. "Here's what you are looking for. Nathan faxed this to us shortly after the meeting. Tony asked for a ninety-day extension so he could complete the Bedford site, and he was willing to put up his home as collateral. Nathan said to accept the offer."

"Such a dichotomy in instructions was common?"

He waffled his hand in the air as he smiled. "There were meetings, and there were meetings. Peter is very much by the book, and Nathan didn't like to meddle in what were day-to-day decisions. Since Nathan married, the banks had become more and more Peter's to run. But on the side, when it wouldn't rock the boat—yes, this was common."

"How did Peter typically react when he found out?" Dave asked.

"Furious, of course. He'd rant on about his authority and order us not to follow such substandard practices, but there was little he could do to enforce that edict. Nathan was *the* boss, after all."

"And Nathan made the banks more human," Kate observed.

"Not always good business, I know. But the personal touches were Nathan's way of doing business."

"Is there a time stamp on the fax, when it was sent?" She asked.

Mr. Tanner scanned the document. "Tuesday, 10:48 A.M."

"Where does Wilshire Construction stand now?" Dave followed up.

"We put through the ninety-day extension when we received the fax Tuesday morning."

"Would you know why Nathan and/or Devlon was raising money?" Dave asked.

"It's not exactly hidden knowledge that Devlon would have liked Nathan to take the Union Group's banks public. The stock he hopes to receive in such a situation would be worth millions. Every few years he was able to convince Nathan to tighten policies, raise more cash, to get the banks ready for such a move."

"Nathan used the cash to go buy another bank instead?"

The manager smiled. "Exactly. Nathan was content to keep the banks under private ownership."

"Thank you, Mr. Tanner. You've been very helpful."

Kate waited until they were back in the car. "Tony didn't have a reason to kill Nathan Young; the loan had been extended."

"He was still being blackmailed, and he couldn't make those payoffs even with a loan extension," Dave pointed out.

"True," Kate conceded, "but who was really blackmailing him? Nathan or Ashcroft? And what do you want to bet Devlon now convinces the widow she would be better off a multimillionaire, that it's time to take the banks public?"

"Probably. But how does that relate to Tony? He's the one getting blackmailed."

Kate sighed. "I don't know."

"Where to now?"

"Back to your place. I want to look at the files again. I missed something; I know it."

"Kate, you need to get some sleep."

"Later."

"Try now. Lean your seat back; you can get a thirty-minute nap on the way back to the house."

"Seriously?"

"Kate, go to sleep."

It was his look as much as his words that made her chuckle and recline her seat.

"Good night."

Kate sorted through the boxes in the formal dining room and pulled out two to take over to the table, following a hunch.

Dave leaned against the dining room table beside her. "What are you looking for?"

"I don't know. I'll know when I see it."

"I'll get you an early lunch."

"Thanks." She barely noticed when he ruffled her hair before he walked away.

He came back with two plates, sandwiches and fruit, and took a seat beside her.

"The explosives." She took a bite of the sandwich he had brought her as she paged through the file. "These are Wilshire Construction's invoices. There should be something here."

"How does that help Tony? Proving the explosives used in the bombing were shipped to Wilshire Construction just tightens the case against him."

"Only if he took them."

She pulled some paperwork from the file with a frown. "They bought two lots of explosives for the same demolition. That's interesting. Look at the dates and project codes."

It took Dave time to trace through the paperwork. "It looks like one shipment went to the subcontractor doing the work; the other appears to have disappeared. It's not in the inventory or the shipment log as being returned. There is a receiving slip for the shipment on April 5; we've got an inventory audit on...April 8. The lot is missing."

"Any signatures?"

"The receiving clerk and the supply manager, nothing unusual. Those signatures are on 80 percent of the paperwork here."

She looked over at the boxes. "Dave, hand me that top far left box. Henry Lott kept all his old timecards."

"You don't think…"

"April 5 to April 8."

They split the stack and thumbed through the timecards looking for the right dates. Dave found two, she found one. "He worked security those three nights."

Dave got to his feet. "Come on, Kate, let's go see Henry."

Kate leaned against the one-way glass as she watched Henry Lott. They had decided it was best if Graham did the interview. Henry still looked angry, bitter, much as he had at the bank. Kate was grateful she didn't have to hide what she was thinking and pretend to like him at the moment.

"Henry, we know the explosives that brought down the plane came from Wilshire Construction. We know you worked security the three nights when they were taken. Do you really want to be an accessory to 214 murders? Who was around the site those nights, Henry?" Graham's voice sounded slightly hollow through the audio feed.

"He told me to look the other way. Paid me a grand. Cash."

"Who, Henry? Who told you to look the other way?"

"Ashcroft."

"Blame a dead guy. That's real smart, Henry."

"I'm telling you the truth. Ashcroft shows up, tells me to look the other way, mind my own business, and he pays me a grand to do it. I don't want the grand, but I don't want the trouble either. He's a mean one, Ashcroft. So I looked the other way."

"Just like you used to do in the old days, huh, Henry? Turn your head and mind your own business? Is that how you knew they were moving drug money back before Ashcroft went to jail?"

Kate glanced at Dave. It was enough. "Ashcroft taking the explosives puts him deeply involved."

"He's still dead, Kate."

They had enough for a warrant to search Ashcroft's home. Kate didn't know what she hoped to find. Evidence being used to blackmail Tony, something to suggest where it was.

What they found was an apartment of a man who had thought he was traveling to New York for a few days. The place was neat, orderly. The draperies had been closed; the refrigerator had been emptied of perishables and the trash taken out.

The answering machine flashed several times showing messages.

A dead man's home always felt slightly…wrong.

She played the answering machine messages, found nothing there, and then played the introduction message, hoping to find she recognized Ashcroft's voice. To her profound disappointment, there was no introduction message recorded, just the recorder beep.

She followed Dave through the rooms as they decided where to begin.

Within an hour, Kate stopped expecting they would find anything. Ashcroft didn't keep even general financial records such as cable bills, magazine subscriptions, and ATM slips. There was no trace of a safe-deposit box key, anything to indicate other places he might store records.

There were no address or appointment books, no calendars. It was possible they had been with him on the plane, but Kate figured it was more likely Ashcroft's habit to write nothing down.

"Anything?"

She looked up from the last drawer in the desk. "No. You?" Dave had begun in the living room, then moved to the bedroom.

"No."

Kate sighed and looked around the room for anything she might have missed. "We've got another dead end."

"The press will show up here soon; we should go. The guys from downtown can finish this."

She nodded, knowing Dave was right. She walked back with him to the car. "This is getting depressing."

"We know a little more. Ashcroft was expecting to go to New York for a few days."

"It's as good an alibi as any. If Nathan had gotten on his private jet carrying that briefcase, he, his wife, and Devlon would have been killed, and we would have naturally been looking at Ashcroft, only to find we had him on security tapes sitting at the MetroAir gate."

"Exactly. I'm sorry, but none of this really helps Tony."

"I know." She sighed. "We've got to explain what happened without Tony being part of the story. I really do think it's there. I just don't see it."

He put his arm around her shoulders and gave her a hug. "You're trying Kate. That's what matters. I'm proud of you."

She really hated the fact she blushed. "Really?"

"You're acting on the hope he's innocent. That can't be easy given how much the evidence suggests otherwise."

"He's family, Dave. Not the kind of relative I would have chosen, but he's family. He's going to get every benefit of the doubt I can give him."

"Jennifer, if you're going to prune my roses for me, at least cut yourself a couple bouquets to take inside. You're embarrassing me." Dave handed her a glass of ice tea as he joined her.

Jennifer smiled. "They are so beautiful. I'm just enjoying the chance to work with them. This is pure therapy. Where's Kate?"

"I hope she's taking a nap, but I somehow doubt it. She's probably back in the files again. I wish I had something to offer her, but I'm just as stumped as she is."

"She's like this when something about a case is bugging her. Don't worry about it. She can conserve energy better than anyone I have ever met."

Dave cut her one of the American Beauty roses. "I'm glad you agreed to stay here. Kate needs the diversion. She literally lit up when she saw you arrive."

"I'm the favorite of all the O'Malleys, didn't you know that?"

He laughed at her tongue-in-cheek reply. "I think you might be, if only because they're relieved you are the youngest, not them."

"Do you have any idea what it was like to have six guardians?"

"Stephen wouldn't be so bad. And having Kate for a roommate had to be an adventure. But Marcus? How did you ever get a date past him?"

"Put them all together and they were pretty intimidating." Jennifer smiled and turned her attention to the white roses. "Could I tag along with you to church in the morning?"

"Sure. Services are at ten o'clock."

"Thanks."

Dave crouched down beside her to gather up the cuttings. "How do you think Kate will react if I invite her to come?" It was a casual question, but one he carefully weighed asking. He was aware Jennifer paused, studying him a moment before answering.

"She's the type who will invite herself if she's interested. But I'm planning to ask her."

"I don't mean to ask behind her back, but is she interested in Jesus, Jennifer? Or has the bombing pushed away that interest?"

Jennifer rocked back on her heels. "Dave, she has to get to the point she can trust Him. She's not there yet. It's not just the confusing realities such as why God allowed the plane to be bombed, or the difficulty in following commands like 'love your enemies.' Those are there, but ultimately, with Kate, it's personal. She has rarely heard 'I love you' where it was meant without strings. Give her some time to realize Jesus means it."

"Her childhood."

"Exactly. It was pretty rough."

"I've been figuring that out."

"There's hope for her. The Lord won't change what He means with 'I love you.' Kate's the type that will keep testing it until she figures that out."

"I had figured it would be understanding justice, mercy, and the rest."

Jennifer chuckled. "Oh, she'll challenge you for answers and explanations on all kinds of tough questions. She's nothing if not logical, and she expects to find out answers to questions or at least understand the theological knot. Giving her a simplistic answer is the worst thing you can do. But the bottom line with Kate is whether someone really is who he presents himself to be."

"I'm sorry God used something so difficult as your cancer to push Kate to look at the gospel."

"You noticed that, too? I didn't mention it to her."

"I noticed. What do you want me to pray for, Jennifer?"

"That God gives me enough time to complete this mission."

He understood it, what would be closest to her heart. "To lead all the O'Malleys to Jesus."

"Yes. Kate's the first nick in the wall. When she comes around, there will be two of us to convince the third. When the third believes, the fourth becomes easier to convince."

Dave chuckled. "And here I thought Kate was the plotter."

"I'm the youngest one in the family, remember? I know how to get things done."

"Here you two are. I wondered where you had disappeared."

Dave turned to see Kate crossing the patio. "Come convince Jennifer to cut herself a bouquet of flowers."

"How about a bouquet of pink ones, Jen? They would look great in the living room."

Jennifer nodded and began to cut the bouquet. "They would."

"Sara and Adam are planning to come over for lunch tomorrow. Anything in particular you two would like fixed on the grill? Ribs? Pork chops?"

"You're brave enough to fix ribs?" Jennifer asked, glancing up.

"Sure. Think Marcus and rest of the family would be willing to join us?"

"Jack and Stephen are off duty; Lisa would be the only question mark," Jennifer said.

"I'll ask them," Kate offered.

Dave heard the pager. It startled him, and he tensed as he realized it was Kate's pager going off.

She reached down and shut it off, reading the number as she reached for her cellular phone. She dialed. "Yes, Jim."

Dave watched her eyes shadow. "Of course. I'm on my way."

She closed the phone and studied it for a moment before looking up at him. "Can I borrow your car?"

"About this case?"

"No. It's unrelated. They've got a standoff, and I'm the closest." She looked at him quietly, waiting.

She couldn't tell him details; he knew that from dozens of his own cases. He wasn't ready for this, but he had to be. She was going back into danger because it was her job to do so. It was a test, not one she had asked to create, but one that was suddenly there between them. "Can you duck the press?"

"Jim said he would make sure my name stays off the radio."

He reached in his pocket, found the keys, and handed them to her. "Switch the radio to your department frequency. It's set to ours. Be careful."

"I will. I may be late for dinner."

He watched her leave and wanted to swear at her for making her last words such a casual comment. If something happened to her...

Jennifer slipped her hand into his. "Relax. She doesn't take unnecessary chances."

"Jennifer, she'd step in front of a bullet if it were necessary, the same way she would step in front of someone going for a basket and take the charge. She would never think about the risk to herself; she'd just act."

"You're in love with her."

His frustration over the situation was intense. "And it's the most miserable reality of my life. My hands are tied."

"She'll believe, Dave. She has to."

"I just hope it's sooner rather than later." He sighed. "She's going to be annoyed, but it will be easier to wait where she is than here. Would you like to come along?"

Jennifer smiled. "No. I've got more practice at this than you have. But call me when you know something, please?"

"I will."

Kate leaned her head back to catch the breeze coming along the side of the brick apartment building, tired but content after two hours spent settling a violent quarrel that had begun over the simple reality of melted ice cream. She wondered how many cases this made that she had resolved peacefully. It was an idle thought since she only counted the ones that had failed. A win was simply to be enjoyed.

Dave sat down beside her on the metal stairs of the fire escape. She was too tired to be surprised that he had found her. She gratefully took the water jug he offered her, drinking half the quart of ice water before pausing. "It was hot up there." She looked over at him. "Any word on Tony?"

He shook his head. "No."

She nodded. "It would have been too good to hope for."

"You settled this one peacefully?"

"Yes."

She finished the ice water. He handed her an apple. She smiled. "I prefer junk food. This is marginally healthy." She took a big bite anyway and wiped away juice running down her chin with the back of her hand.

"Natural sugar. You'll get used to it."

Her smile broadened. "You're trying to change me."

"If I didn't meddle, you wouldn't have anything to complain about."

She grinned and toasted him with the apple. "True."

Her shoulders were stiff, and she rubbed the right one, hoping to relax.

"Let me."

He started to work out the kinks. "Lower to the left." She relaxed. "Right there."

"What were you leaning against? You've got a rust streak down your back."

"Do I look like a skunk?" She tried to twist and see, finding the idea amusing.

"Maybe a red one." He dumped some water on a towel and wiped off the worst of it. "Would you like to go chase the sunset?"

She was working on the apple and wasn't sure she had heard him correctly. "Do what?"

"The sunset is beautiful from the plane. And the weather is perfect. The case investigation won't slow down if you take a couple hours off. It would do you some good to get away from it for a while."

"Tonight?"

"Yes. We can catch it if we hurry."

"I thought we needed to stay away from O'Hare."

"Sara and Adam took the jet to New York. I had them route it back to Milwaukee. It's not too far a drive."

She was ready for a nap, but she could sleep anytime. She looked at him, trying to decide if it was love or just affection that made his face so endearing to her. "What about Jennifer?"

"Lisa came over. They were making brownies and talking about Fourth of July plans when I called."

Kate nodded. Jennifer was in good hands. "I need to change."

"I'll buy you a tourist T-shirt at the airport."

"I could use something for the baseball game." She saw the question in his look.

"The O'Malleys have a game on the Fourth, and my lucky shirt died last year."

"Really?"

"I did this slide into home, and Marcus didn't move out of my way. I need a better shirt."

Dave grinned at the image. "Something that will make him move?"

"Exactly." She tossed the apple core into the trashcan by the house. "Can you afford me?"

"Probably." He held out his hands. "Come on, let's go."

Twenty-two

Compared to the complexity of O'Hare, the Milwaukee airport was a breeze. They parked in the lot across from the terminal, then browsed in the tourist shops. They passed through security and walked out to the private hangars.

"There she is." Dave pointed to a plane by the third hangar.

Kate stopped, stunned. The plane was a gleaming, midnight blue Eagle IV. "It's beautiful."

"She. This lady has her own personality."

The pride in Dave's voice was obvious. Kate looked at the jet, then back at him. "This is what you fly for fun?"

"Yes. Though I do use it frequently for work. It makes it easier for the team to get around. Come on; let's get you settled inside. My flight plan is already filed. Give me twenty minutes to complete the preflight, and we'll be ready to get in the air."

She reached up to slide her hand across the smooth, gleaming metal of the wing. "It's such a sleek, beautiful plane." Not small either. It would take some walking to circle this plane.

"One of the best." He brought down the stairs and offered her a hand.

"Oh, my." Kate had expected nice, but this was *really* nice. No crammed together seats or lack of legroom here. It had been configured with plush leather seats and mahogany side tables, and honest-to-goodness wallpaper and blue carpet. There were even two sketches carefully mounted on the cabin wall. "This is great."

"The cockpit has windows that come all the way down to your

elbows. You'll see what I mean about a great view."

"I can join you up front?"

"I can even teach you to fly it if you would like."

"Don't you have to be certified to instruct?"

He smiled. "Yes. I'm a good teacher, too. Care to find out?"

She let that settle in. He wasn't joking. "I'll think about it."

He ruffled her hair. "Do. Dan said he would stock the refrigerator for us. Make yourself at home. The walk around won't take long." He stepped into the cockpit, came back with a flight log and checklist, and disappeared back down the stairs.

Kate picked up her bag and moved to the back of the plane. She was going to have a hard time flying on a commercial aircraft after seeing this luxury. The lavatory was full cabin width, with marble counters and matching hand towels. In the drawer she found a sewing kit and small scissors and cut the tag off her new T-shirt.

The evidence that the plane was someone's home in the air began to be apparent as she took Dave at his word and looked around. In the cupboard next to the refrigerator was someone's idea of snacks. Not a small bag of peanuts, but a full can of cashews, half a package of pecans and hazel nuts still in their shell waiting to be cracked. They were bracketed by a bag of Oreos and peanut M&Ms.

A sketchpad was tucked in with the magazines, well-worn playing cards in the pocket beside the table, and three paperbacks beside a stack of CDs. There were feather pillows and blankets, even a teddy bear in the back closet. Kate smiled at the whimsical bear before closing the door. They were touches of people's lives. Neat, orderly, but personal. Touches of Sara by the look of them.

Kate laughed when she stumbled upon the stash of sports equipment. Besides the golf clubs, there were very well broken in baseball gloves, a couple scuffed baseballs, a Frisbee, even a Chinese box kite. She could just see Dave taking off for a weekend and flying somewhere to join friends for a game of golf. With this plane, it could easily become commonplace.

"Been up to see the cockpit yet?"

She turned and smiled. "Not yet."

"Grab us a couple cold sodas and come join me. You'll enjoy it."

The electronics were not what she had expected to see based on the movies she could remember. Like the plane itself, the electronics were sleek, modern, well designed, and colorful. "Where did all the knobs and dials go?"

Dave smiled. "I know. The dash looks like a nice piece of sound equipment, doesn't it?"

"Built in radar?"

"Yes. Come on; buckle into the copilot seat. You won't disturb anything."

She slid into the seat carefully, not sure she was ready to have pedals at her feet and a wheel in front of her. You could fly the plane from this seat, and it was intimidating. She carefully put her soda into a holder, fastened on the spill guard top, and quietly watched Dave methodically check settings and work down the checklist on his knee. She recognized comfortable movements that came from thousands of repetitions.

"There are headphones behind you on the right."

She looked around and found them. He showed her the toggle for voice.

She heard him speak briefly with someone over the radio, and a crewman appeared before them on the tarmac. On the signal all was clear, Dave touched one red button, then another, and the two jet engines came to life with smooth, steady power.

He finished working down the preflight checklist, then turned the brace board on his knee and held up his hand to the crewman. He got a smile and wave toward the taxi line with the batons. "We're all set to travel."

She listened as he slipped easily into the tower radio traffic. She wasn't able to understand what was said even though she heard the words, recognized his repeat of the instructions and his acknowledgment. The plane began to roll. Fascinated, she watched him handle it with ease, his hands light on the wheel, and his feet in motion. He took it directly down the centerline of the taxiway and into the queue behind two other planes waiting to turn onto the runway and into the wind for takeoff.

"You use your feet as well as your hands?"

"Rudder and brakes are at your feet. Use the brakes right, and you can turn this plane on a dime."

Minutes later he got clearance for the runway.

It was everything she had hoped for and yet so much more. The plane had much better speed than Kate expected, and Dave handled her with finesse, bringing the nose up and guiding the plane smoothly into a climb.

"I filed a flight plan for us to cruise at thirty thousand feet. Airlines don't usually fly at that altitude. We'll head west toward Denver and be traveling with the sunset for almost an hour, depending on the cloud cover."

He spoke briefly with the tower and moments later reached down and retracted the landing gear. Noise inside the airplane diminished. They traveled through the first cloud bank, coming out above it. The sun was shining on the top of the clouds. "One more cloud bank, and then we'll be leveling off."

Kate yawned to clear her ears as she watched the display climb through twenty-eight thousand feet.

Dave reached down and adjusted the trim, eased forward the nose, then leveled off at thirty thousand feet. "And that's how this baby cruises."

The beauty entranced her. She was looking close up at the top of clouds, not through the scratched Plexiglas windows on a commercial plane. "I can see why you love it."

The top of the clouds came up toward them looking like billowing cotton balls, the high altitude winds tugging wisps of white. She watched new clouds build ahead of them, exploding into the clear air as growing mushroom clouds. "What's it like when these are thunderstorm clouds?"

"If you're high enough to be above the storms, they are a spectacular display. Most of the lightning actually happens up in the cloud, and it will light up like a Christmas tree. The clouds will form very rapidly, shooting thousands of feet into the sky."

"This is already spectacular."

"Just wait. It gets better."

When the sun slipped to the right angle, the clouds suddenly became a blanket of pink below them. "Wow. Have you ever taken a picture of this?"

"A few. But even film can't do the breathtaking color justice."

"How long will this last?"

"We'll be able to stay in this zone of color for probably half an hour. You'll see it paint the canopy of clouds high above us here in a few minutes."

Kate saw the colors of the sky in all their brilliance, from the blanket of pink, to the deep caps of red, and then the deep streaks of blue and gray

as the sun slipped lower on the horizon. Dave banked them south, showing her the color gradients appearing. "If we were closer to the Rockies,
you would see the snow-covered mountaintops being touched with the
color as well."

"Has Sara ever tried to capture it on canvas?"

Dave smiled. "A few times."

"Thank you for showing me this."

"It was my pleasure." He brought the plane back around on a return
heading.

"Would you like to fly her? Now's a perfect time and place for a lesson."

"What would I have to do?"

"Just put your feet lightly on the pedals and your hands on the wheel.
You'll barely have to touch either to keep her on this heading. There's no
major crosswind to deal with."

"Are you sure you trust me with your toy?"

Dave chuckled. "I won't let you fall out of the sky."

Tentatively she reached forward to take it.

"Good. Relax your grip a little more on the wheel; hold it like a feather
you don't want to crush."

It was as easy as he had described to keep it level; the plane barely
seemed to move even though the readout showed them doing over three
hundred knots.

"Try a gentle turn, say about ten degrees to the right."

Beginning to anticipate the responsiveness, she brought the plane into
a bank to the right, coming out at exactly ten degrees and holding it there.

He chuckled. "I already see a budding perfectionist. Good. Level it out
and we'll try a climb."

Kate grinned and smoothly came back level. The fact his hands were
comfortably folded across his chest said he either had confidence or strong
nerves. Either way, she appreciated the compliment. "I think I could get to
love this."

"Hang around, and we'll be dancing around the sky frequently. Bring
the nose up in a climb and watch how it changes your airspeed."

She did and easily saw the correlation. "Is this how they do a hammer-
head? Go into a pure vertical climb and stall out their airspeed?"

"Yes."

Growing more comfortable by the minute with the fact she was playing with a multimillion-dollar toy, Kate smiled over at him. "Show me how the rudders are used."

Dave grinned, scanned the skies and the radar, then took the controls and slipped the plane left. "Feel how I'm moving them?"

She could, and she memorized the sensation. It was the same light touch as with the turns. "Yes."

"Try it."

The lessons continued until the light was totally gone, and then Dave took over, flying by instruments the remaining distance into the airport. When the plane set down with a smooth, rolling flair, Kate was already regretting they were on the ground. "That was really fun."

He smiled. "Don't worry. You'll get a second invitation."

He taxied from the runway back to the hangar, following the directions given by the crewman with the glowing red batons. When the engines shut down, the still, quietness of the night reclaimed them.

In the glow of the one interior light turned on, Dave completed the flight logbook and slipped it back in the map case.

Kate unbuckled her seat belt, loath to call it a day. Dave stopped her move to slide from the seat with a gentle hand on her arm. "Kate." She looked over at him and saw the smile. "You'll make a great pilot. You really should keep taking lessons."

"You're a good teacher."

"I'm also willing to work for free. How about it? Want to hire me?"

His hesitation, so rare in him, made her smile. "You're hired." She wasn't going to let an offer like that pass by.

She watched as Dave completed his walk around the plane, speaking with the crewman. He stepped back on board for a moment, then came off carrying something white. He joined her as the crewman moved the plane into the hangar.

"What's this?" She was amused to realize he was carrying a pillow.

"You're getting some sleep on the trip back."

"I can't stay up and talk?"

He caught her hand in his. "Not tonight."

They walked together to the car. Kate settled with the pillow, reclining her seat back, turning so she could look at Dave. Would this be the norm for days spent with him if they did try to make a relationship work?

Frustrating moments when a case had no apparent solution, tense moments when her pager went off, quiet moments ultimately relaxing together? The idea was getting easier to accept. It was hard to imagine not being with Dave in the middle of a day.

"What are you thinking about?" Dave asked.

"Today."

He glanced over and smiled. "I heard a yawn under that word."

"My eyes are tired." She snuggled into the pillow. "It was a nice evening."

"Yes, I was thinking the same thing. Sleep, Kate."

Her eyes were already sliding closed. "If I don't remember to say good night later, consider it said."

He chuckled lightly and brushed his hand along her cheek. "Sweet dreams."

Twenty-three

D ave stopped at the bottom of the stairs and frowned, then headed down the hall toward the dining room and the smell of coffee. Kate was there, a stack of empty candy wrappers beside her, sipping a cup of coffee, studying the notes on the wall.

"I didn't hear you get up. How long have you been down here?"

She looked over and smiled. "Since about 2 A.M., I guess. I've got something to show you."

She looked…pleased. He pulled out a chair, intrigued.

"Devlon did it."

Where has she gone this time?

She laughed at his skeptical look. "It's all there." She gestured to the wall. "I was almost right yesterday. Ashcroft is the one who started it all. But it was Devlon that helped him, not Tony."

Dave settled down in the chair, willing to give her room to explore ideas. She'd been up most of the night again. She probably had found something. Not what she hoped for but something. "Explain what you've found."

"Ashcroft wanted to kill Nathan because he turned him in and sent him to prison for ten years. He wanted to go after the man who turned evidence against him, Tony Sr., but since he was dead, Ashcroft had to settle for framing Tony Jr. and dragging me down instead. But Ashcroft also wanted to rebuild his drug operation, and that meant the one person he didn't go after was his inside man at the bank." The look that entered her eyes was one Dave had never seen before: fierce, cold, calculating. "Devlon."

She tapped the audit book beside her. "Ashcroft was blackmailing Tony, but Devlon moved that blackmail money to Nathan's account so Nathan would look less than lily-white."

"That makes him a bomber?"

"Yes. Because it means he was doing Ashcroft's bidding. And the evidence suggests he had been doing it for years. With the attempt to convince Nathan to take the banks public, Devlon couldn't afford a whiff of that becoming public."

She tapped the top Post-it note. She had taped up a new easel sheet and done her own Post-it notes. Dave noted her handwriting was atrocious and wondered if she had been filling them out while they were stuck on his wall. He buried a grin; he didn't think he'd win points for asking.

"Are you paying attention?"

"Yes."

She frowned at him. "Pay close attention, buddy; I've been up for hours to figure this out."

"I could use some coffee if this is going to be a long explanation."

She handed him hers without even a comeback, and Dave started paying serious attention. She didn't relinquish coffee easily.

"Nathan turned Ashcroft in, got him sent to jail because of a suspicious account. Guess who brought that account to Nathan's attention?" She tapped a note. "Devlon. He'd probably been handling Ashcroft's drug money for years. When the auditors got too close, he covered his own back."

She tapped the second note. "Ashcroft gets out of jail a decade later and starts blackmailing Tony Jr., squeezing him hard enough he's running out of money. Tony Jr. needs to get the bank to ease up, give him time, but there's Devlon, insuring it's going to play by the book. Tony's looking at bankruptcy, and he can't make the next payment. Ashcroft then moves to pressure Tony Jr. into planting the bomb."

"Which the evidence suggests Tony Jr. did."

Kate shook her head, and Dave was startled at her confidence. "Tony Jr. said no; I'm certain of it.

She walked him through what she thought had happened. "That left Ashcroft with everything arranged, the money moved, Tony Jr. set up to take the fall, the calls made, his alibi established, the perfect opportunity to act, and no one to plant the bomb. But he's got a card with Devlon. So he uses it. Think about it. Ashcroft had enough evidence to push Devlon into moving money around. One step further is planting the bomb in Nathan's laptop. We know Devlon had access; he was the one using it that morning.

"And in the end we get a classic double cross," she continued. "Devlon doesn't like the fact Ashcroft has him over a barrel. But it's pretty easy for Devlon to take care of Ashcroft, he just does some fast talking and puts Nathan on the MetroAir flight as a last minute walk-on. Good-bye Ashcroft. Good-bye Nathan. Devlon has a nice alibi; he was supposed to fly to New York with Nathan until the last second change in plans. Tony Jr. looks guilty; Ashcroft who could implicate him is dead; and he walks away running First Union Group, with the prospect of the banks going public now that Nathan is no longer there to resist the idea."

"So he gets everything but the girl."

Kate smiled. "He could be seeing Nathan's wife, Emily, on the side for all I know."

She looked at the board, then back at him. "Do you see any holes? Because I don't."

"The phone calls."

"We still need to track down the voice on the tape, but I now think it's going to prove to be Ashcroft's. And the location the bomb threat call originated from—I'll lay money when they did the tests, they didn't check the power levels from inside a plane parked at the gate. They'll match the footprint we have."

"And the calls to your apartment? The black rose?"

"Both were Ashcroft. If Ashcroft was smart, and I'm willing to bet he was, the calls would have been made from a pay phone somewhere. We might find a florist who remembers him buying the rose."

"How do we prove this?"

Kate began to pace. "Devlon strikes me as arrogant. What do you want to bet he's already moving some of Ashcroft's secret accounts to his own?"

"We go after Devlon's financial records?"

"I would. And what do you want to bet he's already tried to get his hands on the evidence Ashcroft was using to blackmail Tony with? He's going to have problems if Tony starts to talk."

Dave leaned forward and slowly set down the coffee mug. "Kate, if you're right, Devlon is vulnerable to Tony talking—214 deaths vulnerable.

He's not going to hesitate to make it 215."

He watched her literally pale in a heartbeat.

"Call Jim. We've *got* to find Tony."

Dave shook his head, dialing Marcus instead. "We've got to pick up Devlon first."

"Call Marla, too. If she knows what's going on, she may be able to convince Tony to turn himself in if he calls her."

He nodded, agreeing, even as he gently pushed her back into a chair.

He had always admired Marcus's ability to absorb information. His questions were brief, pointed, and he went to the bottom line much faster than Dave. Marcus would take care of getting Devlon brought in for questioning.

Closing the cellular phone, Dave called Jim next. The cops were already looking hard for Tony, but at least they would know now he was as much at risk of being a victim as he was a possible bomb suspect. The calls made, Dave closed the cellular phone, set it back on the table, and took a hard look at Kate. He crouched down to get at eye level with her. "It's going to be okay. We'll find Tony."

"I'm scared to death something will happen to him before we find him." Their gazes met. "He's innocent. I've got a brother, and he didn't do any of this."

He wrapped his arms firmly around her. "Sometimes there is something wonderful besides mercy and justice."

"What's that?"

"The truth."

Her smile wobbled a bit. She hugged him, hard. "Could we go to church?"

"Really?"

She nodded against his shirt.

"Why?" He didn't want to push too hard, but it desperately mattered.

Her hand settled over his. "Call it curiosity." Her hand tightened at the look of disappointment he quickly tried to mask. "I'm cautious, Dave, despite all that you see in my job. I'm not going to risk my heart without understanding much better who I am giving it to. That direction in Luke of 'follow me' requires a lot of blind faith in who you follow. Give me some credit for wanting to go forward with my eyes open and not half closed."

"I keep hoping faith will be easy."

She smiled. "Give me time. I make it hard because I have a hard time trusting."

"He's trustworthy."

"Yes, I am beginning to think so." She released his hands and got up. "Let me go check on Jennifer."

Kate was glad she had Dave on one side and Jennifer on the other as they walked through the lobby of the church toward the sanctuary. Ben was trailing them half a step back. Dave diverted them to the balcony where fewer people could approach and start a conversation. Kate wondered if it was to make it easier on her or for security reasons. When Ben took up a position at the stairway exit, she figured it was probably some of both. Dave had been edgy this morning as they left the house. As he had quietly reminded her, the only time Devlon had met her, she had been with him.

The music started, and Kate set aside the problem to focus on the service. She had been truthful with Dave; it was curiosity that made her ask to come. Jesus had heard her first prayer and helped her figure out a way for there to be both mercy and justice. She was curious why He had done that. She owed Him something in return, and if it couldn't as yet be an agreement to follow, she could at least say thank you.

Dave settled his hand comfortably around her waist, sharing his bulletin with the words for the songs. Kate knew how important this was to him, how proud he was to at least have her with him. It was Independence Day weekend, and the choruses were about freedom. Freedom in Christ. Was that what Dave and Jennifer had found? Freedom?

She was beginning to understand the distinction between "follow me" and "follow these rules." Jesus was the person who made it all fit together. Mercy, justice, loving others. Jesus had shown her love when He answered that first prayer. There was no reason to do that on His part. Except maybe the desire for her to notice and say thanks.

One of the stories from Luke came back to mind; it had been on the lower left-hand side of a page, toward the back of the book. A story of ten lepers. They had all asked for mercy, and Jesus had healed them all. Only one had returned to say thanks.

Thank You, Jesus.

You're welcome. The soft reassurance was gentle; it felt warm inside like a smile. She let out a soft sigh of relief; at least one instinctive step toward Jesus had mirrored that of another fellow searcher long ago.

The songs ended, and they took their seats again.

Was she ready to take the step she knew was next? She had reached the point it no longer felt like stepping over a cliff to trust God with her future. But was she really ready to answer "follow me" no matter where it might lead? She had been wrestling with it since reading Luke. Some of the pages were now worn with her notes. Knowledge was no longer the issue. Trust was.

Dave had shown her in his life a peace that came from inside, and she knew after weeks of observation that the peace came because of his faith. She wanted to enjoy that peace, but it was a very big step.

She had never been one to step back out of timidity. Her life, certainly her job, would be easier with that resurrection promise to cling to, a guarantee of eternal life. Even a possible future with Dave rested on this decision.

Kate shut out all the pluses and minuses, closed her eyes, and took a slow breath, retreating as she did when in a crisis to the quiet place inside where she could listen to her own heart. Trust. It was there.

Jesus, I'll follow. It's a choice I make, knowing what that means. I will follow where You lead, and do what You teach. I do believe Your love explains Your mercy. I choose to believe it will never waver or burn low, that Your love will be there for me for an eternity. Forgive me for a lifetime of saying not now. Forgive my doubts, my sins, and my stubborn heart. And please, make me a better cop when You place me at the crossroads of another person's life.

If there had been a sparkle of warmth before, now the joy was so intense it felt almost hard to breathe.

"*...for there is joy before the angels of heaven when one sinner repents....*"

She wanted to laugh as she realized the Scriptures had already recorded her journey. She had heard the Bible referred to as a living book, and now she understood. Her journey was one others had taken, yet also uniquely hers, and uniquely understood. The book had been written in preparation not only for others, but also for her.

She felt Dave's arm tighten around her waist, realized there were tears on her cheeks, and reached blindly into her pocket for a tissue.

Lord, I need to find Tony. He's my brother. I would like to say hello. Will You help me?

"Kate, what's wrong?" Jennifer asked softly.

She shook her head, not wanting to disturb the service with a whisper that might travel given they were seated in the balcony.

Dave's arm slid around her and turned her gently into his shoulder. His strength felt so good. She rested her head into that hollow he offered and let the last few moments of emotions be absorbed into the comfort of his embrace.

Was this, too, what it meant to be in love? An embrace that didn't need words to explain the commitment? She knew, in the same way she knew with the O'Malleys, that she could ask Dave for anything she needed, and if it was in his power to do it, he would.

She could do the same with Jesus. He wasn't going to let her down. She took a deep breath, for the realization touched deep.

Thank You, Jesus. I'm going to enjoy meeting my brother. She felt the humor come back as the stress dropped away, and she smiled slightly. *But, Jesus, please, we're going to have to do something about that name. Tony brings back too many memories, and going with simply Jr. is not much better.*

As the sermon drew to an end, she began to pull back from Dave, mop up her eyes. She hoped her face had the same peace she had seen on Jennifer's but was afraid her eyes only looked red. There was more to do. She wanted to talk to Jennifer to be sure she understood what baptism meant. The reason for the urgency Jennifer felt to share what she had discovered was plain. The rest of the O'Malleys had to believe; they couldn't afford the delay.

She turned to Dave as the service concluded and saw the worry on his face. She squeezed his hand. She didn't want to explain until she had a few moments to regain her composure. The crowd in the balcony began to disperse.

Ben stepped aside to let a couple coming toward them through. Kate hurriedly wiped her eyes one last time. Dave's sister Sara trailed closely by her husband; Kate knew them instantly from the pictures around Dave's home. This was so embarrassing.

"Sara." Dave stepped forward and enveloped his sister in a hug. "Come meet Kate," he said turning to make the introductions.

Kate liked the lady at first sight. Beautiful, the pictures had not done her justice; petite, and with an open inquisitive gaze that made Kate aware of just how closed her own expression must be. She had instinctively retreated to the impassive mode of observing as soon as she saw them. She could feel the nerves taking over as she said hello and shook hands.

Jennifer stepped forward, and the awkward moment passed. Jennifer could charm anyone with her smile and her calm manner. It let Kate take a half step back and simply follow the conversation as Jennifer and Sara talked about New York.

Dave touched her arm. "I'm going to bring the car around. Come down the back stairs; Ben knows the way. Sara and Adam are going to follow us."

She nodded.

Two minutes later she was following Ben through the relative quiet of the back stairways, Adam beside her. Kate found Sara's husband to be a confident man, charming, and from his attention to his wife a couple steps ahead of them, very much focused on those he loved. They reached the lower landing.

"Let Ben check for reporters before we go out," Adam suggested when she would have opened the door to the step outside.

"I'm never going to get used to this," she remarked, dropping her hand.

"With time it will become second nature. It's part of the reality of being news."

"Outside of a church?"

"If they had a lead on your location, absolutely." He glanced over at his wife who was still in a discussion with Jennifer, then turned back to Kate. He rested his shoulder against the wall, relaxed, watchful, sharing a smile. "Dave managed to forget to mention you were from the South."

"He's been talking about me." She didn't know whether to be secretly thrilled or embarrassed.

"Not enough to satisfy Sara."

Kate glanced over at her. "Your wife is lovely."

Adam chuckled. "You should see the disaster that is our bedroom. She had absolutely nothing to wear suitable for this occasion. You make her nervous, Kate. Hence the fact she's hiding behind your sister at the moment."

Kate blinked, just once. "I do?"

"You do; so relax. The nerves are mutual." He was making a well-educated guess; there was no way she appeared nervous. She knew how hard the disciplined control had clamped down on her expression. If anything, she appeared distant and aloof.

"I don't have to see them to know they are there. Was that you Saturday afternoon? The early evening news reported the standoff in progress."

She rested her back against the wall, unconsciously positioning herself as a cop would to keep the world in front of her. She decided she liked Adam. "Yes."

"I'm glad you were able to settle it peacefully."

"Almost all situations have peaceful conclusions if there is enough time." She glanced again at Dave's sister and decided it was easier to ask Adam than to try to broach the subject with Sara later. "Is Sara okay with what happened at the bank? I know it had to have been a hard day for her, waiting so long for news. And with her past—"

"A few nightmares, a few old memories, she's dealt with it."

"I wish it hadn't happened." She grimaced. "I never did send a thank-you for the flowers. I honestly meant to."

He flashed her a grin that made her blink for its warmth. "You're forgiven."

Ben came back inside, held open the door, and gave the all clear. Adam moved to rejoin his wife. "We'll see you at the house in about twenty minutes."

Kate nodded and went with Jennifer to Dave's car.

Dave had stepped out to hold the car doors for them. "Thanks, Dave." She slid into the front seat and reached automatically for the seat belt.

Traffic was beginning to build as they drove back to his home. They had just reached the Lake Forest town boundaries when he looked down, startled, his hand going to his waist. His pager set on vibrate mode had gone off, Kate realized.

He pulled it from his belt and looked at the number, immediately reaching for the phone. He punched in the number as he drove.

"This is Richman."

He listened and his expression became grim. "We're on the way."

"They've found Tony. He's holding Devlon at the bank corporate headquarters."

Her throat closed. *Tony had taken the situation into his own hands.* She had found her brother only to lose him. Her face cleared of the churning emotions. She couldn't afford to give in to them. Tony had managed to get himself cornered with the one person who would want to make sure he didn't come out alive. "Is the situation contained?"

"Sealed off to the top floor. Jim wants you there."

"Marcus?"

"On his way."

He started dialing again, glancing back in the rearview mirror to her sister. "Jennifer, I can have Adam and Sara take you back to the house."

"No, I'm coming along. It might be useful to have a doctor on-site."

Kate knew if a doctor were needed it would be one accustomed to digging bullets out of people rather than a pediatrician, but she would never say as much. She wanted Jennifer there simply because she was an O'Malley.

Dave reluctantly nodded. His attention turned to the phone call he had placed. "Adam? We've got a change of plans." He explained what was happening.

Kate tried to suppress the impact of what was happening, found it difficult to do.

Dave hung up the phone.

Kate asked the question that was bothering her the most. "How did Tony get into the corporate bank offices on a weekend?"

"At a guess, Devlon let him in, thinking to resolve the problem. He's arrogant enough he probably thought he could kill Tony and then claim self-defense."

She cringed having Dave confirm her worst fear. "Yes. It's been all over the news that we have been looking for him. Devlon would have seen that as a way to excuse his actions."

She rapidly dug out a pen from her bag and flipped open the pad of paper she had left in the car the day before, forcing herself to action, to the work that she could do. "Do you remember the bank? The layout of that executive level?"

"Two elevators opening onto a wide east-west corridor. Two secretary stations, the one guarding the east wing was Nathan's secretary. Three doors behind her. A conference room, Nathan's office at the end, Devlon's office."

"Who worked in the west wing?"

"I didn't see the nameplates. But it was the same layout. Two offices and a conference room."

"I'm guessing the corridor was about fourteen feet wide?"

"Yes."

"Were the emergency stairs to the left or the right when we stepped off the elevators?"

"Right. There was a large fern, restroom, and then the emergency stairs."

"The offices are on the top floor, so we may be able to get good use of the roof of the building. It's ten floors, and there are taller buildings on all sides, so line of site will favor us. Which room is the most likely for them to be in?"

"If it's just Tony and Devlon, Tony would likely have pushed the confrontation into Devlon's office."

"Even though the room has full windows?"

"He'd pull the blinds but not realize he's still vulnerable. Safer would be to move to the interior conference room."

"Okay. He'll have line of sight down the corridors, but that's also a problem for him. He can't really eliminate a threat to his back, even if he moves into one of the end offices. There are still the windows." Kate could see the situation and knew how good the SWAT team was. They would be able to breach the floor if it was required. "Did you notice the ceilings?"

"Plaster."

"The rooms are large, not much furniture. An assault team would be able to come in with clear lines of fire."

"Kate, a peaceful conclusion will be found. Trust that."

"I'm praying Jim lets me do the talking."

"You're too deeply involved in this case. Don't get your hopes up. You're going to be on the sidelines for this one."

"You're relieved at that fact."

"Are you going to hate me if I say yes? Devlon isn't exactly a friendly hostage to protect."

"How are they going to handle this? That the one being held hostage is the one probably responsible for blowing up the plane?"

"*Probably* is the operative word. We've got a theory, but not airtight proof against Devlon. And he *is* the hostage."

"Tony is in deep trouble."

He didn't respond. He didn't have to.

Twenty-four

The block around the bank had been sealed off. Media vans and their journalist teams were along the perimeter, trying to get the best vantage point or interview. From the numbers present, word must have leaked that this standoff was related to the airline bombing. Police had to control the crowd of spectators at the barricades. Overhead, the steady thumping beat of police helicopters guarded the scene. Kate scrambled for her badge and hurried through the crowd of cops to the forward command post, Dave jogging along beside her. There were so many different agencies here, men from her unit, the FBI, some of the ATF people. The task force had descended. It was a noisy, busy environment. Exactly what she expected.

"Jim."

He broke free from the cluster of men to join her. "I'm sorry it's going down like this, Kate."

She kept her voice cool. "I've never met him." She had to keep her distance if she was going to have any hope of being involved before this was over. "Where are things?"

"Come take a look at the blueprints. I could use your firsthand knowledge, both of the environment and the two men." She followed, well aware of the less-than-comfortable looks coming from others in the command center. As far as most of them were concerned, she was related to a suspect and therefore a security risk. She was grateful to have Dave beside her. She sensed when someone else joined them and saw the men around the room abruptly shift their gaze away. Kate glanced back. Marcus. Between

Dave and Marcus there was an implicit warning being issued to others in the room. It felt nice to know they were protecting her back.

She turned to look at the blueprints as Jim identified locations. "We've got the elevators shut down, Graham and a team in position on the stairs, more on the roof. It appears to be only Tony Jr. and Devlon on the tenth floor. Shades are drawn, lights are off, but snipers in the surrounding buildings have picked up movement—" he tapped a location—"here."

"Devlon's office."

"Yes. The security guard downstairs said Devlon cleared Tony Jr. to come into the building. Franklin and Olsen are working to get us video optics snaked in through the ductwork along here so we can see what is happening. Phones have been isolated; we've already shut down the air-conditioning, and we're preparing to shut down electricity and water."

Kate nodded, having expected all of those steps. "Tony Jr. arrives at the bank, and Devlon clears him to come up. What happened when he got up there? Were shots fired? How did we get word about what was going on?"

"That's what's so puzzling. Fifteen minutes after Tony Jr. went upstairs, Devlon called the security guard to say he was being held hostage and told him to call the police."

"Tony Jr. *wanted* us brought in?"

"Yes."

"Have you made contact?"

"Christopher. He's gotten through by phone. Tony Jr. wasn't in the mood to talk, said to call back in an hour. We're still twenty minutes away from that time."

If Kate had to pick someone to handle the negotiations in her place, Christopher would have been her choice. "Is everyone aware Devlon is a suspect in the bombing?"

"They know. But Tony Jr. is not making this easier for his own defense."

"If Tony Jr. dies, the ability to prove it was Devlon who planted that bomb gets more difficult."

"I know that, too." Her boss looked at her. "I can clear you to work with Christopher, but as much as I'd like to, I can't give you the phone."

It was more access than she thought she would get. "I'll take it."

"Get him up to speed. You've got about fifteen minutes before that next call."

Kate nodded and turned to scan the room. She spotted Ian in the corner, and he waved her over. Leaving Dave and Marcus talking over the tactics of the situation with Jim, she crossed the room; where Ian was, Christopher would be. She was right. Christopher had made a private corner for himself tucked behind the communication gear. He was lighting his pipe, ignoring the commotion. It was so traditionally Christopher that she couldn't help but smile.

He spun around a chair for her. "Nice mess, this one is lass."

"How much do you know?"

"Not nearly enough. The FBI profile," he lifted the pages from his lap, "is worthless. It assumes Tony is the bomber, something I understand you doubt; therefore, its conclusions are probably wildly wrong. From that kid's shaky voice it is clear he's petrified."

She let out a deep breath. "Innocent, but so terrified he's going to get himself killed by doing something dumb."

"Lass, you and I are going to make sure that doesn't happen. Tell me everything you think happened."

Since she didn't have much time, she sketched in the case. The facts did look incriminating. There had to be a reason to look deeper and see that Devlon was the one who had actually helped Ashcroft. Tony was her brother. No one was going to get away with framing him for something he didn't do. "Tony probably went after Devlon thinking the only way to clear his name was to make the man confess."

"Rather naive of him."

"Yes."

It was time to make the call. Ian set it up for those in the room to hear it. Kate wished she were the one reaching for the phone instead of Christopher.

Come on, Tony, pick up.

"Hello, Tony, it's Chris again."

"Why did you shut off the electricity?"

To keep you from seeking safety in the restroom, maybe get you to crack a window blind. That wouldn't be said of course. Christopher was right. Tony sounded young…and frustrated. Frustrated was not good.

"The alarm inside the bank was ready to sound, and we knew that would be rather distressing for you to hear. We didn't have the codes, so we shut down the system the only way we could."

There was a pause. "I want to speak with Marla."

Wife. Kate scrawled the word for Christopher. He nodded. "We can try to arrange something."

"When she gets here, call me. In the meantime, start looking for the combination to Devlon's office safe."

"What are you looking for?"

"Just get me the combination." Tony slammed down the phone.

Kate winced. "An hour hasn't eased that sound of panic."

Christopher reached over to replay the conversation. "He gave himself an hour to search the place, and he didn't find whatever he expected. What's he looking for? And what happens if he doesn't get it?"

She ran her hand through her hair. "He was being blackmailed. Maybe he is looking for something he thinks Devlon acquired."

"I'm surprised he wasn't pleading his innocence."

She looked at Christopher and saw it was an observation, nothing more, and agreed with him. "I think he's given up believing someone will listen."

Christopher nodded. "Then we'll just have to convince him otherwise."

"We've got video," one of the technicians across the room announced.

Kate pushed back her chair so both she and Christopher could see the screens being turned on. They had one camera with a view of the corridor, another that had been lowered into the corner of Devlon's office.

"Are the tactical teams getting this?" Marcus asked.

"Yes."

Devlon sat in a chair that had been pulled to the center of his office. Kate leaned toward the screen. "What's that around Devlon's wrist?"

"Looks like he's handcuffed to the chair," Christopher speculated.

"Tony made a mistake leaving Devlon in a chair with rollers. If things get interesting, his hostage can move on him. And he left the other hand free."

"He should have used a phone cord, an electrical cord, something," Christopher agreed. "The kid's not thinking things through."

Tony stood in the doorway of the office, trying to watch both directions of the corridor, a gun in his right hand. He had made a few changes to the furniture arrangements. One of the secretary's desks had been pulled over to give him access to the phone. The other desk had been moved in front of the stairway door.

The two men were arguing about something, Kate could see Tony's growing anger and Devlon's belligerence.

"Can we get audio?" Kate asked.

"Franklin is laying down the relays. You'll have it in another minute," Olsen promised.

Dave rested his hand against her shoulder. Kate appreciated the silent support. Tony was pacing. Having seen too many situations like this, she could read the growing storm. Audio sputtered on, the first words broken by static. "…you framed me with that meeting! Now I want those tapes you took from Ashcroft's apartment."

"What tapes? I was never near Ashcroft's apartment."

"I saw you coming out! Now where are the tapes?!"

Kate flinched an instant before Tony fired the handgun wildly over Devlon's head.

The chatter over the secure mikes was instantaneous as the SWAT teams positioned to swarm in.

"No! Everyone stay in place. Do not breach! Repeat, do not breach!" It took shouts from the team leader to get over the vocal traffic and freeze them from moving. "We're still secure!"

Christopher had his hand on the phone. Jim nodded at him. It rang for almost a minute before Tony stormed back across the room to pick it up.

"Tony, what's going on up there? Is anyone hurt?"

"Everything is just fine. Just keep away from me and get me what I want!" In the monitors, Kate could see him still pointing the gun at Devlon.

"You've got a lot of nervous cops around you. It's not a good thing to fire a gun in this situation."

"Where's the combination?"

"We're still checking, Tony."

"I want that combination!"

Kate watched the monitor, worried at the agitation. Was he on something? The situation would be impossible to stabilize if he was.

"Calm down. If we can't locate it, we can drill the safe for you."

Kate wrote. *Tell him we know it's Devlon.*

"Tony, we know you are innocent. We know that Devlon is the one who planted the bomb."

"He's trying to frame me for it."

Ashcroft.

"We know Ashcroft planned this entire thing, that he and Devlon set you up to take the blame." Christopher looked over at her. "Tony, he framed your sister, too. Come out peacefully and let us sort this out."

"I don't have a sister."

"She's sitting right here. Kate Emerson, thirty-six—although she doesn't look it, a decent cop for someone who no longer walks the beat. You want chapter and verse on your parents? The house where you grew up?"

There was silence. "She died years ago."

"Hardly. She changed her name, but she's been here in town all her life. Her name is Kate O'Malley. Maybe you saw her on the news lately."

"I don't believe you."

Christopher covered the phone. "Kate, I need you up there."

Thank you, Christopher. His word was gold unless they went tactical. She looked at Jim for agreement. "Go. Join Graham on the stairs."

The gear was ready. She shoved her feet into the boots.

"What are you doing?"

She didn't spare the seconds to look up at Dave. "My job." Olsen handed her the vest. She pulled in a deep breath to snug down the straps. The gear was custom designed for her, and she got it on fast.

"Ian, audio check."

She nodded as she got a good clear signal through her earpiece.

"You're going to negotiate this?"

"Christopher is. But I'm the proof."

"Give me a minute. I'm coming with you."

She could argue with him, but it would take time she didn't have. "Hurry." She saw Christopher hang up the phone.

"Kate, get in position. Marla is about five minutes out. I'll put her on the phone with Tony, then try to work it so you can open that stairway door and chat with him."

"Can we do anything on the safe combination?"

"Even if we could, the risk is too great that it's empty. If Devlon did ever get his hands on evidence that somehow could incriminate him, you can bet it's long since been destroyed."

Kate knew he was right, but it would be so much easier to have something in hand to convince Tony he could safely end this standoff.

Marcus touched her shoulder as she went past. The pressure was a silent message of support. He was listening in to the same tactical chatter she was. She squeezed his hand in return and moved to the door. She was about to meet her brother for the first time. She could think of much easier places to do it.

She looked over at Dave as they entered the building. He had borrowed gear, was decked out much as she was. His face was grim, and she didn't need that additional stress. He had volunteered to come along. She didn't mind him protecting her back, but added pressure was not something she welcomed or needed. A cop stationed in the bank building lobby pointed toward the stairwell.

Kate glanced over at Dave as they entered the stairwell. "Ten flights. Bet I beat you to the top."

"This is hardly a race."

She took the first flight, going up two stairs at a time. "It's not a major war either. He's not going to shoot his sister."

"Really? You know that for a fact?"

He was afraid for her. How was she supposed to deal with that? She didn't want to deal with it. He shouldn't be putting her in a situation she had to deal with it. "Didn't you say prayer made a difference?"

"Yes."

"Well then quit raining on my prayer. I intend to meet my brother and get him out of this mess." She turned the corner and sprinted up the next flight. "It's just like a kid brother, digging a hole I have to get him out of."

"That's what this morning at church was about?"

"Part of it. I'm okay if something happens. Quit stressing out, or you're going to be worthless to me if this does go bad."

"You believe?"

She took a moment in the turn at floor five to look over at him. "You don't have to sound so skeptical about it."

"Sorry. You took me by surprise."

She took a deep breath and sprinted up the sixth flight. "You get what you wished for and you're surprised. Where's the logic in that?"

He grinned at her. "There is none. It's pure relief."

"Then catch up. You're slowing me down."

She slowed as they reached the eighth floor, and by the turn into the tenth, walked the last flight to eliminate the noise. Graham had six men with him. They had taken positions away from the door, against the concrete wall. Graham smiled when he saw her and whispered over his mike, "Good to see you. No real change. Thompson has the video feed."

She nodded and stopped beside Thompson to get a look. The situation looked much as she had left it. Except now Tony was fifteen feet away on the other side of this door. The nervousness had as much to do with the uncertainty of meeting him as with the danger in the situation.

Christopher's voice came over the command circuit. "Kate, Marla is here. I'm going to patch the conversation onto channel three."

"Switching to three," Kate acknowledged. She leaned against the concrete wall beside Graham. He wordlessly handed her a piece of gum. She smiled and accepted it. She knew even as she unwrapped it that it would be Juicy Fruit. Graham was accustomed to long waits.

Marla's voice came over the channel, strained and worried. "Tony, the building is surrounded with cops. Give yourself up before you get hurt. Please."

"It doesn't matter. I've got Devlon, and one way or another he is going to pay." Kate frowned at Tony Jr.'s choice of words. They were definitely running out of time.

"Tony, Marcus O'Malley is down here. He's with the U.S. Marshals, and he knows about Ashcroft and Devlon. You can trust him."

"If they know what happened, how come I'm the one being hunted? No, Devlon is going to confess. He's going to tell them what he did."

"Tony, please."

"Did you meet this sister that I've supposedly got?"

"No, she's not here. But they tell me she's the one who actually figured out what happened."

"Put Chris back on the line."

"Here he is."

"Marla says this Kate isn't there. Are you lying to me? You said she was beside you. If she's real, put her on the phone."

"Better yet, why don't you meet her? She's at the stairway door."

"I'm not opening any door to the cops! What do you think I am, a fool?"

Kate folded the gum wrapper into a nice foil square.

"Tony, she really did figure out what was going on. I've got one of the calls Ashcroft made to her right here. Hold on, I'm going to play it."

"Hello, Kate O'Malley. I've been looking for you, and what do I see—you made the news last night. We'll have to meet soon."

"That's her answering machine tape, Tony. That's Ashcroft's voice, isn't it?"

"Yes."

"He was dragging her into this. Besides this tape, we've got others. He used her name in the bomb threat. Kate O'Malley is very real; she's a cop, and she's your sister. When she says it was Devlon and Ashcroft, she knows what she's talking about."

"I open this door, the only person I want to see on the other side of it is her. Her hands better be in the air, and she better be motionless. I see anyone else and I'm going to shoot."

Kate flipped back to the command channel. "Got it, Chris."

The others with Graham had been listening in. Given the way the door would swing open, they didn't have to shift far to be out of the line of sight. Dave put himself within reach of her.

She calmly took a breath and keyed her mike. "I'm in position."

The doorknob turned with a sound as if it needed to be oiled. Thompson held the small display so she could see Tony stepping back to the center of the room, gun raised, pointed at the door. Chris gave the green light. "Any time you're ready, Kate."

She opened the steel door with her left hand, as it would let her right hand be in the air when he first saw her.

He took another step back, both hands coming up to grip the gun. "So you're my sister."

"I don't know if it's a pleasure to meet you or not, but yes, I'm your sister."

Her calm words surprised him. When she said nothing else, she saw a puzzled look and his hands adjust themselves on the gun grip. He could only keep the gun sighted like that thirty to forty seconds before the fatigue would force him to either get mad and create some more adrenaline or lower his arms and the gun. His body couldn't produce more adrenaline, a simple fact of how long the crisis had been going on. She waited him out.

"How come you never came back home and bothered to tell anyone you were alive?" The gun lowered a fraction as his arms began to tire.

"I hated our dad. And no one bothered to tell me about you." She looked past him into Devlon's office and nodded toward Devlon. "Would you believe he was the one to first mention your name? That was not a pleasant experience, thank you very much."

"You really are my sister?"

"Yes. I haven't been called Emerson since going on forever. My name is legally Kate O'Malley, but I'm not dead, despite what Tony Sr. said."

He pulled the desk forward several inches, keeping the gun aimed at her. She watched him and made a simple decision. She took one step inside the room.

"Kate, get back here!" The words were hissed at her over the earpiece.

She moved to the left, past the desk, and sat down against the wall. "Close the door, Tony. I think it's time you and I talked."

"Kate, when you get out of this—" Dave sounded more than just angry.

"What are you smiling at?" Tony demanded, nervously shutting the door.

"My boyfriend is yelling in my ear."

"Take that mike off."

"No."

He stared at her. Kate calmly stared back.

"Tony, sit down," she said mildly, just to give him the means to save face. She leaned her head back against the wall, relaxing to make herself comfortable for what might be a long day. "I hate that name, by the way. You got a nickname?"

"What?"

"I have no intention of calling you Tony."

"Junior."

"Get real. You're related to an O'Malley. Have some class." Marcus tried to cover his laugh with a cough and nearly made her deaf. She turned down the volume on the command circuit with her thumb.

"Mom used to call me Will."

"Will." She tried it on for size and found she liked it. "Not bad. Okay, Will. Rule one in the O'Malley world: Don't mess with your older sister."

"That's you."

"Since I'm the one who believes you're innocent, lose the sarcasm. Why did you run? It made you look guilty."

"I didn't. I heard about the bomb, and I went to Ashcroft's to try and recover the video he had. Only Devlon here got there first. I couldn't come forward after that because everything I needed to prove Devlon was Ashcroft's partner was on that video."

"So you came here today to get it."

"He has it."

"Tony, Devlon would have destroyed it the same day he got his hands on it."

"Then give me one reason I shouldn't just shoot him now."

"You may have moved drugs because of pressure from our dad; you may have been stupid enough to let Ashcroft blackmail you; and today is going to give a prosecuting attorney a delight, but you have not killed anyone. Devlon in that office has killed 214. I need justice, not your idea of vengeance, thank you very much. He screwed up my life, too, you know."

"I've turned over a new leaf. You can ask Marla. I haven't even had a parking ticket in years. It was just easier back then to do what Dad said than to fight him. And Ashcroft was framing me with it. He stole explosives from the construction site. Everything pointed to me."

"You only look guilty. I figured it out." She looked at him, trying to decide the best tactic. "Ashcroft knew more about O'Hare security than you did. The cops investigating his organization sent eight people to jail, got you and two others fired, but the evidence they have developed suggests Ashcroft was rebuilding his network since he got out of jail. He didn't need you to get the bomb into O'Hare, but you were a great fall guy. He was already blackmailing you; why not frame you, too? Who set up that Tuesday morning appointment at the airport?"

She smiled as she saw his eyes narrow. "Yes, I thought so. Devlon. There will be a phone record of the call he placed to you, showing it was Devlon and not you that set up the meeting at the airport. What about that fax the bank manager received, extending your loan—who stood at the fax machine and sent it, you or Nathan?"

"I did."

"From the business lounge."

"Yes."

"Did you know you are on tape doing so?"

"Security cameras are there?"

"Yes. The fax came through at 10:48 A.M. It's there in black and white on the top of the page. But someone else had just called in the bomb threat, and I wrote down the time we were paged about it. 10:48 A.M. You were busy, Tony, and you're on tape being busy."

"That's not much."

"There are electronic fingerprints on the money Devlon had been han-dling for Ashcroft. It's pieces of a puzzle, Tony. We've only been looking at Devlon a short time, and we've already turned over some ugly things under the rocks. You'll have to trust me when I say there will be more." She was pleased to see him lean against the desk, relax ever so slightly. "Why were you letting Ashcroft blackmail you? Why were you paying him off?"

"It wasn't for me. It was for Marla. She's on one of the security tapes with Ashcroft. She didn't know. She was just delivering a package. She had no idea what was in it."

"I believe you."

"I couldn't take a chance a jury might not. She's the best thing that ever happened in my life. And once I paid the first blackmail money, Ashcroft had me."

The phone began to ring.

"You had better get that Tony. And listen to what they have to say, okay?"

Tony took a step toward the phone.

She heard something fall. She came away from the wall and to her feet in less time than it took Tony to turn toward the office, but the error had been made. They had been talking too long without either checking on Devlon, and his chair had been on rollers. She heard a faint whisper in her ear that was someone screaming for her to get down and felt her heart stop. She'd turned her mike down too low for them to warn her when Devlon began to move. Her own instincts now screaming at her, she hit Tony with a blindside tackle just as gunshots split the wood of the desk.

Devlon was shooting at them.

Tony tried to bring his hand up with the gun to return fire, and Kate did the thing that seemed most logical. She hit him.

She knew enough to shut her eyes. The flash grenades went off as bril-liant repeating strobes, and the decibel level of their noisemakers made her ears ring. Two figures in black came across the desk still partially blocking the stairway door, took firing positions by Devlon's office, and in went another flash grenade.

The assault was finished before Kate could sort out the players. She sat up, wincing with pain she didn't bother to mask.

Lord, this wasn't in my plans.

She coughed up blood.

"Don't move." Dave's face wavered in and out of focus.

"Broke a rib."

"And a few other things."

"The vest took the hit." She could feel the radiating bruise, had to suck in air to make the world stop swimming. "I told you a younger brother was trouble." She tried to laugh at the observation but couldn't. The vest that had saved her life was too tight. She reached for the straps with hands that didn't seem to want to coordinate their movements.

"Kate."

She looked up. "Marcus, I'm not dead." He was pale as a ghost.

"Get Jennifer up here." The order from Marcus over the command circuit made her grimace.

"I don't need the full family for a busted rib."

"What you're going to get is a doctor, so shut up."

"You may have punctured a lung," Dave said quietly, supporting her against his shoulder.

She was beginning to get her breath back. "I bit my tongue, rather badly, with that blindside tackle. The slug hit nothing but Kevlar, but it packed a punch. I need my ribs strapped and something cold to drink." She saw the relief cross Dave's face. "Remember to tell Jennifer I want the cherry lollipop."

He kissed her forehead. "I'll do that."

"Good." She looked at Tony Jr., now coming around with a groan. "He's got a jaw like a rock. I nearly broke my hand."

"Be glad you did. If he'd had that gun in his hand when the team came through, there would have been little choice."

"I know. I guess I've now officially got more family."

"I know a good lawyer."

"He's going to need one."

"Don't scare me like this again, Kate." Dave ordered. "You weren't supposed to enter the room."

"I don't take chances lightly. I figured this time the stakes were high enough."

Dave brushed back her hair. "Maybe."

"You're just annoyed you couldn't take a bullet for me."

He grinned. "I've already got my scars."

"Do you?"

"Yes."

"Forget to duck?"

"Insuring someone else did."

Jennifer had joined them, and Kate didn't want to lose this moment. "Jennifer, come back in about an hour."

Dave choked back a laugh. "Would you behave? I'm not going anywhere. That's a promise."

Twenty-five

Kate speared an olive from the dish with her toothpick. They had a beautiful day for their Fourth of July bash. The park pavilion was perfect for the massive spread of food they had brought with them. There was something about a family picnic that restored her faith in the better things about life. She looked over at Jennifer, and then back at the rather brutal game of horseshoes going on. "I really think you should just plan to elope with Tom before the family scares him off."

"No need. He's winning."

Kate turned to pay more attention, her hand cushioning her taped ribs. She had a hairline fracture, a nuisance, but it was going to bench her from the baseball game that afternoon, and that had her really annoyed. In the last decade she had missed only two O'Malley baseball games, and both of them had been due to pages. "Really? No one is throwing the game?"

"Tom just nailed another ringer."

Kate grinned. "I bet that's giving Stephen fits."

It felt good to finally have a day to just hang out with the family and not have to worry about what was going to hit her the next day. Tony Jr. was working on a plea bargain with the DA, and Peter Devlon would eventually be facing one of the biggest trials in U.S. history.

She was still getting used to the reality she had a brother. Will, she refused to think of him as Tony Jr., was still very much of a mystery to her. They had forged a tentative acceptance of the fact they were related, but any sense of a personal relationship was going to take time. She had met

Will's wife, Marla, and had liked her immediately. Time. She would need a lot of it, so would Will.

Dave dropped his arm around her shoulders. "Hey, beautiful. What's happening?"

"Just chatting. I thought you were watching Jack and the steaks."

"He's burning them," Dave replied cheerfully.

Jennifer got to her feet with a laugh. "I'll go."

Dave nudged Kate over, and she made room for him on the bench. She smiled at his slight sunburn and feathered her hand through his hair. "Is the day everything you expected?"

He slowly leaned in against her, invading her space, before kissing her, taking his time to purposefully drive her crazy. "Pretty much." He grinned. "What's the blush for?"

"My family is watching." *And you've been driving me crazy the last few days.*

"They've unanimously decided I should stick around."

She grinned. "Have they?"

"Yes." He interlaced his fingers with hers. "What about you?"

"You mean I have a choice?"

"No."

"I didn't think so." She rolled a shoulder, pretended to think about it, and finally caved in. "You can stick around. I've decided I rather like your company. Besides, I know better than to go against the family."

He studied her for a moment, and the smile became tender. "I was thinking along the lines of something serious."

"How serious?"

"How about, for now, a promise that you'll be my girl for at least the next year? The guys think it's a good idea."

"What?"

"Is it the proposal or the fact I asked their permission?"

She blinked, hard. *Jesus, I was expecting this question in a few months, not now. Dating a cop is a big deal.*

Dave was God's man. And she had learned to trust Him.

She knew what she wanted.

She turned toward him and leaned her arm back against the picnic table. "We have an unwritten rule in the family, you know."

"What?"

She smiled. "Never turn down an invitation to an adventure."

He relaxed. "Good. We'll have one."

"That's a guarantee?"

"You can take it to the bank." He looked at her. "Not First Union."

"I already don't know if I can handle your sense of humor."

"You'll learn."

"That's easy for you to say." She leaned her head against his shoulder, made herself comfortable. His arm settled around her shoulders. "You can handle the pages?"

"I've survived three. By my calculations, I've only got about a thousand to go before you retire."

She chuckled. "You're going to count them?"

"Absolutely."

"Do I get keys to the jet?"

"Is it a deal breaker?"

She grinned.

He ruffled her hair. "Okay, they're yours. Along with lessons."

"Thanks." She rested her hands against his chest, watching his eyes as he studied her, as he smiled. "I love you, you know."

His hands cupped her face. "I know." His arms comfortably encircled her waist. "I love you, too."

Hearing the words still made her blink; no man had ever said them to her with that confident certainty. She studied him, feeling for the first time uncertain, and trusting him enough not to mask what she was feeling. His expression softened, and the growing warmth in his gaze flooded over her. He barely had to lean forward to kiss her. "Trust me, Kate. I love you."

His reassurance settled deep inside. She rested her hands against his chest to give a cheeky grin. "Good."

"You haven't actually answered my question yet," he pointed out.

She wanted to laugh. "Yes, I'll be your girl."

"Good."

"That's an awfully smug look."

"Marcus said if I could get you to agree before game time, I could be team captain."

Her elbow caught him in the ribs as she moved back.

"Hey!"

"Where's Marcus?"

He rubbed the sore spot. "Probably getting out of the line of fire."

"He should."

"I'm unofficially part of the family, Kate. Leave your brother alone."

"I don't need him arranging my life."

He caught her as she moved to get up. "As if anyone could. Sit." His arms closed around her ribs below the wrap to make sure she did. "He's got a party planned for tonight for Tom and Jennifer. He thought I might like to come celebrate with you."

She blinked and what had been annoyance changed to a concerted effort not to let a tear fall. "Marcus planned a party?"

Dave gently hugged her. "Yeah. He thought it would be a nice O'Malley tradition." He kissed her softly. "I agree with him."

Kate leaned into the kiss. "There will be fireworks at the party."

He smiled. "I think we've got some fireworks right here."

"Fireworks and love. Nice combination."

"Break it up, you two. It's lunchtime."

Kate leaned back, blinked, and realized the family had joined them. She smiled. "Jack, did you burn my steak?"

"I tried my best."

She laughed. "Dave, are you sure you're ready for this family?"

"I wouldn't miss this adventure for the world."

Dear Reader,

Thank you for reading this book; it was such a pleasure to write. I fell in love with Kate O' Malley. After spending time with Dave in *Danger in the Shadows*, I knew he was one of the few people who could handle Kate! They have a bright future together.

A cop is driven by a need for justice. I was curious to find out which would be more poweful—a need for justice or a need for mercy—if the dilemma became very personal. I sketched a story that let me explore the subject, and found Kate's journey through the questions fascinating. Even I found the solution to her dilemma a surprise. Any time the character of God becomes the basis of a story, I have found it to be a wonderful book to write. I hope you enjoyed the story.

As always, I love to hear from my readers. Feel free to write me at:

Dee Henderson
c/o Multnomah Fiction
P.O. Box 1720
Sisters, Oregon 97759
E-mail: dee@deehenderson.com
Web site: www.deehenderson.com

Thanks again for letting me share Dave and Kate's story.
Sincerely,

Dee Henderson

THE O'MALLEY SERIES

The Negotiator—Book One: FBI agent Dave Richman from *Danger in the Shadows* is back. He's about to meet Kate O'Malley, and his life will never be the same. She's a hostage negotiator. He protects people. Dave's about to find out that falling in love with a hostage negotiator is one thing, but keeping her safe is another!
ISBN 1-57673-819-1

The Guardian—Book Two: A federal judge has been murdered. There is only one witness. And an assassin wants her dead. U.S. Marshal Marcus O'Malley thought he knew the risks of the assignment...He was wrong.
ISBN 1-57673-642-3

The Truth Seeker—Book Three: Women are turning up dead. Lisa O'Malley is a forensic pathologist and mysteries are her domain. When she's investigating a crime it means trouble is soon to follow. U.S. Marshal Quinn Diamond has found loving her is easier than keeping her out of danger. Lisa's found the killer, and now she's missing too...
ISBN 1-57673-753-5

The Protector—Book Four: Jack O'Malley is a fireman. He's fearless when it comes to facing an inferno. But when an arsonist begins targeting his district, his shift, his friends, Jack faces the ultimate challenge: protecting the lady who saw the arsonist before she pays an even higher price...
ISBN 1-57673-846-9

The Healer—Book Five: Rachel O'Malley makes her living as a trauma psychologist, working disaster relief for the Red Cross. Her specialty is helping children. When a school shooting rips through her community, she finds herself dealing with more than just grief among the children she's trying to help. There's a secret. One of them witnessed the shooting. And the murder weapon is still missing...
ISBN 1-57673-925-2

It was a good night for a sniper, Marcus realized as he checked with the men securing the perimeter of the church property. They were running behind schedule and Marcus could feel the danger of that. Twilight was descending. In the dusk settling in the open areas around the church across the clusters of towering oak trees, the shadows themselves spoke of hidden dangers.

It was time to move.

Marcus raised Luke on the security net. "I'm changing the travel plans. We're going to take the family out the back entrance. Cue us up to leave in five minutes."

"Roger."

He reentered the church.

Marcus had been too occupied during the last hour to really look at Shari, an unfortunate reality that went with the job. It was everyone else who was the threat. He looked now and what he saw concerned him. She was folding, he could see it in the glazed expression, the lack of color in her face, the betraying fact her brother had noticed and now had his hand under her arm.

Definitely time to leave.

Marcus moved to join them and relieve Craig.

Shari saw him coming and broke off her conversation to join him. "Marcus, could—"

The window behind her exploded.

Shari heard someone gasp in pain and the next second Marcus swept out his left arm, caught her across the front of her chest at her collarbone, and took her feet right out from under her.

She felt herself falling backward and it was a petrifying sensation. She couldn't get her hands back in time to break her fall and she hit hard, slamming against the floor, her back and neck taking the brunt of the impact. His arm had her pinned to the ground, his hand gripping her shoulder. He wasn't letting her move even if she could.

"Shari—"

She couldn't respond, her head was ringing so badly.

That had been a bullet.

She wheezed at that realization; her lungs feeling like they would explode. Around her people were screaming.

Another window shattered.

Marcus forcibly pulled her across the floor with him out of the way. "South. Shooter to the south!"

She could hear him hollering on the security net, and it was like listening down a tunnel. Who was bleeding? Someone was bleeding, she could see it on his hand.

It was coming home to her now, very much home. Someone was trying to kill her…again.

Available now from
DEE HENDERSON

THE TRUTH SEEKER
ISBN 1-57673-753-5

Women are missing. It's been happening for years.
Lisa O'Malley's found the killer, and now she's missing too.
U.S. Marshal Quinn Diamond is not about
to lose the woman he loves to the man he hates...
The drama continues with book three in the O'Malley series.

Lisa O'Malley was sitting on the side step of the fire engine, silent, one tennis shoe off as she'd stepped on a hot ember and burned the sole, her stockinged foot moving slowly back and forth in the soot-blackened water rushing down the street toward the nearest storm drain. Her gaze never leaving the dying fire. Her brother Stephen had wrapped a fire coat around her, and she had it gripped with both hands, pulled tight.

Quinn Diamond kept a close watch on her as he stood leaning against the driver's door of a squad car, waiting for a callback from the dispatcher. She was alone in her grief, her emotions hidden, her eyes dry. She'd lost what she'd valued, and Quinn hated to realize how much it had to resonate with her past.

Kate sat down beside her.

Quinn watched as the two sisters sat in silence, and he prayed for Kate, that she would have the right words to say.

Instead, she remained silent.

And Lisa leaned her head against Kate's shoulder and continued to watch the fire burn, the silence unbroken.

Friends. Deep, lifelong friends.

Quinn had to turn away from the sight. He had so much emotion inside it was going to rupture into tears or fury.

He found himself facing a grim Marcus O'Malley.

"Quinn, get her out of here."

"Stephen has already tried; she won't budge."

"No. I mean out of here. Out of town," Marcus replied grimly. "The killer goes from notes and phone calls to fire. He's not going to stop there."

Marcus was right. Lisa had to come first. "The ranch. She's going to need the space."

"Thank you."

"I'll keep her safe, now that it's too late."

"Quinn—we'll find him."

That wasn't even in question. He was going to hunt the guy down and rip out his heart.

THE PROTECTOR
ISBN 1-57673-846-9

The house was a total loss. Firefighter Jack O'Malley shone his bright light on the dripping walls, looking for anything that would provide a source for the smoke he was still chasing. Second-floor beams above him groaned as the building settled. Fire had shattered what was once a beautiful home. It was like walking around inside a sarcophagus. The place felt like it was dying.

The kitchen smelled of something nasty, the sharp smell of burnt cleaning supplies making Jack's eyes water. Limp bananas now hung over a bowl whose apples looked like cooked mush. Coupons fluttered from the counter to the floor, turning to a sodden mass in the standing water. Pictures on the refrigerator had bled away color in the heat, leaving behind the ghosts of people barely discernible.

He was grateful the family had not been caught in the inferno. This was so incredibly senseless. The fire looked like it had been set.

Weariness washed over him again. He'd like to find the man responsible for this and deck him.

A wisp of gray caught his attention as the house breathed. Some smoke was coming through the central air ductwork. Jack touched his radio. "Nate, check the utility room again."

"On it."

Jack walked through what had once been the patio door, stepping out into the night. The massive spotlights from the fire engines in front of the house cast strange shadows onto the backyard through holes in the house.

Popcorn.

Jack stopped in his tracks when he spotted the white kernels lying at the edge of the deck. The building anger surged and fury swept through him. Someone had stood and watched the house burn, had come prepared to enjoy the sight. It was a signature he'd seen before.

The kernels were scattered, dropped as though stragglers from an overflowing fistful. Jack searched the area. He had hoped this particular arsonist was going to stick to his nuisance fires of grass and trash. Instead, he'd just escalated to his first house.

He hated arsonists. Painful experience from his own past had taught him how ruthless a fire starter could become. Destruction of property.

Innocent victims. Injured firefighters. They had to find this guy before someone got hurt.

He could fight a fire, but fighting a man— Jack felt like his hands were tied and he hated the feeling of being helpless. He was an O'Malley. He wasn't one to duck trouble. He preferred to go after it. And this was clearly trouble. How was he supposed to go after a man who chose to be a coward and hide behind a match?

Around him the firefighters from Company 81 were pulling hose and shouting to be heard over the sound of a power saw. They were aggressively searching for hot spots within the house, trying to find the source of that smoke still rising like a wavering cobra into the air.

Somewhere in the ruins this fire was still alive. Jack pulled back on his gloves and looked over the house with an experienced eye. A decade of fighting fires had taught him well, for it was not a forgiving profession.

Fire was an arrogant beast. If in control, it challenged anyone who approached with ferocious disdain. If forced to retreat, it liked to lie low, patiently waiting, then exacting a painful revenge.

They'd find it. Kill it. And another dragon would be slain.

"Cole." Jack got the attention of the fire investigator.

There were few men who could dominate a fire scene just by being present; his friend was one. Cole Parker had made captain at thirty-six, a decade before most. He now led the arson group. Jack trusted the man in a way he trusted few outside his family.

"What do you have, Jack?"

With his flashlight, Jack illuminated the popcorn.

Cole, a big man with a big shadow, stilled for a moment, then walked over to the deck.

"He's escalating," Jack said.

Cole bent to pick up a kernel. "We knew he eventually would. Five fires in seven weeks, he's not a patient man."

"He's ringing fires around the new boundaries of the fire district." Jack knew it was at least a clue to figuring out who the arsonist was.

Cole just nodded. "A dangerous man playing a dangerous game." He ate one of the popped kernels. "Salt. He's bringing his own refreshments."

"I really didn't need to know that."

His friend rose gracefully to his feet. "I thought this had the sound of one of his. Late at night, edge of the district." He looked over at Jack. "Gold Shift."

The implication that Jack's shift was being targeted hadn't escaped his attention. They worked twenty-four hours on, forty-eight hours off, yet all the fires had been fought by his shift. Jack would not easily admit he'd started to sweat when the tones sounded. It was hard to hold his trade-mark good humor when someone out there appeared determined to make sure he was going to face flames.

Cole brushed his hands on worn jeans. "Tell me about this fire."

"It was in the walls."

First on the scene, Jack had pushed his way into the front hallway, shining his light, and had watched the paint bubble from the heat inside the walls. No flames had been visible, but as soon as he poked his ax into a wall, the dragon leaped out, roaring. "We had a hard time getting water onto the face of it."

They slogged across the yard now turned into mud by the hours of streaming water. "Think he's after the press attention?" Jack asked.

"Bold enough to stand around after the fire starts and flick popcorn into the flames, arrogant enough to set fires frequently. Now he's escalating in the type of fires he sets. He wants the attention—ours, the press's, and ultimately the public's."

"We'll have a panic on our hands if we don't stop him before the press connects the fires."

"Not to mention copycats."

Smoke twisted in their direction, the heavy ash particles making Jack cough. "What time is it?"

Cole sent him a sympathetic smile. "After 2 A.M."

Two and a half hours. Jack felt like he had run a marathon. The turnout coat sat heavy on his shoulders, and it stuck and rubbed at his neck as he moved. The last hours had turned his shirt into a sweaty mass. Jack knew he could forget any idea of sleep tonight. It would be dawn before they got the fire mop-up complete.

He'd kill for a shower. The smell of smoke and sweat was a stench he didn't mind as long as he was moving and downwind of himself.

"You did a good job of knocking it down."

He was pleased at the praise, for Cole didn't give it lightly. "Thanks."

Jack scanned the few remaining spectators—neighbors hurriedly dressed, a couple kids entranced at the sight of the red engine and ladder truck, local media, a cop blocking the street from thru traffic.

Some firebugs were watchers. They acted just so the firefighters would get called out. They'd stand and watch the battle, their own personal entertainment. No one stood out among those watching.

Jack turned back to the house and watched guys turn a nozzle back on to deal with a pocket of fire found smoldering in the wall between the garage and the breezeway. "This isn't going to be his last fire."

"Safe wager."

"Any ideas?"

Cole shook his head. "No ideas, no assumptions, no conclusions. You know how this job is done."

Jack did. It took patience he didn't have. "My men are at risk." Cole reached over and squeezed his shoulder.

"Lieutenant, O'Malley?" A firefighter from Truck 81 stepped to the open front door. "You're going to want to see this."

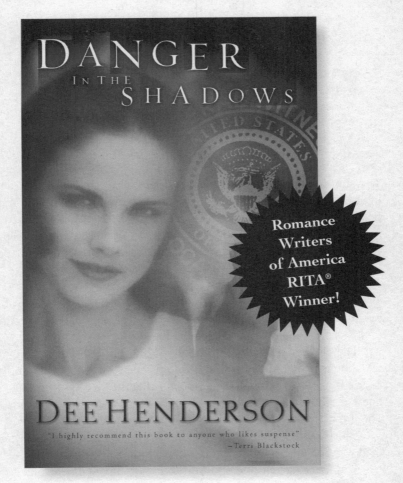

Don't miss the prequel to the O'Malley series!

Sara's terrified. She's doing the one thing she cannot afford to do: fall in love with
former pro football player Adam Black, a man everyone knows. Sara's been hidden away
in the witness protection program, her safety dependent on being invisible—and loving
Adam could get her killed.

ISBN 1-57673-927-9

Available now from
DEE HENDERSON
DANGER IN THE SHADOWS

RITA Award Winner—the highest national award given
for excellence in romantic fiction
National Reader's Choice Award Winner
Bookseller's Best Award Winner

The summer storm lit up the night sky in a jagged display of energy,
lightning bouncing, streaking, fragmenting between towering thunder-
heads. Sara Walsh ignored the storm as best she could, determined not
to let it interrupt her train of thought. The desk lamp as well as the
overhead light were on in her office as she tried to prevent any shadows
from forming. What she was writing was disturbing enough.

The six-year-old boy had been found. Dead.

Writing longhand on a yellow legal pad of paper, she shaped the
twenty-ninth chapter of her mystery novel. Despite the dark specificity
of the scene, the flow of words never faltered.

The child had died within hours of his abduction. His family, the
Oklahoma law enforcement community, even his kidnapper, did not
realize it. Sara did not pull back from writing the scene even though she
knew it would leave a bitter taste of defeat in the mind of the reader.
The impact was necessary for the rest of the book.

She frowned, crossed out the last sentence, added a new detail,
then went on with her description of the farmer who had found the boy.

Thunder cracked directly overhead. Sara flinched. Her office suite
on the thirty-fourth floor put her close enough to the storm she could
hear the air sizzle in the split second before the boom. She would like
to be in the basement parking garage right now instead of her office.

She had been writing since eight that morning. A glance at the
clock on her desk showed it was almost eight in the evening. The push
to finish a story always took over as she reached the final chapters. This

tenth book was no exception.

Twelve hours. No wonder her back muscles were stiff. She had taken a brief break for lunch while she reviewed the mail her secretary had prioritized for her. The rest of her day had been spent working on the book. She arched her back and rubbed at the knot.

This was the most difficult chapter in the book to write. It was better to get it done in one long, sustained effort. Death always squeezed her heart.

Had Dave been in town, he would have insisted she wrap it up and come home. Her life was restricted enough as it was. Her brother refused to let her spend all her time at the office. He would come lean against the doorjamb of her office and give her that look along with his predictable lecture telling her all she should be doing: Puttering around the house, cooking, messing with the roses, something other than sitting behind that desk.

Sara smiled. She did so enjoy taking advantage of Dave's occasional absences.

His flight back to Chicago from the FBI academy at Quantico had been delayed due to the storm front. When he had called her from the airport, he had cautioned her he might not be home until eleven.

It wasn't a problem, she had assured him, everything was fine. Code words. Spoken every day. So much a part of their language now that she spoke them instinctively. "Everything is fine"—all clear; "I'm fine"—I've got company; "I'm doing fine"—I'm in danger. She had lived the dance a long time. The tight security around her life was necessary. It was overpowering, obnoxious, annoying...and comforting.

Sara turned in the black leather chair and looked at the display of lightning. The rain ran down the panes of thick glass. The skyline of downtown Chicago glimmered back at her through the rain.

With every book, another fact, another detail, another intense emotion, broke through from her own past. She could literally feel the dry dirt under her hand, feel the oppressive darkness. Reliving what had happened to her twenty-five years ago was terrifying. Necessary, but terrifying.

She sat lost in thought for several minutes, idly walking her pen through her fingers. Her adversary was out there somewhere, still alive, still hunting her. Had he made the association to Chicago yet? After all these years, she was still constantly moving, still working to stay one step ahead of the threat. Her family knew only too well his threat was real.

The man would kill her. Had long ago killed her sister. The threat didn't get more basic than that. She had to trust others and ultimately God for her security. There were days her faith wavered under the intense weight of simply enduring that stress. She was learning, slowly, by necessity, how to roll with events, to trust God's ultimate sovereignty.

The notepad beside her was filled with doodled sketches of faces. One of these days her mind was finally going to stop blocking the one image she longed to sketch. She knew she had seen the man. Whatever the cost, whatever the consequences of trying to remember, they were worth paying in order to try to bring justice for her and her sister.

Sara let out a frustrated sigh. She couldn't force the image to appear no matter how much she longed to do so. She was the only one who still believed it was possible for her to remember it. The police, the FBI, the doctors, had given up hope years ago.

She fingered a worn photo of her sister Kim that sat by a white rose on her desk. She didn't care what the others thought. Until the killer was caught, she would never give up hope.

God was just. She held on to that knowledge and the hope that the day of justice would eventually arrive. Until it did, she carried a guilt inside that remained wrapped around her heart. In losing her twin she had literally lost part of herself.

Turning her attention back to her desk, she debated for a moment if she wanted to do any more work that night. She didn't.

As she put her folder away, the framed picture on the corner of her desk caught her attention; it evoked a smile. Her best friend was getting married. Sara was happy for her, but also envious. The need to break free of the security blanket rose and fell with time. She could feel the sense of rebellion rising again. Ellen had freedom and a life. She was getting married to a wonderful man. Sara longed to one day have that same choice. Without freedom, it wasn't possible, and that reality hurt. A dream was being sacrificed with every passing day.

As she stepped into the outer office, the room lights automatically turned on. Sara reached back and turned off the interior office lights.

Her suite was in the east tower of the business complex. Rising forty-five stories, the two recently built towers added to the already impressive downtown skyline. She struggled with the elevator ride to the thirty-fourth floor each day, for she did not like closed-in spaces, but she considered the view worth the price.

The elevator that responded tonight came from two floors below. There were two connecting walkways between the east and west towers, one on the sixth floor and another in the lobby. She chose the sixth floor concourse tonight, walking through it to the west tower with a confident but fast pace.

She was alone in the wide corridor. Travis sometimes accompanied her, but she had waved off his company tonight and told him to go get dinner. If she needed him, she would page him.

The click of her heels echoed off the marble floor. There was parking under each tower, but if she parked under the tower where she worked, she would be forced to pull out onto a one-way street no matter which exit she took. It was a pattern someone could observe and predict. Changing her route and time of day across one of the two corridors was a better compromise. She could hopefully see the danger coming.

Sara decided to take the elevator down to the west tower parking garage rather than walk the six flights. She would have preferred the stairs, but she could grit her teeth for a few flights to save time. She pushed the button to go down and watched the four elevators to see which would respond first. The one to her left, coming down from the tenth floor.

When it stopped, she reached inside, pushed the garage-floor parking button, but did not step inside. Tonight she would take the second elevator.

Sara shifted her raincoat over her arm and moved her briefcase to her other hand. The elevator stopped and the doors slid open.

A man was in the elevator.

She froze.

He was leaning against the back of the elevator, looking like he had put in a long day at work, a briefcase in one hand and a sports magazine in the other, his blue eyes gazing back at her. She saw a brief look of admiration in his eyes.

Get in and take a risk, step back and take a risk.

She knew him. Adam Black. His face was as familiar as any sports figure in the country, even if he'd been out of the game of football for three years. His commercial endorsements and charity work had continued without pause.

Adam Black worked in this building? This was a nightmare come true. She saw photographs of him constantly in magazines, local newspapers, and occasionally on television. The last thing she needed was to be near someone who attracted media attention.

She hesitated, then stepped in, her hand tightening her hold on the briefcase handle. A glance at the board of lights showed he had already selected the parking garage.

"Working late tonight?" His voice was low, a trace of a northeastern accent still present, his smile a pleasant one.

Her answer was a noncommittal nod.

The elevator began to silently descend.

She had spent too much time in European finishing schools to slouch. Her posture was straight, her spine relaxed, even if she was nervous. She hated elevators. She should have taken the stairs.

"Quite a storm out there tonight."

The heels of her patent leather shoes sank into the jade carpet as she shifted her weight from one foot to the other. "Yes."

Three more floors to go.

There was a slight flicker to the lights and then the elevator jolted to a halt.

"What?" Sara felt adrenaline flicker in her system like the lights.

He pushed away from the back wall. "A lightning hit must have blown a circuit."

The next second, the elevator went black.

UNCOMMON HEROES SERIES

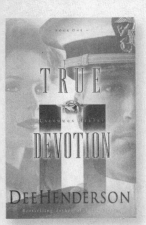

True Devotion, Book One

Kelly Jacobs has already paid the ultimate price of loving a warrior: She has the folded flag and the grateful thanks of a nation to prove it. Navy SEAL Joe "Bear" Baker can't ask her to accept that risk again—even though he loves her. But the man responsible for her husband's death is back, closer than either of them realize. Kelly's in danger, and Joe may not get there in time . . .

ISBN 1-57673-886-8

True Valor, Book Two

Air Force Pararescueman Bruce "Striker" Stanton spends his life rescuing pilots downed behind enemy lines. Grace "Gracie" Yates spends hers flying an F/A-18 Hornet for the Navy. With dangerous jobs, often away from home, they exchanged love letters. Now a fight between Turkey and its neighbors is spiraling into a confrontation. For the military deployed in the region, it's not just the occasional news headline—it's their daily problem. When Grace is shot down behind enemy lines, Bruce has got one mission: get Gracie out alive...

ISBN 1-57673-887-6

True Honor, Book Three

For CIA officer Darcy St. James, the terrorist attack on America is personal: Friends died at the Pentagon. She's after a man who knew September 11 would happen and who chose to profit from the knowledge. Navy SEAL Sam "Cougar" Houston is busy: The intelligence Darcy is generating has his team deploying around the world. Under the pressure of war, they discover the sweetness of love, and their romance flourishes. But it may be a short relationship—for the terrorists have chosen their next targets, and Darcy's name is high on the list...

ISBN 1-59052-043-2

Available now from
DEE HENDERSON

TRUE DEVOTION

Uncommon Heroes—soldiers standing in the gap for
honor…and love.
Don't miss book one in this exciting new series!

Kelly slipped her hand into Joe's as they strolled down to the water's edge
then turned north to follow the beach toward the Hotel del Coronado
where their evening had begun. Music from the Ocean Terrace restaurant
at the hotel drifted toward them, the colorful lanterns lit around the
Terrace reflecting on the water. It was a festive mood.

"One of the last memories I had in the water before you rescued me
was from the last time we walked this beach."

"Really?"

She nodded. "Friday night after dinner. You indulged me with a walk
down to the Terrace to buy a frozen fruit smoothy. Remember?"

"I remember the smoothy—it gave me an ice cream headache."

"I had forgotten that."

"I haven't."

"What I remember is holding your hand while we walked, deciding
how nice it was not to be walking alone."

He squeezed her hand gently. "Thank you. You're welcome to hold my
hand anytime you like."

Kelly returned the pressure, communicating without words her pleasure, and they walked in silence along the shore. This was the best memory maker of the evening. The restaurant, the movie, roses, and the bear—
of all the images of the evening, this was the one she treasured most. She
had walked this beach with Joe before, but this time it was different. This
time in a new way she belonged beside him and it felt that way: special.

The evening was going to end eventually, and she didn't want that to
happen. Would he kiss her good night? There were already stars in her
eyes; that would certainly cap this evening with the best ending possible.

The moonlight flickered as clouds skimmed over the sky.

Joe stopped.

She looked at him, puzzled, and saw his eyes narrow as he gazed ahead.

There was only the dark shadow of the surf and the resulting white breakers. The sound clued her in, an odd interruption in the withdrawing surf as it pulled back to sea.

They both began to run.

A limp body was rolling in the surf, being thrown by the sea to the shore.

TRUE VALOR

He stood out in his flannel shirt and jeans, but so far none of the sailors had made the mistake of assuming he was a civilian. Air Force Major Bruce "Striker" Stanton warily watched them continue to arrive and crowd into his sister's backyard, and he wondered how many sailors Jill had invited from the aircraft carrier USS *George Washington* to come to the predeployment party. It would be like her to invite them all so as not to leave anyone out. All five thousand plus of them.

He felt like he had invaded enemy country. The sailors, the average age of which was twenty-one, looked like children. They got younger every year. A few of his friends cut from Air Force cloth were also here but had long ago been swallowed up in the sea of white.

Striker maneuvered through guests to the chair he had staked out on the patio. His dog was curled up asleep under the chair. A party, food, and many willing hands to offer treats, and what did his dog do? Sleep. He had yet to figure out this yellow lab he had acquired two months ago from the pound.

Bruce nodded a greeting to one of the Navy SEALs he knew as he settled into the chair and prepared to stay put for a while. Sprinkled in the mix among the young sailors were a few grown-ups. The ship's officers, SEALs, and naval aviators stood out by the self-assured way they staked out their space.

Bruce had driven up from Pensacola, where he was based, to Norfolk, center of gravity for military operations in the state. He'd come for the weekend because his sister had invited him.

And he'd come to see Grace.

He didn't have to search to find her; he'd kept track of her in his peripheral vision throughout the afternoon. Grace stood out in red, the sweater a bold splash of color in a sea of white. His sister's best friend had been in his sights for years. Jill had introduced him to Gracie. Lieutenant Grace Yates was one of those self-assured naval aviators. She was going to spend the next six months deployed in the Middle East, catapulting off the deck of the USS *George Washington* in an F/A-18 Hornet.

He watched her mingle and chat with the other squadron pilots; she'd long ago been accepted into their exclusive ranks. Gracie loved to fly and she turned that passion into a single-minded focus to be the best.

She rarely talked about herself. How many layers were there to the mystery of who she was? He was determined to find out. He was on a mission. Grace was the objective. And his profession had taught him well the value of good reconnaissance.